D0568862

Practicing Organization Development

**The Change Agent Series
for Groups and Organizations**

MISSION STATEMENT

The books in this series are intended to be cutting-edge, state-of-the-art, innovative approaches to organization change and development. They are written for and by practitioners interested in new approaches to facilitating effective organization change. They are geared to providing both theory and advice on practical applications.

SERIES EDITORS

**William J. Rothwell
Roland Sullivan
Kristine Quade**

EDITORIAL BOARD

**David Bradford
W. Warner Burke
Edith Whitfield Seashore
Robert Tannenbaum
Christopher G. Worley
Shaolin Zhang**

Other Practicing Organization Development Titles

Consulting to Family Businesses

A Practical Guide to Contracting, Assessment, and Implementation

Jane Hilburt-Davis

W. Gibb Dyer, Jr.

JOSSEY-BASS/PFEIFFER
A Wiley Imprint
www.pfeiffer.com

Practicing
Organization
Development

Copyright © 2003 by Jane Hilburt-Davis and W. Gibb Dyer, Jr.

Published by Jossey-Bass/Pfeiffer
A Wiley Imprint
989 Market Street, San Francisco, CA 94103-1741   www.pfeiffer.com

No part of this publication, except the exhibits as noted below, may be reproduced, stored in a retrieval system, or transmitted in any form or by any means, electronic, mechanical, photocopying, recording, scanning, or otherwise, except as permitted under Sections 107 or 108 of the 1976 United States Copyright Act, without either the prior written permission of the Publisher or authorization through payment of the appropriate per-copy fee to the Copyright Clearance Center, 222 Rosewood Drive, Danvers, MA 01923, (978) 750-8400, fax (978) 750-4744. Requests to the Publisher for permission should be addressed to the Permissions Department, John Wiley & Sons, Inc., 605 Third Avenue, New York, NY 10158-0012, (212) 850-6011, fax (212) 850-6008, e-mail: permreq@wiley.com.

The exhibits that appear in this book (except those for which reprint permission must be obtained from the primary sources) may be reproduced for educational/training activities. We do, however, require that the following statement appear on all reproductions:

Consulting to Family Businesses by Jane Hilburt-Davis and W. Gibb Dyer, Jr.

Copyright © 2003 by Jane Hilburt-Davis & W. Gibb Dyer, Jr. Published by Jossey-Bass/Pfeiffer, San Francisco, CA.

This free permission is limited to the reproduction of material for educational/training events. Systematic or large-scale reproduction or distribution (more than one hundred copies per year)—or inclusion of items in publications for sale—may be done only with prior written permission. Also, reproduction on computer disk or by any other electronic means requires prior written permission. Requests to the Publisher for permission should be addressed to the Permissions Department, John Wiley & Sons, Inc., 605 Third Avenue, New York, NY 10158-0012, (212) 850-6011, fax (212) 850-6008, e-mail: permreq@wiley.com.

We at Jossey-Bass strive to use the most environmentally sensitive paper stocks available to us. Our publications are printed on acid-free recycled stock whenever possible, and our paper always meets or exceeds minimum GPO and EPA requirements.

Jossey-Bass also publishes its books in a variety of electronic formats. Some content that appears in print may not be available in electronic books.

Acquiring Editor: Josh Blatter   Senior Production Editor: Dawn Kilgore
Director of Development: Kathleen Dolan Davies   Manufacturing Supervisor: Becky Carreño
Developmental Editor: Susan Rachmeler   Interior and Cover Design: Bruce Lundquist
Editor: Rebecca Taff   Illustrations: Richard Sheppard

ISBN: 0-7879-6249-X

Library of Congress Cataloging-in-Publication Data

Hilburt-Davis, Jane
    Consulting to family businesses : a practical guide to contracting, assessment, and implementation / Jane Hilburt-Davis, W. Gibb Dyer.
        p. cm. (The practicing organization development series)
    Includes bibliographical references and index.
    ISBN 0-7879-6249-X (alk. paper)
    1. Family-owned business enterprises—Management—Handbooks, manuals, etc. 2. Business consultants—Handbooks, manuals, etc. I. Hilburt-Davis, Jane. II. Title. III. Series.
    HD62.25.D936 2002
    658'.04—dc21

2002007172

Printed in the United States of America
Printing   10 9 8 7 6 5 4 3 2 1

Contents

Part 2: Consulting to Family Businesses

Part 3: The Family Business Consultant

List of Figures, Tables, and Exhibits

Acknowledgments

WE **WOULD LIKE TO THANK** those who willingly and enthusiastically participated in the interviews and our colleagues at FFI, who both challenged and offered ideas and support. We would also like to thank those participants at the Cambridge Center's seminars who, through their excitement with the learning, challenged us and helped develop these ideas, in particular, Joseph Inskeep, who is director of the Center's training programs. We would also like to thank Roland Sullivan for bringing us together and encouraging us on this project, along with the other series editors, Kristine Quade and William Rothwell, and the support staff at Jossey-Bass, Kathleen Dolan Davies and Josh Blatter. Susan Rachmeler, development editor, also provided important input on the final draft of the book.

We would also like to thank our clients over the years, who have provided us with unique training grounds to hone our consulting skills. While we have had the daunting responsibility to help them, we have also gained much-needed experience and insight as we have worked with them to improve their businesses and their families. Finally, we would like to thank members of our own families, who have helped us to understand the importance of family in our lives.

Preface

THE REASON THAT WE WROTE THIS BOOK is quite simple: It had not been written yet. Until a few years ago, only a handful of books had been written about family businesses. The last few years have seen an explosion of books on the subject, but only a few of them have been for the family business consultant and they typically concentrate on only one aspect of the process, that is, strategic planning, process consulting, or relationship issues in family businesses. Also missing has been a systematic approach to the skills and competencies needed and the career development resources that are available for the consultant who works with these unique systems. It was just a matter of time before this book would be written and, with the encouragement and support of the series editors, we began.

This book, while based on sound theoretical material, is intended to be practical. It provides a roadmap to effective change management when working with family businesses. The book takes the reader step by step through the consulting process, with additional information about the systems ideas and interventions that work. To help apply the concepts, we have provided exercises, worksheets, and resources for further study. The examples used in the book are case-based and focus on the problems most frequently found in family businesses. (One important note: All of the cases in this book are disguised.) Our consulting framework is based on the traditional organization development (OD) methodology of action research, while introducing new ideas and theories from the evolving body of knowledge about family businesses.

The field of OD has largely ignored family businesses, and this book was originally conceived to address that gap. However, it soon became clear to us that the breadth and depth of the book should serve a larger group of readers. Although the book is grounded in an OD framework, it is targeted to a much broader audience of professionals from accounting, finance, law, and the behavioral and management sciences who are entering the field or who have been advising family businesses for years and want to update their thinking. This book emphasizes the interplay of systems and the importance of a multidisciplinary approach to family business consulting.

The challenge is always to keep up with the field. As family businesses become more sophisticated and aware of best practices, they will challenge their advisors. Their advisors, in turn, challenge their own assumptions and build on them. Through this process, the field will continue to evolve. We have not written the last word, but hope that our book will provide a foundation on which each consultant, through time and experience, can build. We hope to educate the new generation and challenge the old.

Authors' Backgrounds

Jane Hilburt-Davis has a background in both family systems therapy and OD, and she has used the action research model as a framework for her consulting to family businesses. She has also been teaching and supervising family business consultants for over a decade and is founding principal of Key Resources, a consulting group that specializes in family-owned and closely-held businesses (based in Massachusetts). Jane, along with Jack Troast, established the Cambridge Center for Creative Enterprise, a nonprofit institute dedicated to teaching the best practices of consulting to family firms and winner of the Family Firm Institute's 2000 Interdisciplinary Achievement Award for outstanding contribution to the advancement of interdisciplinary consulting to family businesses. During these years, she has been piecing together reading and case material from various sources for teaching, as well as creating her own teaching materials. To a large extent, this book has grown out of that need, again proving that necessity is the mother of invention.

Trained originally as a biologist and then as a systems therapist and organization development consultant, Jane has been fascinated with interacting, evolving systems and particularly with planned and spontaneous changes in human systems. None has been more challenging in her professional life than the family business system, in which there is much to lose as well as much to gain. Freud once said that all one needed for happiness is to find fulfillment in "love and work." Both are at stake with our family business clients. They deserve the best from us.

As a doctoral student at MIT, Gibb Dyer was introduced to the field of family business by his professor and mentor Richard Beckhard. Dick was one of the founders of the field of organization development, and he was intrigued with the challenges he faced as an OD consultant to family businesses. Dick enlisted Gibb as his research assistant to work with some of his clients to investigate the problems they were facing. As a result of this research, Gibb wrote his dissertation on cultural change in family-owned businesses, and from that research came his award-winning book, *Cultural Change in Family Firms: Anticipating and Managing Business and Family Transitions*, which was published by Jossey-Bass in 1986. From MIT, Gibb moved to the Marriott School of Management at Brigham Young University, where he currently is the O. Leslie Stone Professor of Entrepreneurship. As a professor at Brigham Young, Gibb continues to do research on the problems facing family businesses and teaches and counsels students who work in family businesses. He also regularly serves as a consultant to a variety of family firms, which furthers his understanding of how to consult effectively with these types of organizations. In his consulting practice, he collaborates with Roger Peay, a family counselor and therapist, along with professionals from other fields in a multidisciplinary effort to help his clients.

We began our collaboration on this book after we were introduced to each other by Roland Sullivan, one of the Practicing Organization Development series editors. We both felt the need to write a book to provide guidance for family business consultants, for, as we started in this field, we generally had to learn the hard way—through trial and error. Over the past year as we have been developing our ideas, we have communicated via e-mail, fax, and phone to encourage one another's thinking in regard to this book. This has been a stimulating experience for both of us. We bring to this project similar orientations to the practice of consulting, but we also have significant differences in our backgrounds that have encouraged each of us to challenge our own thinking and to think more deeply about what it means to be a family business consultant.

How This Book Is Organized

We have divided the book into three parts. Part 1 will help the reader to understand the unique nature of family businesses. Part 2 is about how to consult effectively with family firms, and Part 3 is focused on the knowledge and skills that are needed to be a successful family business consultant.

Part 1: The Family Business System

Chapter 1, Why Family Business Consulting?, introduces the reader to the topic of family business and the development of the field. It contains a discussion of both the uniqueness of family businesses and the problems they present to family business advisors. This chapter also has a description of family business systems, with a comparison of the systems of families and businesses and the unusual position of consultants who work within the boundaries of the interacting systems.

In Chapter 2, Characteristics of "Healthy" Family Businesses, we describe healthy and unhealthy family business systems and compare and contrast strengths and weaknesses along several dimensions, such as culture, leadership, roles, time, and family involvement.

Part 2: Consulting to Family Businesses

In Chapter 3, Contracting and Assessment, we describe the methodology of the action research model, followed by a discussion of the contracting and assessment phases of the process and appropriate issues to consider and questions to ask in each phase. In this chapter you will also find a description of the genogram and its uses and a discussion of transactional dynamics and boundaries.

Chapter 4, Feedback and Planning, contains the stages of data feedback, including suggestions for organizing and presenting data to a family and for generating solutions. There is also a suggested format for a retreat with a family. The chapter concludes with a comparison of simple and complex conflicts and effective strategies to deal with each.

In Chapter 5, Intervening in Family Firms, we explain the implementation phase of the action research model. In this chapter are examples of interventions, a discussion of types of change models, and the intervention process. We distinguish between emotional and technical interventions and the level of intervention that is needed for each, while emphasizing the interactional dynamics of each. We also include an intervention grid and tips for dealing with resistance to change.

Chapter 6, Helping Family Firms Make Developmental Transitions, contains a description of the interacting systems of the individual, family, and organizational life cycles. Whether these systems are in or out of synch can determine their success. Relevant to this is our discussion of crises and changes, both normal and accidental, and the importance of rituals, with suggestions for helping the client system deal with changes and stress. Succession planning is also included in this chapter.

Part 3: The Family Business Consultant

In Chapter 7, Skills and Ethics of the Family Business Consultant, we discuss the knowledge and skills that are unique to those working with family businesses. We have also included the Family Firm Institute's self-assessment questionnaire that each certificate program applicant completes and uses as a map on the journey to becoming a family business consultant. Also included are suggestions for gaining support and setting fee structures, as well as a discussion of ethics for family business consultants.

Chapter 8, Special Situations and Challenges, includes special situations presented by the family business client. The topics discussed are copreneurs, emotions, addictions, gender issues, nonfamily managers, family offices and foundations, and ethnicity. This chapter serves as a resource and overview for each of the issues. There are additional resources suggested at the end of each section.

Chapter 9, The Rewards and Challenges of Consulting to Family Businesses, includes material from interviews with twenty experts in the field. Their responses describe what makes consulting to family businesses unique, its challenges, lessons learned, and effective interventions.

Jane Hilburt-Davis
Lexington, MA

W. Gibb Dyer, Jr.
Provo, UT

March 2002

Part 1
The Family Business System

Why Family Business Consulting?

FAMILY BUSINESSES ARE the most common form of organization in the world. They are found in virtually every sector of the world's economies and range from small "mom and pop" enterprises to giants like Levi Strauss and Company. While all family businesses are unique in some way, they typically experience common problems and dilemmas that often require the help of a consultant. The problems confronting leaders of family firms are generally not found in other types of organizations and therefore require a consultant who is attuned to the unique features of family enterprises. The following descriptions of a few of the problems facing leaders of three family firms will help to illustrate this point.

▶ CASE 1.1

One mother operated four different businesses with her three daughters. One of the businesses, a retail establishment, was started several years ago, primarily to give the oldest daughter an opportunity for gainful employment (she'd had some difficulty holding a job in the past). The mother felt that the business was rather small, in a narrow market niche, and wouldn't require much of her attention. Unfortunately, the oldest daughter was not very good at running the business, and the business was losing money year after year, while the three other businesses were doing well and the profits from those businesses had to be used to subsidize the losses incurred by the retail firm. In desperation, the mother called a consultant and described the situation. Finally she inquired: "What do I do? I love my daughter and want her to succeed, but I can't afford putting cash into a business that is a loser. Also, my other daughters seem to resent the help that I'm giving my one daughter. They think I'm playing favorites. How do I keep family harmony and still run a profitable business?" ◄

► CASE 1.2

The CEO of another family business was hoping to retire soon. He had proposed that his four sons take over the business from him, although he wanted his wife and himself to retain ownership of most of the firm's plant and equipment. His sons could then lease these assets from him and his wife. The sons didn't know what to make of the offer, so they called in a consultant. They had several questions for the consultant:

- "Do you think Dad really wants to turn over the business to us, or is he keeping control of the assets so he can still be in charge?"

- "Can we trust him?"

- "What percentage of ownership of the business should each of us have?"

- "Who should replace Dad as the next CEO?"

- "How much should each family member working in the business be paid?"

- "Should our sister who is not working in the business be compensated in some way?" ◄

► CASE 1.3

A CEO of a successful family firm had a difficult dilemma. In the early days when he was just starting his business, he relied on several of his brothers and sisters to get the business off the ground. Much of the business's success was due to the hard work and dedication of family members. Now that the business was growing and successful, he realized that many of his siblings did not have the skills or abilities to take the business to the next level of growth and development. The company needed more specialized technical and managerial skills for it to continue to grow. What should he do? Should he attempt to have the family members trained in the skills the company needed? Should he fire incompetent family members? Should he replace the family employees with "outsiders" who had more experience and expertise and find another role for the family members? How would the family respond if professional managers were brought into the firm? However, the most important question for the CEO was: How do I get answers to these questions? ◄

These are the kinds of issues facing the leaders of family businesses that often require the help of a consultant. The questions raised in these three cases are not easy to answer. However, we believe that consultants, armed with appropriate theory and proven practices, can make a difference in helping family businesses successfully answer these kinds of questions.

Thus, the purpose of this book is to describe the unique problems facing family firms, present strategies that consultants can use to help family firms, and discuss the unique skills that are required of consultants who work with them.

What Is a Family Business?

Before we discuss what it means to consult successfully with family businesses, it is important to define what we mean by "family business." There are various definitions of family business that we might use; however, for our purposes we will define a family business as "an organization where ownership and/or management decisions are influenced by a family (or families)" (Dyer, 1986). We find that there are a variety of family firms that fit this broad definition. In some family firms, the family controls both the ownership and the management of the business. Thus, the family is able to exert great influence over the behavior of the firm (and vice versa). In other family firms, the family controls the firm's ownership, but hires nonfamily managers to run the enterprise. In these types of family firms, the family is typically interested in influencing the firm's mission and goals, occupying seats on the board, and receiving a financial return for their ownership, but do not want management responsibilities. Still other businesses, like IBM, are often not considered family businesses since they are publicly held. However, family influence at IBM was evident in key personnel decisions as Thomas Watson, Sr., made sure that his son, Thomas, Jr., succeeded him as president and that his other son attained a high position in the company. Thus, even a large, publicly traded company like IBM could be considered a family firm. Finally, there are some organizations in which there appear to be no family connections to the business. However, over time as the firm's leaders have children who mature and want to join the business or as a family begins to have interest in the firm's ownership and management decisions, the business can evolve into a family firm. Indeed, we have sometimes discovered that a founder of a business will declare that his or her firm is not a family business, only to take actions that would indicate otherwise. Moreover, some business leaders like to avoid defining their businesses as family firms, as they are afraid that such a label implies that they encourage nepotism and have a less than professional attitude about business.

The variety of family firms and the ambivalence that some leaders may have in viewing their businesses as family firms creates a unique set of issues for consultants who work with these types of firms. While we do see family firms following certain ownership and management patterns, each firm is unique, with its own history and family dynamics. Therefore, one important function of a family business consultant is to assess accurately what kind of relationship the family has with the business. To do this, however, requires the consultant to understand the family firm from a systems perspective.

Family Firm Systems

We have found that a systems framework is helpful in building good theory regarding the functioning of family firms. It is important to see a family firm as being comprised of three separate, but overlapping systems: (1) the business system; (2) the family system; and (3) the ownership or governance system. These systems and their relationships are illustrated in Figure 1.1.

Figure 1.1. Systems of a Family Firm

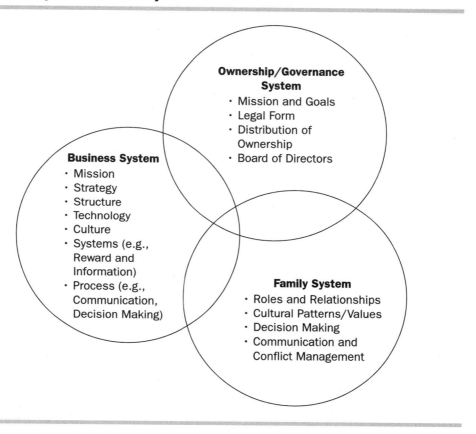

Source: R. Tagiuri & J.A. Davis (1982). Bivalent attributes of the family firm. Working paper. Harvard University Press, Cambridge, MA. [Reprinted in *Family Business Review, IX*(2), pp. 199-208.]

The *business system* encompasses the organization's mission and strategy. It also includes the various design elements that support the business strategy, such as the organization's structure, systems, and technology, along with the key processes that help the organization achieve its goals. The *ownership* or *governance* system includes the firm's legal form (for example, Limited Liability Company [LLC], C-Corp, and so forth), the distribution of its ownership, the board of directors or other governance mechanisms, and the goals and aspirations of those who own and govern the business. Finally, the *family system* involves the family (or families) connected with the enterprise. The family's goals and aspirations, its roles and relationships, its communication patterns, and its cultural values are all parts of the family system.

Family Values Versus Business Values

The unique dynamics of a family business arise as these three systems overlap one another. Many of the conflicts, issues, and dilemmas facing family firm leaders who attempt to manage all three systems successfully are the result of differing values that are found between businesses and families. These differences are listed in Table 1.1.

Table 1.1. A Comparison of Family and Business Systems

Areas of Conflict	Family Systems	Business Systems
Goals	Development and support of family members	Profits, revenues, efficiency, growth
Relations	Deeply personal, of primary importance	Semi-personal or impersonal, of secondary importance
Rules	Informal expectations ("That's how we've always done it")	Written and formal rules, often with rewards and punishment spelled out
Evaluation	Members rewarded for who they are; effort counts; unconditional love and support	Support conditional on performance and results; employees can be promoted or fired
Succession	Caused by death, divorce, or illness	Caused by retirement, promotion, or departure
Authority	Based on family position or seniority	Based on formal position in the organization's hierarchy
Commitment	Intergenerational and lifetime; based on one's identity with the family	Short-term; based on rewards received for employment

Conflicts between business and family values are often very apparent to the consultant trying to help a family business. A business primarily exists to increase shareholder wealth by being profitable and efficient. Growth is also frequently the aim of shareholders who want to increase their wealth. Families, on the other hand, exist to develop and support family members and achieve strong bonds of emotional support. Relationships in families are of primary importance, typically last a lifetime, and are deeply personal. In contrast to the relationships in family businesses, business relationships are generally short-lived, of secondary importance, and are largely utilitarian in nature. Businesses often articulate clear rules of conduct. Rewards and punishments are meted out depending on the employee's behavior. Employees can be fired or laid off depending on the circumstances. Family rules tend to be in the form of unspoken expectations that also strongly influence the behavior of family members. While family members may break family rules, such behavior rarely results in a family member being permanently cut off from familial affection or participation in family activities. Moreover, family members are generally rewarded for who they are—not merely for what they do. Effort counts and a healthy family provides family members with unconditional love and support. Businesses reward employees for results and employees are advanced in the company based on their performance. Succession in a family occurs when there is a death or a divorce. Succession in a business occurs when managers retire, are promoted, decide to leave, or are fired. Authority in the family is based on one's position in the family (mother, father, oldest son, and so on) and seniority, while authority in the business rests with those key positions in the organization's hierarchy. Commitment to the family spans generations and lasts a lifetime. Strong identification with the family strengthens this commitment. Commitment to the business tends to be short-term and contingent on the rewards one receives for participating in the organization.

These divergent values between business and family are found at the intersection of these three systems. Thus, the challenge for the family business consultant is to help the client manage these conflicts and help maintain healthy business, family, and ownership systems. This is not easy when the goals and values of the business and family are at odds with each other. Family business consultants often find themselves helping their clients sort out the tradeoffs in managing these differences.

Family Business Consulting

We have found family business consulting to be significantly different from working with nonfamily enterprises. The field of organization development, where we both have received our training, has historically focused on *action research*, where the consultant helps the client generate data about the client's problems that is then fed back to the client. This feedback is then used to develop a plan for change, and the consultant's role is then expanded to serve as a *change agent* to help the client manage the change process. In this book, we describe how this framework of action research is used to help family businesses.

Traditionally, the organization development (OD) consultant has focused on helping the client manage the *process* of change. In family business consulting, the consultant must not only be versed in managing process, but in providing *content* information for the client as well. Clients have specific content questions that need to be answered. For example, if a consultant is trying to help the head of a family business plan for ownership and leadership succession, the consultant may need to gather data about the current state of the family business and help the client manage the changes needed as the business moves to a new future where there is new leadership and there are new owners. While managing the process of such a transition is certainly important, the consultant may also need to help the family change its estate plan, its legal form, and its distribution of firm ownership in order to solve the key problems. Thus, content knowledge and technical expertise are needed as well to make these types of changes. In this regard, we find family business consultants coming to the field from a variety of different professions, such as accounting, law, family therapy, and estate planning, for each of these professions has a body of knowledge and technical expertise that can help those in family firms. We have found that most change efforts in family businesses are not likely to succeed unless there is the right combination of both content and process knowledge on the part of the consultant (Hilburt-Davis & Senturia, 1995). That is why multi-disciplinary consulting teams should often be the rule, rather than the exception, in working with family businesses, as no single person is likely to have all the content and process knowledge needed. As we do our work with family firms, we often have to "hand off' critical aspects of the change process to other consultants or collaborate with them to come up with effective solutions.

For example, in one family business, one of two brothers who started the business died unexpectedly from cancer, leaving his spouse as his brother's partner.

The surviving brother and his sister-in-law didn't trust one another, which led to a variety of family and business problems. To resolve this issue, an OD consultant was asked to help mediate between the two. After a day-long series of interviews and emotional meetings, the two antagonists agreed to create a new partnership agreement and develop a buy-sell agreement were one of them to die. Once this agreement was made, the OD consultant contacted the family's attorney, whose role it was to work through the legal issues related to the agreement and put the agreement into a legal document. Without this collaboration between the OD consultant and the attorney, an effective change would not have taken place.

This example of conflict between a brother and his sister-in-law highlights another unique feature of consulting with family business—the issue of *emotion*. While emotions influence individuals in all workplaces, family businesses are particularly emotionally charged. Clients may become angry, scream, cry, and express feelings denoting depression. Entrepreneurs, who often lead family businesses, are noted for being rather volatile and can prove difficult to work with. Changes in a family firm often shake up previously established patterns of behavior, causing emotions to rise to the surface as power, prestige, role definitions, and self-esteem are altered during a consultation. Thus, consultants to family firms, who work with the owners and the family as well as the business, must be prepared to help their clients work through the emotions they experience as they make changes to improve the health of both the families and their businesses. Professionals who consult to the business only, and not other systems (that is, family and ownership), are not working as family business consultants.

Given the importance of having both content and process knowledge, along with the ability to deal with emotions in helping family businesses, one of the arguments of this book is that consultants from various disciplines should work together to help family businesses. Regardless of the consultant's profession, we believe that the action research framework from the field of organization development provides the best approach to help family firms manage the difficult changes they need to make. And armed with content knowledge from the needed disciplines, the consultant (or consulting team) can apply that knowledge to help leaders of family firms understand their options and move forward to make those technical or content changes that are needed.

Through the theories, models, and change strategies presented in this book, we hope that consultants from various disciplines will develop a common frame of reference and a common language with which to collaborate and learn from one another as they work with family firms. Without the development of such a common paradigm for working with family firms, consultants will likely be frustrated in their efforts to help these firms, and their family firm clients will not be well-served.

The Development of the Field

Interest in family business consulting has grown significantly in the last decade. It has become a "hot," if relatively young, field with an influx of professionals from the disciplines of mental health, law, finance, accounting, management, and organization development. Research regarding family businesses has also been accelerating. In describing the brief history of family business consulting as a profession, Kelin Gersick (1994), past editor of the *Family Business Review,* wrote that the earliest information on the subject dates to "occasional articles or lectures that grew out of the idiosyncratic interests of individuals in the 1950s and 1960s." The 1970s saw an occasional article on the topic, which often focused on wealth transfer or such problems as family conflicts or nepotism. As interest in helping family businesses continued to grow, the field of family business was finally born in the early 1980s.

In the 1980s, professionals and academics began to identify with the "family business field" and began to identify themselves as "family business consultants" or else defined themselves as professionals in a particular discipline with family business as their specialty. Family business advisors seem to take varied paths into family business consulting. Some "back into it," noted the late Richard Beckhard: "One of my first clients back in the 1950s was a small family-owned corporation. I found that as I worked with the firm over the years I became involved with the family—its ownership and its role in the firm" (Lansberg, 1983, p. 29). Recently, however, family business consultants have taken a more deliberate route into the field. Accountants and attorneys often find that most of their clients are family businesses. More and more therapists, either through frustration with managed care or a desire for new challenges, are expanding their practices to larger systems and are discovering family business consulting. Management and organization development consultants are attracted to the challenge of consulting in these complex systems. Thus, family business consulting began as an interdisciplinary field.

The consultant to family firms will find out very quickly that family firms are not just small businesses or a small minority of organizations worldwide. Recent statistics on family firms have noted:

- Over 90 percent of the businesses in North America and the majority of businesses worldwide are family-owned;

- Nearly 35 percent of all Fortune 500 firms are family firms; and

- Family businesses in the United States account for 78 percent of all new job creation, 60 percent of the nation's employment, and 50 percent of the gross domestic product. (Source: ffi.org/looking/facts.html)

Despite the dominance of family firms in the world economy, journalists, such as Thomas Petzinger, have noted that since the industrial era a stigma has been attached to family businesses because of the perception that family businesses are unbusinesslike and irrational. However, Petzinger, in *The New Pioneers*, notes that perceptions are starting to change: "What's important to understand is that the family business has become a model for all business. The reason is that business, today more than at any time in a century or longer, is built on relationships—the very stuff of which families too are made" (1999, pp. 216–217). And Alvin Toffler predicts in *Powershift* that, "Wherever family relationships play a part in business, bureaucratic values and rules are subverted, and with them the power structure of the bureaucracy as well. This is important, because today's resurgence of family business is not just a passing phenomenon. We are entering a 'post-bureaucratic' era, in which the family firm is only one of the many alternatives to bureaucracy" (1990, p. 178).

Despite this "rise of the family firm," there are clearly problems for these organizations on the horizon. For example:

- They have a striking failure rate: approximately 30 percent survive into the second generation and only 12 percent to the third generation;

- In the next five years, 39 percent of family firms in the United States will experience some change in leadership, and over the next twenty years, $4.8 trillion will be transferred from one generation to the next in the largest intergenerational transfer of wealth in U.S. history; and

- Twenty-five percent of senior family business shareholders have not completed any estate planning other than writing a will; 81 percent want the business to stay in the family but 20 percent are not confident that the next generation is committed to the business. (Source: ffi.org/looking/fbfacts_us.html)

These problems suggest that there is much work to do to help family businesses succeed in the future.

In addition to meeting the needs of like-minded professionals who were working with family businesses, the founding of the Family Firm Institute in the United States in 1986 and of the Family Business Network in Europe in 1990 was, in many ways, a response to the challenges facing family firms. These organizations have been instrumental to the development of the field. Their membership includes academics and consultants and family businesses, and they have helped to define the "state-of-the-art" practice in the field. Since their founding, the study of family businesses and the practice of consulting to family firms have attracted professionals from many fields. There are now approximately 1,100 family business consultants around the world, and there are more than 150 family business forums, providing continuing education for family businesses. (Source: ffi.org/looking/fbfacts_us.html)

The need for more information regarding family businesses is critical given the dynamic nature of these enterprises. For example, Sharon Nelton (1995) in *Nation's Business,* notes that over the past decade family businesses:

- Have become more knowledgeable about what it takes to be successful;
- Are more likely to identify themselves as a family business;
- Are run or know they should be run more professionally;
- Are increasingly run by women;
- Are more global in their outlook and are gaining political clout; and
- Are reflecting the changing definitions of the family.

Because of these changes, we have seen a surge of interest in studying and helping family business by academics and consultants.

Consulting at the Boundaries:
The Role of the Family Business Consultant

Different types of consultants work in the three systems of family firms—often as if the systems were separate and distinct from one another. Figure 1.2 illustrates where these consultants often do their work.

Figure 1.2. Role of the Family Business Consultant

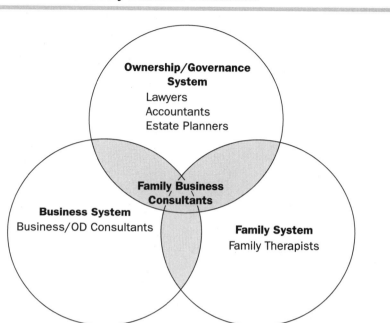

As Figure 1.2 suggests, business consultants in areas such as strategic planning, marketing, and operations only attempt to improve the functioning of the business system. Organization development consultants also find their work largely within the business system. Lawyers, accountants, and estate planners often find themselves concerned only about how the firm is owned and governed. Family therapists, on the other hand, are primarily concerned about the health of the family. They typically want to improve relationships in the family and the functioning of individual family members.

What distinguishes family business consultants from these other consultants who work within only one system is that family business consultants work at the boundaries where there are overlaps between these systems. For example, family business consultants may help a family that is in conflict because family members can't decide whether they should treat one another as family members or as employees. They may engage in succession planning with the client to ensure that the needs of the family, the business, and the shareholders are taken into account. They may also work with a family to ensure that the family is properly represented on the board of directors and to monitor the effectiveness of that board.

To illustrate why the family business consultant must have a systems perspective to advise family business leaders effectively, we will turn to the case of Georgia and John White (names disguised) (Dyer, 1992). John and Georgia had created a very successful retail business that was growing rapidly and was worth several million dollars. John and Georgia traveled frequently in their private plane and were worried about what might happen to their business were they to die in a plane crash. They contacted a CPA firm that advised them that they should transfer 49 percent of the firm's shares to their children so that inheritance taxes would be avoided should they die. So each of their five children—most of them teenagers—received one-fifth share of 49 percent of a multi-million-dollar business. Of course, John and Georgia believed that they wouldn't die in an accident and that their children would not receive any of their inheritance until they were much older. Unfortunately, neither the Whites nor the CPAs took into account the volatility of the firm's industry or the maturity level of the White's children. Due to unforeseen economic reverses, the Whites were forced to sell their business, and their children, who now owned almost half the company, became millionaires overnight. Georgia White commented on how this affected her family:

"The number one change that we would make today, had we known that we were going to sell the company, would be to not give our children 49 percent of our business in stock. Our children would have to earn their own money, get an education, go into careers of their own choice, buy their first homes, struggle to buy their furniture, have direction, and accomplish goals. To actually know the thrill of what it is to achieve success on their own. We feel that this is an area that we as their parents totally lost control of and that we have done a big disservice to our children, and it is a big concern to us. Of course, they would be shocked at hearing me say this. They are thrilled to have this wonderful opportunity to have new houses, to go golfing every day, to be able to do whatever they want. But they received too much money too soon, and it could really be a curse to them in the future. [That's] the biggest worry that John and I have. They will never know or understand the true value of achievement." (Dyer, 1992, pp. 199, 200)

The case of the White family illustrates what can happen when a consultant sees only one system. The CPAs' goal in advising the Whites was to reduce their tax burden. They didn't examine the possibility that the firm might need to be sold given the conditions of the market, nor did they think through the impact on the children of receiving a windfall inheritance. Thus, the Whites were poorly served and now must contemplate the "What if?'s."

In the next chapter we will explore the characteristics of "healthy" and "unhealthy" family businesses to provide the consultant with a framework for assessing the effectiveness of the family businesses he or she is attempting to help.

2

Characteristics of "Healthy" Family Businesses

BECAUSE THEY ARE COMPLEX SYSTEMS and the consultant is working inside the boundaries, consulting to family businesses requires a unique understanding of these enterprises. Acknowledging the complexities of family businesses, Sal Minuchin, family therapist and consultant, in an interview in *Family Business Review*, describes family businesses as "like Russian novels—there are many subplots that make up the story, and they are all being played out simultaneously" (Lansberg, 1992, p. 312). The challenge is to appreciate these subplots and manage our own reactions to them. To reduce them to the simple story lines of a sit-com will greatly limit our ability to create and manage collaboratively the changes in these often Shakespearean-like dramas. Even now, as family businesses are advertising themselves proudly as family-owned businesses, they are understandably wary if they think that their needs are not fully appreciated or understood.

In this chapter, we will more fully explore the dynamics of family businesses by describing the strengths and weaknesses of family enterprises. In particular, we'll describe the characteristics of "healthy" and "unhealthy" family businesses. For consultants to begin to help family firms, they need to develop a normative framework of system-wide health in order to compare their client's condition with that of a healthy organization.

Healthy Family Businesses

To understand how best to advise family businesses, it is essential to understand what a healthy and successful family business looks like. Lansberg (1999), in *Succeeding Generations*, defines success as "Having fun making money together." A healthy business family is not tied up in knots with tension; the individuals have trust in each other and the future and are able to make use of each other's abilities and knowledge.

The following list includes attributes of a healthy family business system:

Functioning of the Family

- Individuals can manage themselves and relationships with others;
- Family has the ability to resolve conflicts with mutual support and trust;
- Boundaries between work and family are appropriate and respected;
- Knowledge is used wisely and isn't blocked by unresolved relationship problems;
- Communications are open and clear;
- Individuals are flexible and able to use advisors wisely;
- Family has the ability to make decisions and move forward;
- Family is clear about goals and navigates toward the goals;
- Family has good direction and leadership;
- Transitions are managed and marked by rituals; and
- Intergenerational boundaries are appropriate and respected.

Management of the Business

- Knowledge is developed and mobilized as collective intelligence;
- Organization and its members make use of knowledge to adapt to changing environment and produce a sustainable, competitive advantage for the business;

- Decision making is based on knowledge and expertise;
- Organizational learning develops new competencies and effective behaviors;
- Responsibility and authority are balanced;
- Leadership is spread throughout the company/family; and
- Succession is planned early.

Development of the Governance and Ownership System

- The mission and goals are clear;
- There is a functional board of directors with outsiders on it; and
- There is a sound plan for succession and transfer of ownership over the generations.

Effectiveness of the Boundaries Between the Family Business Systems

- Business uses family values in strategic planning;
- Boundaries are porous and allow appropriate exchange of information between systems;
- Each system uses goals and values to steer the course;
- Business issues are not acted out in the family and vice versa;
- Mutual learning exists between the systems (family's learning flows to the business and vice versa) and is put into action; and
- Individuals understand core competencies of one another and of the company.

An example of a healthy family business would be the Williams family. This family business is run by three sisters and led by the mother, who is chair of the board. The family members love and respect one another. They have grown up in the family business and each understands the others' roles. They communicate on a regular basis and, although they may have disagreements at work, such conflicts do not spill over into their family lives. Thus, they enjoy family reunions and vacations together on a regular basis. The business has been growing, and the sisters meet regularly to assess the performance of the business and to solve problems. They have brought in expertise from outside the family—particularly in the field of finance—to help run the business. They also have a functioning board that includes some nonfamily members who have specific expertise to help provide direction for the firm's senior managers. Family values are communicated between family members and shared with nonfamily employees. In many ways, the firm has become an extension of the family's values. The family has also taken steps to protect itself against unanticipated events, such as a death or the disability of a key family member, and they have developed a process that will help them plan for leadership succession in the future. Family members often express the pride they feel in being part of a family business as well as the satisfaction and joy of working with other members of the family.

Unhealthy Family Enterprises

In contrast to the Williams family, the Davis family has a different story. The founder, Jim Davis, described his situation to a family business consultant this way: "I have had my son working for me in the family business for some time. Recently, I felt that he was behaving unethically so I fired him. My wife was so upset with me that she kicked me out of the house. Now, I have to sleep on the sofa at my office. Furthermore, my business hasn't grown over the years, and I feel overwhelmed at times with the amount of work I have to do. I don't have a board of directors or someone else to turn to for help. What should I do?" Jim's description of his family business highlights some of the key features of those family businesses that are not healthy. These unhealthy conditions can be summarized as follows:

- The family has poor communications skills and is unable to manage conflict;
- There is low trust between family members;
- The goals and values of the family are unclear;
- Family members' roles and obligations are unclear;
- The business lacks a sense of direction and does no strategic planning;
- The business lacks sufficient expertise—the family tries to do it all;
- There is little thought to succession planning;
- There is little collaboration between the family and nonfamily employees;
- There is not a functioning board of directors;
- There is no one to turn to for advice and help with key problems;
- Family issues spill over into business issues (and vice versa); and
- Boundaries between work and family are unclear.

These are a few of the key warnings signs that the family business may be in serious trouble. In Chapter 3 we will explore in greater detail how to diagnose the health of a family business.

Strengths and Weaknesses

While it is helpful to understand the conditions that lead to healthy and unhealthy family businesses, most family businesses cannot be classified either as completely healthy or unhealthy; each has certain strengths and weaknesses. Indeed, the uniqueness of family businesses is best understood by examining their strengths and weaknesses, often different sides of the same coin. Whether a particular dimension of a family business is a strength or a weakness depends on three factors: (1) the degree to which the boundaries between the family and the business are managed; (2) the health of each system; and (3) the degree to which adaptability and learning are inhibited or encouraged in the boundary interface. The dimensions of a family business and the strengths and weaknesses associated with them are found in Table 2.1.

Table 2.1. Strengths and Weaknesses of Family Firms

Dimension	Strength	Weakness
Infrastructure	Informal; flexible; entrepreneurial; innovative	Unclear; confusing; boundary problems; indecisive; resistant to change; lack of management development; no organization charts
Roles	Often play multiple roles; flexible; dual relationships; quick decision making	Role confusion; jobs aren't done; nepotism; dual roles interfere with learning and objectivity; family birthright can lead to unqualified family members in jobs
Leadership	Creative; ambitious; informal authority; entrepreneurial	Autocratic; resistant to structure and systems; avoids letting go

Table 2.1. Strengths and Weaknesses of Family Firms, Cont'd

Dimension	Strength	Weakness
Family's Involvement	Employees committed; loyal; shared values and belief system; family spirit; family name; family dream; strong sense of mission/vision	Can't keep family issues out of business; inability to balance family's and business's need for liquidity; lack of objectivity; inward looking; emotionally charged decision making; can't separate work and family; rivalries
Time	Long-term perspective; committed; patient capital; loyalty; deeper ties; trust built up over time	Hard to change; tradition bound; history of family affects business decisions; trust affected by early disappointments
Succession	Training can begin early; mentoring a life-long process; can choose when to leave	Family issues get in way; unwillingness to let go; inability to choose a successor
Ownership/Governance	Closely held; family owned; high degree of control; earnings are motivators	May sacrifice growth for control; do not have to answer to stockholders; often no outside board of directors; high premium on privacy
Culture	Innovative; informal; flexible; creative; adaptable; common language; efficient communications	Founder's role stifles innovation; inefficient; highly emotional; resistant to change; reactive; high risk for conflicts
Complexity	Can foster creativity; rich interplay of roles and goals	Must be managed to avoid confusion; can be a drain of resources and energy

We'll now discuss each of these dimensions listed in the table in turn.

Infrastructure. The *infrastructure* of family businesses is often casual and face-to-face and may even include "pillow talk"! This creates an atmosphere of informality and high contact which, when managed, can foster creativity and innovation. The weakness is that roles are often unclear and there may be duplication of work and conflicts about who does what. Casual may become careless. Career paths may be unclear. Whether it comes from a dislike of bureaucracy or a lack of knowledge about formal operating systems, the resulting informality can exacerbate family conflict, interfere with efficiency, and encourage a crisis-based, reactive approach to the world.

Roles. Family members play at least four *roles.* There are the family and business roles, and for each of these there are task and emotional roles. Task roles are the jobs assigned; emotional roles are those usually taken up by the personalities of the people. One may be the peacemaker, one the comedian, one the pessimist, and one the optimist. Birth order may also influence the roles one takes and plays (Forer, 1977; Leman, 1992; Toman, 1976). Additionally, family members are often willing to do whatever is necessary for the success of the company. It is not unusual, especially in a young, small company, to find the owner making sales calls, running errands, and trying to obtain funding. This is also expected of other family members and employees. Role conflict can be detrimental when family roles are confused with work roles. Sibling issues can fester in the family and explode in the boardroom or in the management team meetings. Stew Leonard, who once called a son who wasn't performing well into his office, gives an example of balancing multiple roles. He pointed to two hats on his desk—one with "boss" written on it and the other with "dad." Stew put on the "boss" hat and said, "I've given you plenty of warning about your poor performance, and you haven't improved. You're fired!" Then, he put on the "dad" hat and said, "Son, I heard you've just been fired. What can I do to help?" (Davis, 1990).

Leadership. *Leadership* in a first-generation family business is the entrepreneurial founder who often leads informally and resists structures and systems. Schein (1983) describes entrepreneurs as being intuitive, impatient, and easily bored. Such a leader tends to discourage independence in the next generation, even though their success depends largely on training, mentoring by the first generation, and the effectiveness of the succession plan. Usually, in later generations, leadership evolves into a more professional, managerial-like style or even sibling teams or cousin consortiums (see Lansberg, 1999). Although the rewards for effective sibling teams can be high, the work to get there is daunting. As one client who was trying to work with her siblings asked, "How are we ever going to work this all out? We're all trying hard, but I think it was much easier when father was the only boss. He didn't have to share responsibility and check in with three others!"

Family's Involvement. The role of the *family* provides a critical dimension. Unlike nonfamily firms that usually discourage family involvement and have policies against nepotism, the family in the family business plays an integral role. Family members care about the family name in the community and the industry; they share values and a belief system, defining who they are, who they want to be, and what kind of legacy and business they want to leave. This commitment is not without its price, however. Sometimes family members work long hours for low pay. Resentment can build; perceived inequities by the second generation may create rivalries. Too much togetherness has often been the cause of conflict and of failure of the family to see the bigger picture and to recognize changes in the environment. This is especially true in family businesses, as they tend to be more closed systems, less willing to look outside for help or even to see the larger economic environment. For example, in the film, *Substance of Fire*, often used in teaching about family businesses, the father refuses to listen to his children, who warn him that his present project is too expensive and will ruin the company. He wants to stick to the old ways and vision and denies that his project will bankrupt the company. He sees his children's opposition as treacherous and, in doing so, brings near ruin to the company and the family. (This film is available for rental at most video stores.)

Time. *Time* has several dimensions: the history of the family; dreams and plans for the future; and the present situation. Often family businesses' informality promotes quicker adaptations to market conditions. Although the business may be young, the family has had a much longer history together, which adds a long-term perspective and the individuals' loyalty to one another and their dreams for the business. Moreover, family owners may be willing to forego short-run financial returns in order to encourage the future growth and stability of the business. However, the traditions of the family may or may not be appropriate for the business. The family history also adds an emotional level that can affect major decisions and roles that individuals play in the business. Time as a metaphor is useful in family retreats for honoring the past and building on the present to create the future.

Succession. Poor *succession planning* is one of the major reasons cited for the high mortality rates of family businesses. Strikingly, CEOs of family businesses typically serve six times longer than their counterparts in public companies (Cliffe, 1998). A long CEO tenure enables informal succession planning to begin years before the formal process. The downside is that succession is a voluntary act that requires a letting go by the founder, the courage to choose the right successor or successors, and support from the family of the succession process. Despite some evidence that family businesses are becoming more financially sophisticated, according to Ross Nager, director of the research project of the Arthur Andersen Center for Family Business, CEOs have not improved their willingness to engage in succession and strategic planning (Cliffe, 1998). An interesting discovery by Collins and Porras, in their classic study of the habits of visionary companies, *Built to Last,* is that "Home-grown management rules at the visionary companies to a far greater degree than at the comparison companies. Time and again, they have dashed to bits the conventional wisdom that significant change and fresh ideas cannot come from insiders" (1997, p. 10). The potential for developing fresh leaders within the family business exists when doing succession planning.

Ownership/Governance. Since early-stage family businesses are usually closely held and *privately owned,* the owners have total control over their companies. The *governance* structure is based on the founder's decisions and dependent on his or her ability to lead and his or her style of leadership. John Ward (1997) notes that resistance to an outside board may be based on fear of the unknown, fear of losing control, a bureaucratic encumbrance, or too much work. However, research has shown that boards with outside advisors are critical to the long-term success of a growing family business.

Culture. An organization's *culture,* its personality, is complex and of several levels. Schein (1983) explains that the family business embodies the founder's values, style, and spirit in the early stages. It is often creative, informal, and capricious. But it can also reflect the dysfunctional aspects of the founder's personality as well. Often, communication is based on mutual understanding, and members see no need for employee handbooks or operating manuals. The knowledge remains below the water line, rarely questioned or evaluated

Complexity. The level of *complexity* in a family business can be both a liability and an asset. On the one hand, it can lead to a rich interplay of goals and roles, both business and family. On the other hand, it provides the ingredients for a clashing of business and family values. The management of many feedback loops and much complexity can lead to growth, or it can produce stagnation by checking the family business system's ability to learn and adapt. Family functioning and business organization deeply affect each other. In an interesting study in *Family Business Review*, Danes, Zuiker, Kean, and Arbuthnot (1999) found that the level of tension between firm and family affects their success in achieving business goals. However, the overlap of roles, relationships, ownership, management, and family subsystems, and the increased emotionality does not necessarily lead to an increased level of dysfunction. The key is the family business system's ability to manage the tension and to be open to adjacent possibilities (Sherman & Schultz, 1998) and available opportunities. In order to accomplish this, the family and business must be able to function efficiently and effectively together.

This discussion of the relative strengths and weakness of family firms should begin to sensitize the consultant to the issues that often arise in the attempt to ascertain the health of a family firm. Now we will turn our attention to the process of consulting with family firms.

Part 2
Consulting to Family Businesses

③

Contracting
and Assessment

AT AGE SEVENTY-FIVE, Mort Thomas has worked in the jewelry business for almost fifty years. He first worked with his uncle, and then opened his own store forty-five years ago. Over the years, the business has grown and Mort now owns a total of eight stores with total annual sales of approximately $12 million. Mort's wife, Shirley, died six years ago after battling cancer for two years. Mort was considering "cutting back" when Shirley became ill. He was devastated by her death and changed his mind about retiring. He was left wondering, "What should I do with all this time on my hands?" He and Shirley had planned to move to the Southwest, where they owned a condominium and where their oldest daughter, Harriet, age fifty, lives with her husband and three children.

The two younger children, Mark, forty-eight, and Steve, forty-four, are in the business. Mark is the general manager and Steve is in charge of marketing and sales. Mort is president and owns all the equity in the company. Although he has told everyone that Mark will succeed him as president, he has not done any formal succession or estate planning. The brothers argue constantly in the office. They each report every argument to Mort, who tries to resolve their disagreements, usually without success. Mort says that the current conflicts are "killing him" and that he can't even think about succession planning until his sons begin to act more "like adults" and get along better. The nonfamily employees are often dragged into the siblings' battles and report that morale is at an all-time low.

Mort comes to the office every day, even though he no longer has any formal duties. Mark notes that Mort is "driving me nuts" because he still wants to be involved in day-to-day operations. In spite of all this, the business continues to expand and be profitable, providing a good living for Mort and his two sons. But the family issues are beginning to spill over into the business. The manager of one of the stores, Tom, who has been with the company for fifteen years, is now threatening to leave. The HR director has tried to get the brothers to hold executive management meetings, but each one ends in an argument. Mort has little in savings or retirement; his assets are all in the business. His attorney, David, has worked with him for thirty years and has given up trying to convince him to create an estate plan. Over the years, Mort has made secret deals with his kids, lending them money as they ask. He says he just "can't say no." One of Mort's friends, also in the jewelry business, had heard Jane speak at an estate-planning meeting. He knew about Mort's problems and had given Mort Jane's number. The request for consultation came from Mort just after Mark asked for a $21,000 loan.

This case is typical of a family business referral. The issues presented are complicated and raise the following questions for the consultant:

- Can I handle this alone? If not, who else needs to be on the team?
- Where do I start?
- Who is the client? Do I begin with the family? Do I begin with the business?
- How do I help them work through these conflicts?

The Consulting Process

There is no single map for consulting to family businesses, but one approach that we use is a modification of the *action research* method of assessment and change commonly used in organization development. Because these steps are iterative, we've outlined them in a circular fashion in Figure 3.1.

Figure 3.1. The Consulting Process

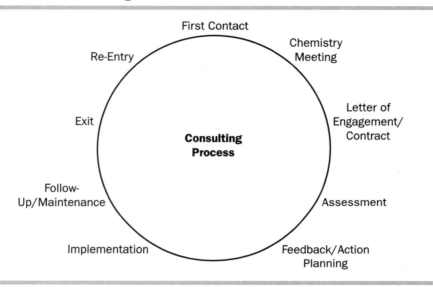

In this chapter we will discuss the first four phases of the consultation process: (1) first contact, (2) the chemistry meeting, (3) contracting, and (4) the assessment. (Note, however, that the change process does not usually happen in a linear manner. It is necessary, however, to understand the fundamentals to be prepared for surprises, emerging events, and, seemingly, random events.) In Table 3.1, we have outlined the goals, questions, outcomes, and risks associated with each of these steps in the consulting process.

First Contact

The first contact for help usually comes to us over the telephone. Typically, the persons requesting help have either attended a seminar taught by the consultant, read something written by the consultant, heard about the consultant from an acquaintance, or been referred by another consultant. In this initial conversation with a prospective client, there are several questions that need to be answered:

1. Who is calling? What is his or her role?
2. Who/what is the source of the referral? Does the source of the referral affect how you might work with the client?

Table 3.1. The First Four Phases of the Consulting Process

Phase	Goal	Questions	Desired Outcomes	Risks
First Contact	To assess the motivation for change and to understand the major players	Who owns the problem? Who has leverage? What is the referral source? How have you been introduced? What has just happened to prompt this call?	Appointment for chemistry meeting	Underestimating the complexity; overestimating your abilities
Chemistry Meeting	To assess whether the issues and personalities are a good match. Construct a rough genogram with the family	What is the problem? How do they describe it? How do others see it? What are the goals/desired outcomes? What resources are the family business willing to invest in the change process? What expectations do they have about you and your work? Where is the energy for change?	Agreement to work together; transition from referral to engagement; beginning to build trust	Rushing to judgment; not getting enough information needed to contract; not stating your own biases (such as democratic participation, fairness, open communication, importance of conflict)
Contract	To write a contract that defines the scope, time frame, products of the work, and expectations of client and consultant	What is the mutually agreed on work? How will fees be charged? What is the scope of the work?	Signed contract	Underestimating the work, time, and fees; too narrow a focus
Assessment	Complete picture of business, governance, and family; understanding of the presenting and real problem; broaden the perspective; provide map for change process	What is the family's vision? What are the presenting themes? Where's the energy (positive and negative)? What is the real problem? How well can they manage/handle/use the data (meta-assessment)? What is the work to be done and what will get in the way?	Understanding of the problem and suggestions for interventions	Having preconceived ideas about the problem; not getting information about the whole system; not seeing technical solutions; not appreciating multiple realities; inability to take systems perspective; having too narrow a focus

3. What is the request? What is the problem?

4. What types of consulting skills are required? Is the caller asking for technical advice (information) or process guidance (teaching processes and procedures)?

5. What does the family "look like" (basic family structure and relationships)?

Finally, it's important to remember the adage: "Clients call not to change but as a result of change." Potential clients call because they've experienced some change in their lives that has motivated them to call a consultant. Most of the clients are experiencing rather significant pain related to recent events that have influenced them to come for help. Thus, it is important in the initial contact to ascertain the source of that pain. In our experience, the most frequent requests for help by family businesses fall into the following categories (Habbershon & Astrachan, 1997):

- Family conflict;
- Lack of clarity about goals and values;
- Family communication and behavioral problems; and
- Succession problems.

The first contact with Mort was a phone call just following another heated argument between the brothers. He said that he had obtained Jane's name from a friend of his. He wanted help "stopping the fighting between Mark and Steve and getting them to show me some respect." He did not have a succession or estate plan, nor were there clear delineations in the job descriptions of Mark, the heir apparent, and Mort. He said that those problems could easily be solved "if the fighting would stop." Jane explained that she would like to come in and meet with Mort, Mark, Steve, and Harriet in order to see as complete a picture as possible. She also described the consulting process, and a family meeting was arranged. However, if Jane hadn't had the requisite knowledge or expertise to help Mort and his family deal with the problems they were facing or felt that Mort's goals were inappropriate, she would either have told Mort to find another consultant or referred him to someone whose expertise was consistent with the help that they needed. Some of the best decisions we have made as consultants have been to turn down potential clients or refer them to someone else when we don't feel qualified or comfortable with the problems that they want to address.

Chemistry Meeting

After the initial contact with the client, a meeting is set up to discuss the issues facing the client in more detail. In some cases, it is possible that several individuals in the family firm may be invited to this meeting to clarify the problems and identify the "client." The goal of this phase of the engagement is first *to define the client*. This is not as easy as it seems, since each professional may define the client differently. As the family business consulting evolves, there is a growing appreciation that the family business is best served by the consultant who defines the *family business system* as the client. Many therapists who consult to family businesses, however, define their work as consulting to *families in business together*. The legal profession has clear guidelines on the definition of the client, but these are being challenged by the needs of family business systems. In the past, much time at conferences and seminars has been spent on the questions: "Who is the client? Is it the family? Is it the business? Is it the owner?" We think that it is the family business system. For each consulting assignment, however, this needs to be thought through carefully, for defining the client affects our effectiveness and our work. After the client is identified, the next goals are to negotiate the scope of the work, clarify expectations of the client and the consultant, raise concerns about the change process and resistance, come to an agreement, clarify the consultant's role, and define the product that the consultant will deliver.

In this initial meeting, it is important to establish an atmosphere of trust and safety to lower the defensiveness that is often present. The unconscious processes and issues—the topics that remain "under the table"—will only surface in an atmosphere of trust. In the case of the Thomas family, these issues were (1) Mark's gambling, a habit that was revealed during the chemistry meeting and that Mort had been supporting with previous loans; (2) a growing frustration among the senior employees, who felt that the family was creating a "hostile environment" at work; and (3) Harriet's anger and fear that her father and brothers would destroy the business. Unless we raised these issues to a level of consciousness to be examined, they would remain hidden and unresolved. Defensiveness in the form of denial, avoidance, repression, displacement, scapegoating, and projection all serve to help clients avoid the real issues. Trust reduces defensiveness, and thus gaining the trust of the client is crucial at the first meeting. The consultant begins to create an environment of trust and safety by (1) establishing ground rules of confidentiality ("What we say here stays here, unless otherwise agreed on"); (2) defining rules of behavior ("Everyone gets a chance to speak"); (3) building a collaborative process ("We'll work on this together"); and (4) directing energies at the problem, not at one another ("I need to know about the problems, and then we will begin to focus on solutions"). By doing these things, the consultant begins to create an environment for the family to communicate in new ways—more openly and more effectively.

Because the consultant often opens the "hermetic seal" (Jonovic, 1984) that has kept problems from being discussed and has also served to keep these problems resistant to outside influences or help, this forum creates an opportunity not only for the beginning of the resolution of old family conflicts but also for gaining updated perceptions of each family member and his or her family. We should always be aware of our impact on the system. In fact, it is not unusual to see shifts (toward either health or dysfunction) in a family business as we start a consultation.

In the chemistry meeting, the consultant, as change agent, should describe the roles she/he plays in the change process. These roles include the following:

Coach. As coach, the consultant works with individuals to teach new ways of communicating, setting personal and career goals, and determining whether these goals are compatible with the goals of the family business. A coach may also provide leadership training and assist with problematic relationships, keeping boundaries between family and business clear. Coaching also involves referrals to other professionals, such as a therapist, career counselor, or financial advisor.

Conflict Manager. In this role, the consultant works with members of smaller groups in the family or business who have the most difficulty working together or who are trapped in a conflict that blocks the work. This effort will include dialogue building, conflict resolution, and improving communications.

"Container" or Holding Environment. Introduced by Winnicott (1987), who studied the nature of the mother-child bond, the "holding environment" provides a balance of safety and challenge, of protection and vulnerability for the infant. Eventually, the child internalizes these elements and develops a robust sense of self. Key to healthy development, with the ability to grow, learn, work, and love, is the quality of the holding environment. To provide this, the consultant must be able to tolerate ambiguity and anxiety while the system changes.

Transitional Object for Change. This role is similar to that of "container" and requires that the consultant be able to stay calm and manage his or her own feelings during the change process while encouraging the client and being available for support and encouragement. This role requires an ability to differentiate between normal anxiety associated with change and signs of pathological reactions. For example, if during the succession process the founder's anxiety increases, that's normal. If, however, during this process there are clear signs that the succeeding generation is unable to take over, or the founder continues to sabotage the process by staying actively involved in work, the consultant must be more than a transitional object, but must take an active role in helping the family business to find solutions. For example, he or she might assess whether the successors are capable of taking over and willing to do so, or he or she might help the owner to let go and move on.

Teacher. The family business consultant teaches throughout the process. We find that, at the first meeting, a short teaching module on the uniqueness of a family business and some of the statistics of success and failure help to normalize the situation and help the family see that they are not as unusual as they fear. The three-system model (Figure 1.1) is useful to help families see the complexity of their situation. We will often have each family member put an X on the circle or circles that best describes his or her role or roles. Teaching and education are integral parts of the entire consultation, from issues of healthy communication, fair compensation, and how to run a family council meeting to setting up a board of advisors or addressing the needs and concerns of nonfamily business managers.

Asking the Hard Questions. Early on in the consultation, it is important to establish your role as the one who asks the tough questions ("Why does Mark think he can get $21,000 just for the asking?" "What does Harriet think of how her brothers and father are behaving in the business?" "Is anyone worried that the employees will leave?" "Who was aware of Mark's gambling?"). Introducing this concept in the beginning is critical; the family is warned that it is part of your job.

As soon as work starts with the client and the consultant has established trust and a set of ground rules for interaction between family members, the consultant continues to help the client by the following means:

1. *Clarifying Communications.* For example, each person speaks for himself or herself and differentiates among "what you think, what you feel, and what you know for a fact." The consultant may initially repeat what he or she has heard each individual say.

2. *Encouraging a Positive Problem-Solving Approach.* For example, if there is a disagreement, we will agree to solve it by this method (which could be voting, consensus, whoever is most affected decides, or other ways);

3. *Challenging the Family's Way of Seeing the Problems and Proposing Solutions.* These solutions might include holding regular family council meetings or executive management meetings, learning how to conduct effective meetings, and making fair decisions. If we take care of the process and the procedures in the family's interactions, we hope they will begin to solve their own problems and create structures. Then we build and enforce structures and mechanisms in each of the systems—family, ownership, and business—to generate healthier interactions, enforce healthy boundaries, and offer methods and mechanisms for planning, solving problems, and managing conflict. Structures are an integral part of the consultation process. For example, if a conflict begins in a meeting, we will already have instituted a mechanism for dealing with it so that it can be managed and not divert people's attention from the agenda. These mechanisms may include an "offline" conflict coaching session with the consultant, a fishbowl dialogue during the meeting (with coaching from the consultant), or stopping the conflict with a "Deal with that outside the meeting" admonition. In the ownership system, the structures may include an outside board of directors; in the business system, performance reviews for family members and fair compensation mechanisms are other examples. The assessment will determine what structures are needed.

The two-hour chemistry meeting with the Thomases included Mort, Mark, Steve, and Harriet. The agenda was as follows:

- Introductions and Ground Rules
- Three Systems Model
- Description of the Problem
- Description of the Consultation Process
- Goals
- Next Steps

During and after the chemistry meeting, the consultant should answer the following questions:

- Who is the client?

- Are you and the client a good fit? Do your skills fit the client's needs? Do you need to add additional members to your team?

- Do you like the family and its members?

- How do they define their issues?

- Is there enough energy/commitment for change? Where is the energy for change?

- Who has the most authority, formal power, and informal power?

- Are they willing to commit resources (time, money, personnel) to the change process?

- How should you create a sense of safety (for example, "You are to be commended for seeking help for this") or urgency ("If you don't deal with this, it will get much worse")?

- Will the client understand the collaborative nature of consultation? Clients must realize that their participation is an integral part of the consulting process.

If, after answering these questions, you find that you and the client are a good "fit," you then move to the next stage and write the proposal/engagement letter. If you have trouble answering these questions, you may need to gather more data or even meet again with the client to better understand his or her needs, issues, and orientation to a consulting engagement. If you find there is a poor fit between you and the potential client, either decline the engagement or refer the client to a more appropriate consultant.

Proposal/Engagement Letter/Contract

The proposal/engagement letter is designed to clarify the relationship and nature of the contract between the consultant and the client. This letter forces the consultant to identify the client, which is often difficult for attorneys and family therapists, who may need to identify a single individual as the client, even though they are working for the benefit of the entire family system. The letter should outline the work to be performed and the expectations that the consultant has for the client. The time, money, and effort to be expended are described, along with the method of payment to the consultant. Finally, the letter should describe who would serve as the liaison (administrative, scheduling, meeting preparations, and so forth) between the client and the consultant. Exhibit 3.1 shows a typical proposal/engagement letter.

Exhibit 3.1. Sample Engagement Letter

October 4, 2002

Dear Mort,

It was a pleasure meeting with you, Harriet, Mark, and Steve. This letter outlines my understanding of your needs and a proposal for work on the areas that you wish to address in your family business. I found the meeting challenging. Having had an opportunity to reflect on it, I would like to outline a plan tailored to your needs. The purpose of the proposed scope of the consultation process is to guide your family's decision making and strategic planning regarding the future of the family and the business. When providing services described in this proposal, my client is the family business system. This allows me to work in the interests of the business *and* of the family that owns the business.

The Context

You began Sparkle Jewelry approximately forty-five years ago, and you and your family have worked hard at creating the business it is today. The specific issues that you are seeking help with are

1. Improving the relationship between Mark and Steve so that the business can be run more effectively by the second-generation family members working in the business.
2. Negotiating with Mark your respective roles in the business.
3. Professionalizing the business so that the business is run like a business and the family like a family. This includes, but is certainly not limited to: clear job descriptions, hire and fire policies, compensation and benefits packages, employee handbook, and executive/management team building.
4. Developing a succession plan that includes an estate plan and considers Harriet, Mark, and Steve.

Every family business faces unique challenges. Only one-third of family companies survive to the second generation and less than 15 percent succeed into the third generation. *As in many family businesses, the family issues have affected business decisions and vice versa.* Any consultant you engage should have both education and experience in working with family businesses.

Exhibit 3.1. Sample Engagement Letter, Cont'd

To address these issues, I have found it useful and effective to think of the consultation as a process (not an event) to be considered in phases. I suggest the following for your situation:

Phase I: Assessment, Planning, and Design

1. *Individual Interviews and Onsite Visit to the Business.* This would include a series of individual interviews with you, Harriet, Mark, Steve, their spouses, your key advisors (accountant and attorney), board members, and key employees. This would be done as soon as possible.

   Prior to conducting the interviews, I would like materials related to the business to be made available for me to make a complete assessment of the business environment. These materials would include a brief history of the business; basic financial information; any past consultants' recommendations; and other information that you feel is relevant. This, along with the interviews, allows me to have as complete a picture as possible.

2. *Feedback Meeting/Action Planning.* I will prepare a report with an assessment and recommendations that can serve as a guide for you. This will address both family and business concerns. It will include a framework for both formalized business undertakings and suggestions for effective communications, conflict management, and decision-making techniques. These guidelines will serve as practical suggestions for subsequent meetings with me. The summary report will be presented at a family-only meeting. If it seems appropriate, I will invite Marcia Green, HR director, your attorney, David Richards, and Donald Whitley, your accountant, to present their recommendations early in the schedule for the day. Following the presentation, I will facilitate a discussion with the family on the issues raised and attempt to come to a consensus on the long-term and short-term steps to take. It is important to remember that the action plan we develop to solve your problems will be *your* plan for improvement, and therefore your input and participation are very important.

Phase II: Implementation

During this phase, I will work with the family in continuing the proposed changes that were adopted at the planning retreat. I want to emphasize, however, that the format of Phase II will be determined during the Phase I assessment. During implementation, I will distribute teaching and training materials for your use.

Phase III: Follow-up Assessment

It is difficult to establish an exact time frame that would allow for a comfortable initial transition. Typically, within the first year, we find it useful to convene a group meeting to review the progress. In your situation, this meeting may be with you and/or the entire family. This component of the work will provide further assessment as to the overall goals and objectives and reinforce positive changes that have occurred.

Exhibit 3.1. Sample Engagement Letter, Cont'd

Fees and Billing Arrangements

My professional services are billed at a rate of XX per hour, plus expenses. I estimate that the scope of services for the *first phase* outlined herein could be provided for an amount not to exceed XX. I will, however, render time and material summaries and bill you on a regular basis to keep you up-to-date on the financial picture. This is my best estimate and I will continuously communicate with you regarding the schedule.

The scope of services beyond the first phase will be determined by your needs, although it has been my experience that the subsequent stages are essential in ensuring positive changes for the family and the business over time. This is a collaborative process between the client and the consultant. I do request that a retainer be paid at the beginning of the work. Please indicate your approval of this proposal by returning this signed letter and a retainer of $XX. I believe that a commitment of time and resources is critical for the best chance of success.

Please keep in mind that this proposal includes a range of services. I would be pleased to make adjustments consistent with your expectations. This proposed work plan involves consultation that includes *both* content, *what* is decided, and process, *how* it is decided. Each is important in a change process and all relevant family members are essential. I hope that this outline clearly presents my thoughts on the process and one means by which we could proceed. I can understand your frustration with the need to speed up the process. To obtain deep and lasting changes, however, I have found the best way is not to skip any of the necessary steps. I have also found that some relief can be gained early on in the process with small, but significant, changes. I think that our process will accomplish this.

You are to be commended on your willingness to look ahead, learn from the past, consider what is best for *both* the family and the business, and move forward in a thoughtful and strategic manner. I welcome the opportunity to work with you and your family business.

Sincerely,

Assessment and Diagnosis

Once the client has agreed to engage you as a consultant, the real work begins. An assessment of the family firm's systems is the first step to diagnose the client's problems effectively. This assessment has several objectives: (1) to provide the family and consultant with a roadmap; (2) to complete a realistic picture of the situation;

(3) to give the members of the family and business an opportunity to tell their stories; (4) to prepare feedback for the family to prioritize the problems to solve; (5) to evaluate any discrepancies between the *presenting* problem and what you understand to be the *real* problem; (6) to understand what it's like to work in the boundaries; (7) to assess the impact of the consultant's presence in the system; (8) to determine how effectively the family can use the feedback; and (9) to identify any special problems, such as addictions, personality problems, or ethical, legal, or financial issues that require a referral to a specialist.

The consultant should also recognize that the assessment is an important intervention in and of itself. It affects the systems being studied. For example, after Jane finished a series of phone interviews of a two-generation family in business, the oldest son, who had contacted her originally, called to say that, "The interviews got us talking again. We think we can figure out what to do to solve this problem." Jane replied that that is not unusual, and in some situations the family, on its own, can see the problem all the way to the solution. It is more likely, however, that old behaviors and patterns will reemerge as family members are faced with the changes. She said that she hoped the family could do it, but encouraged them to call her if things stalled, if they had questions, or if they needed outside help. Conversely, opening up the system may produce negative reactions. Members of one family business had a serious argument as a reaction to the question: "What is the problem?" Finding out what helped or what ignited the fire provides many clues that are helpful in doing the assessment.

The Genogram

A valuable tool developed and used by intergenerational family therapists, the genogram organizes large amounts of information in a concise and efficient manner. McGoldrick, Gerson, and Shellenberger's (1999) book *Genograms: Assessment and Intervention* provides a clear and comprehensive discussion of their use, illustrating the stories of families such as the Kennedys, Freuds, and Roosevelts. The genogram, typically drawn early in the assessment phase or with the family in the chemistry meeting, enables the consultant to understand and explain the transmission of problems, coping skills, and family strengths and weaknesses from one generation to the next. It resembles a family tree, with additional symbols to depict the interactional dynamics. Figure 3.2 illustrates the various kinds of information that can be represented in a genogram.

Figure 3.2. Reading a Genogram

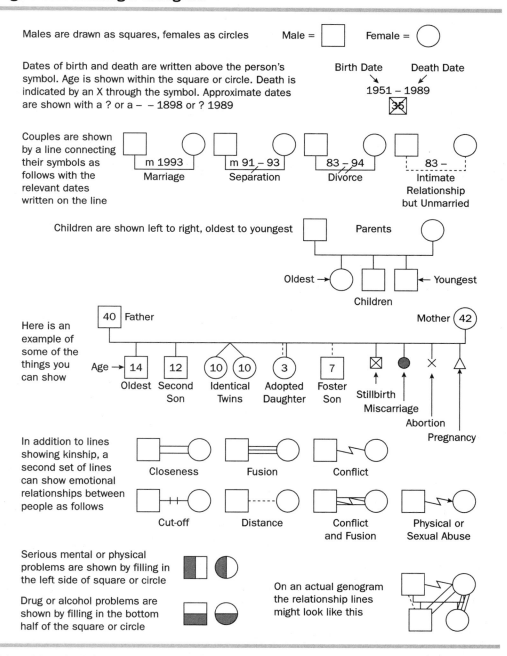

Males are drawn as squares, females as circles   Male = ☐   Female = ○

Dates of birth and death are written above the person's symbol. Age is shown within the square or circle. Death is indicated by an X through the symbol. Approximate dates are shown with a ? or a – – 1898 or ? 1989

Birth Date   Death Date
1951 – 1989

Couples are shown by a line connecting their symbols as follows with the relevant dates written on the line

m 1993
Marriage

m 91 – 93
Separation

83 – 94
Divorce

83 –
Intimate Relationship but Unmarried

Children are shown left to right, oldest to youngest   Parents

Oldest →   ← Youngest
Children

Here is an example of some of the things you can show

40 Father   Mother 42

Age →
14
Oldest
12
Second Son
10 10
Identical Twins
3
Adopted Daughter
7
Foster Son
Stillbirth
Miscarriage
Abortion
Pregnancy

In addition to lines showing kinship, a second set of lines can show emotional relationships between people as follows

Closeness   Fusion   Conflict

Cut-off   Distance   Conflict and Fusion   Physical or Sexual Abuse

Serious mental or physical problems are shown by filling in the left side of square or circle

Drug or alcohol problems are shown by filling in the bottom half of the square or circle

On an actual genogram the relationship lines might look like this

Adapted from: McGoldrick, Gerson, Shellenbarger (1999). *Genograms: Assessment and Intervention.* New York: Norton Company.

By adding the history of the business to the genogram, the consultant can demonstrate the effect of the business on the family and vice versa. Family members in the business are drawn in one color, with ownership and management in another color. It is useful to map a family's structure and processes over at least three generations, with significant, "nodal" events highlighted (illnesses, critical life changes, deaths, start of business, repetitive patterns, shifts in family relationships). We often find that nodal events are concurrent (for example, the start of a business shortly after a parent's death or a divorce shortly after the birth of a special needs child).

While demonstrating behavior patterns over time and across generations, genograms can function as assessment, educational, predictive, and intervention tools. Through them, families begin to understand and put behaviors in context and come to appreciate their legacy and history. Genograms also serve as a way to neutralize attitudes about negative behaviors such as "Granddad's stinginess," which can be seen as a result of being raised in the Depression. Also, the family may demonstrate a predictable reaction to stress or change that might help it prepare for future developmental and accidental crises. As you develop and review the genogram with family members, useful questions to ask are: "Where do you think you learned that?" "Who are you most like?" "What was happening in your family and in the world when she started the business?" "What do you know of your grandparents' life?" "What patterns of entrepreneurship do you see?"

In summary, the genogram illustrates that:

- Families repeat problems and solutions;
- Family behaviors have to be seen in their sociocultural, historical, and economic contexts;
- Individual behavior is related to several factors: age, place in family, gender, biological inheritance, and so on;
- Nodal events and how a family reacts to them continue to influence the family over time and can be predictive; and
- Families and their businesses are interwoven over generations.

Figure 3.3 is a genogram for the Thomas family.

Figure 3.3. Thomas Family Genogram

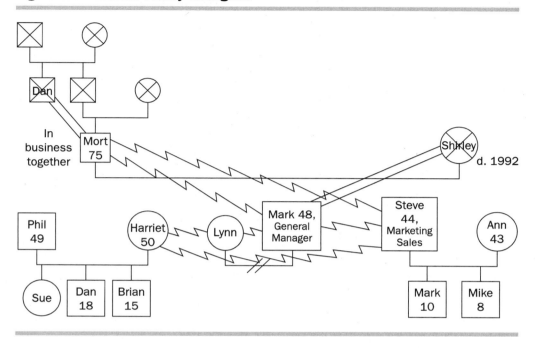

Interviews

Interviews are invaluable for helping to understand the three systems of a family firm and to help answer questions raised by the genogram. We can identify the key people who might be interviewed by examining the roles played by individuals in the business, ownership/governance, and family systems. These groups of people and their relationships to the various systems can be seen in Figure 3.4.

Figure 3.4. Whom to Interview in Family Firms

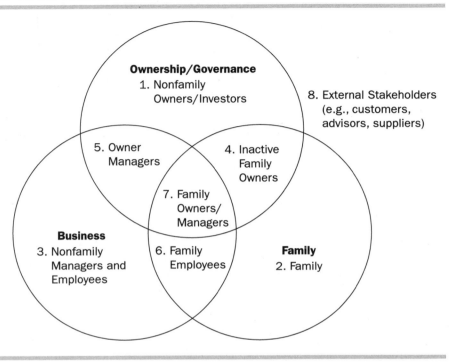

The people in the following roles are generally those who can provide the consultant with the best information:

1. Nonfamily owners/investors: owners who are not family or involved in the business;

2. Family: members of the family who do not own or work in the business;

3. Nonfamily managers and employees: nonfamily who work in the business;

4. Inactive family owners: family members who have ownership but do no work in the business;

5. Owner managers: nonfamily who have ownership and are active in business;

6. Family employees: family members who do not have ownership but who are active in the business;

7. Family owner/managers: family owners who also work in the business;

8. External stakeholders: customers and suppliers or other nonfamily, non-owner stakeholders, other advisors, attorneys, accountants, and other consultants involved.

Tips for Interviews

The following are several tips that we've found useful when doing interviews:

- Interview data should be anonymous when possible but not confidential. Themes/issues/problems should be organized and presented at a family-only meeting in summary form. It can be difficult to maintain anonymity as there are very few "oldest sons" in a family business. Thus, those interviewed must recognize that their input will likely be identified by others.

- Consultants should encourage interviewees to own and share information. If interviewees do not feel that they are willing to have you, the consultant, report an issue back to the rest of the family, you can allow the person to give information that is *off the record.* This information may help you in working with the family, but should not be shared by you with other family members, unless of course the individual brings the issue up in an open setting. It is important to discuss the issue of *secrets* before the interviewing process begins. We make it clear that it is usually not useful for consultants to hold secrets. If family members have something they want to tell us, they need to understand that we will decide whether or not it needs to be discussed openly. The decision to share the information is theirs. However, helping members of the client system to "own" their feelings, ideas, and beliefs is often essential to create a more open, problem-solving atmosphere.

- Develop a picture of the whole system, from multiple realities.

- Understand the difference between the presenting problem ("Mark and Steve fight all the time") and the real problem (no plan for succession; sons being given mixed messages; Mark's gambling).

What Information to Gather

In Chapter 1, we described the various facets of each of the three systems. During the interviews, the consultant should attempt to gather information about the areas of assessment listed in Table 3.2.

Table 3.2. Areas for Assessment

Family	Business/Management	Ownership/Governance
Roles and Relationships	Mission	Mission and Goals
Cultural Patterns/Values	Strategy	Legal Form
Decision Making	Structure	Distribution of Ownership
Communications	Technology	Board of Directors
Conflict Management	Culture	Leadership
	Systems (such as reward and information)	
	Processes (such as communication and decision making)	
	Leadership	
	Finances	

Assessment Questions

Before the interviews, we usually prepare the interviewees by asking them to think about the following questions:

- What do you see as the strengths and weaknesses of the family and the business?
- What do you see as your present and future roles in both the family and the business?
- What would you like your role to be?
- What are your personal goals? Your goals for the family? For the business?
- If you could change three things in the family business, what would they be?
- What solutions have been tried for the problems in the family business?
- Have they worked? Why or why not?

If we are including nonfamily individuals, we will tailor the above for them. The questions that we typically ask regarding the three systems are found in Exhibit 3.2.

Exhibit 3.2. Interview Questions*

FAMILY

Roles and Relationships

- What task and emotional roles do family members play?
- Is there flexibility with these roles?
- Are the relationships cooperative, competitive, or contentious?
- Is there mutual trust?
- What are some of the family's rules, norms, or understandings about behavior?
- Do family members have a life outside the company? Hobbies? Interests?

Cultural Patterns/Values

- What are the core values of the family and the business? Are they compatible?
- How is the family culture learned? Taught?
- How are the values expressed in the infrastructure, resources, and legal and financial decisions?
- How is unethical behavior handled?
- What is the family's ethnic background and how does this affect its style and culture?
- How is the family seen in the community? What is their reputation?
- Is individualism encouraged? Is family togetherness more important?

Decision Making

- How are decisions made?
- Are communications open? Is privacy respected when appropriate?
- Are tough decisions ignored? Postponed?
- Are the infrastructures maintained to encourage a spirit of openness and accomplishment?

Communications and Conflict Management

- How is conflict managed?
- Is there a history of unresolved conflict?
- How do the family and business deal with differences of opinion? Style?
- Is there confidence that differences will be handled in a safe and productive manner?
- Are sensitive issues openly discussed?
- Are there listeners as well as talkers?
- Are the parents giving mixed messages? ("We want you to grow up and be independent, but not to take over" [Queen Elizabeth/Prince Charles syndrome])

Exhibit 3.2. Interview Questions, Cont'd

BUSINESS

Mission

- What is the vision of the family? The mission of the business? Are they compatible?
- Do the leaders in the family and business take into consideration the ideas and goals of others?
- Is the larger context considered in planning?
- Is the vision agreed to and examined on a regular basis?
- Would family members and employees know what the mission is?
- Has the family examined the choices they have made regarding the company's mission and goals as the business has evolved over time?

Strategy

- Are management and governance systems compatible with the size of the business and the challenges it faces?
- Are these systems based on family dynamics or business requirements?
- Are there fair and clear policies about compensation, hiring and firing, job definitions, and decision making?
- Are regular business meetings held?
- Has succession been dealt with, planned for, and understood?
- How is authority developed, exercised, and transferred?
- Are advisors used appropriately?

Structure

- What is the company's structure?
- Is there an organizational chart? What form is it in?
- Is there a human resource system? Is it adequate?
- Has the business been professionalized, that is, have infrastructures and procedures been developed to build consistency and fairness?

Technology

- What is the company's technology?
- Is it up-to-date and suitable for the work to be accomplished?
- What are the measurement systems?

Culture

- What is the family's work ethic?
- Are there generational differences? If so, what?

Exhibit 3.2. Interview Questions, Cont'd

- What is the organizational culture?
- Does the business culture reflect the family's values?

Systems (Reward and Information)

- What are the reward systems?
- Are there performance norms?
- Are there entry and exit strategies and plans for both family and nonfamily?
- Are advancement and promotion based on merit or on family position?

Processes (Communication, Decision Making)

- How are decisions made?
- Is communication open and timely?
- How is conflict managed?
- Is there confidence that differences will be tolerated and diversity encouraged?

Leadership

- Is the leader of the business the right person for the job?
- What is the leadership style?
- Is the leader respected?

Finances

- How profitable is the company?
- What is its worth?
- What are the annual sales? What are the trends?
- What does the balance sheet show?
- What are the compensation and benefits packages of the family and nonfamily managers and employees?

GOVERNANCE

Mission and Goals

- What is the mission? What are the goals?
- Are they agreed to by the owners and communicated to family?
- Are family values reflected in the goals?
- Has ownership succession been planned for? Is the ownership succession plan consistent with the needs of the family and the business in the future?

Exhibit 3.2. Interview Questions, Cont'd

Legal Form

- What is the legal structure?
- Is this understood by the next generation?
- Is this the right one for the present business? For the future?

Distribution of Ownership

- Is there a written succession plan for a transfer of ownership?
- Is the owner's estate plan known and understood by the next generation?

Board of Directors

- Is there a board of directors? How effective is it? Is it composed of only family?
- Is there an outside board that is comprised of some nonfamily directors?

Leadership

- Is the board's leadership supported by the family?
- Does the leader have the skills, training, and experience for the job?
- Is he or she the right person?

*Some of these questions are asked of interviewees and some are asked of the consultant.

Transactional Dynamics

While gathering information from the right people is indeed important in constructing a picture of the family firm's systems, the picture must describe the key dynamics that are at work. Some of the important dynamics concern (1) boundary functioning, (2) balancing processes, and (3) feedback loops.

Boundary Functioning. Boundary functioning describes the quality of *both* the connection *and* the separation between the family and the business and between the family business and the consultant. It is not a barrier but, like a healthy cell membrane, is semipermeable and regulates the exchange of substances (energy, information, emotions, values). It is through this regulated exchange that each system can grow, change, adapt, and, paradoxically, maintain its identity. Rigid boundaries cut off contact, starving and suffocating the system. Examples include not using resources or consultants wisely, failing to do market research, or not knowing trends or the latest information. On the other end of the spectrum, overly diffuse boundaries fail to maintain the system's identity, allowing information from the outside to engulf it (that is, values don't guide the vision; there's no strategic plan; the concept of the business becomes muddy). The ideal is a delicate balance of both the separation and the connection in which the interactions are mutually invigorating. Family businesses often exhibit diffuse boundaries; an extreme of this was a family that Jane began to work with. The father/owner was paying his middle daughter just to show up, to come to the office. He occasionally gave her pointless jobs to do. He was worried about her and didn't think she could make it on her own. He wanted to make sure she had a place to go every day. Everyone knew about and resented the situation. His role as father was confused with his role as boss. (Even his role as father was inappropriate for a twenty-three-year-old!) The father was encouraged to fire the daughter; she was sent to a career counselor. Father and daughter together were helped to redefine their relationship, and a plan was put in place for the daughter to be completely out of the business and on her own in four months. Another example is the Davis family from Chapter 2 (see page 22). (Where would you start in that case to establish healthier boundaries between business and family?)

During times of crises or change, living systems tend to move *temporarily* toward the extremes of functioning. That is, they tend either to "hunker down" and keep the problem to themselves *or* they may panic and call in many advisors haphazardly. As they readjust and adapt, they return to a balance, although perhaps one different from in the past.

This concept is important for family business consultants to understand because we are usually called in *after a crisis.* Often procedures and processes are needed that manage the boundaries as the consultant works in the boundaries. It is the negotiation, compromise, exchange of ideas, and collaboration between families and businesses that sustain both firm and family over the long run. Too often families and businesses are encouraged to keep family and business issues separate. This is unrealistic and a nonproductive use of energy. Forged through the management of difference and exchanges, these connections can withstand the ever-changing, turbulent world within which family businesses can thrive.

Some Questions to Delineate Boundaries Between the Systems

- How often do you discuss business issues at home?

- How often do family disagreements spill into the business arena?

- What did the disagreements within the family look like before there was a business?

- Are you speaking now as mother or as president?

- Are the boundaries between the family and the business respected?

- Are the family members clear about their roles in the family and business?

- Are boundaries of time, space, and opinions respected?

Balancing Processes. A balance of power and influence between the family and the business systems helps create an environment of stability and adaptability. Like the planets in our solar system, family business members are constantly moving in relationship to each other, but are in a delicate balance. If the balance is upset, the results can be disastrous. If one system or the other dominates, there will be an effect on the overall functioning. It may be "the system under stress that normally begins to dominate" (McCracken, 2000, p. 10), but it may also be that the dominant system is growing quickly and requires significant time and resources. Whether it is the family or the business, it will begin to drain energy from the other. If one system dominates, the influence of the other is diminished. These families, as in Case 1.3 in Chapter 1, have had the business take over their lives; they made career decisions early on based on their loyalty to their brother. If the family overpowers the business (Figure 3.5B), because of family dysfunction, stress, upheaval, crises, or inability of the family to manage its stress, the business may be unable to adapt to the ever-changing marketplace, encourage innovation, and stay competitive. These families play out all the emotional dramas in the workplace; this was what was happening to the Thomas family. If the business overwhelms the family (Figure 3.5A), the family concerns take second place to business goals. These are the families that eat, drink, and sleep the business. They have few outside interests and all of their time together is spent thinking about or working on business matters. The more functional system may not be the one that overpowers; it may in fact be the weaker or more dysfunctional one that drains energy from the other.

Figure 3.5. Equilibrium

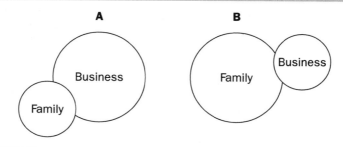

Source: Adapted from K. McCracken (2000). The family business client: Managing the complexity. *The Family Business Client.*

Questions to Determine Equilibrium

- Which system is dominant at the moment? Why?
- What, if anything, should be done about it?
- What systems should be developed to keep the family business system in balance?
- Which functions of the business are being undermined by the family issues (and vice versa)?

Feedback Loops and Process Mapping. Process mapping is a technique, taken from systems thinking, of drawing a picture of feedback loops or behavioral interactions in which the actions and reactions of individuals are inextricably intertwined. Identifying these transactions is critical to understanding what keeps a problem going and helps the consultant avoid blame and stay neutral in the boundaries. We can observe a meeting, watch a heated argument between two sisters, or listen to Mort complain about his sons, but we cannot know what caused the fights, what started first, and what determines the end and beginning of the interaction. We can only speculate and describe the sequence of events. The crucial questions are: "What is happening now?" "What happened just before?" "What happens just after?" "Is the problem in the individuals, the family, the business, or the feedback between them?" These observations enable the consultant to think in patterns of behavior that repeat themselves over time, over generations, over a lifetime. Behavior patterns include at least two actions occurring in sequence in an endless cycle. It is critical to take the long view and offer a fresh perspective on old problems. In Figure 3.6 we describe a behavioral feedback and reinforcing loop in Mort's family. (Balancing, the second type of loop, describes a regulating, not escalating, feedback system.)

Figure 3.6. Reinforcing Loop

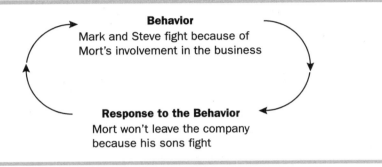

The process for drawing such a reinforcing loop is as follows:

1. Start with the behavior or action. (Mark and Steve fight constantly about Mort's involvement in the company.)

2. Insert the response to the behavior. (Mort won't leave the company because he sees his sons fighting.)

3. Then describe the reoccurring behavioral response to this response. (Mark and Steve continue to fight.)

Of course, as you map such behaviors in various family firms, you may find other, more complex reinforcing loops with different behaviors and responses. Uncovering this "vicious circle" of reinforcing behaviors and responses is the key to understanding the problems in the family firm and to developing strategies to break these negative cycles.

Some of the questions that were used to uncover feedback loops in the Thomas family included:

- What do you (the son) do when Mort begins to interfere?

- What do you think Mort thinks when he sees his sons fighting?

- What does Steve do when Mark goes to Mort for money?

Consultants should find that answering the following questions helps us to remain focused on the key issues and generally leads to a more successful consultation.

Questions to Ask During the Assessment

1. *What is the real problem?* Often what people describe as the problem is only a symptom. And if you focus on the symptom without uncovering the real problem, you are wasting your time and are bound to fail. A doctor not only treats the rash, but conducts a series of tests to find out what is causing it. That is exactly what you must do with a *presenting problem* in the family business system. To get beyond treatment of the symptom, take a series of steps to uncover the real problem. These steps include hearing all sides of the story; getting family members to talk together in a safe, structured and neutral setting; and keeping all options open.

2. *How long has this problem existed?* Problems manifest themselves in three ways: (a) same old stuff; (b) something brand new; and (c) same old stuff in a new package. If the symptom has persisted for a long time, it reflects a deeper problem embedded in the system. This is where genogram drawing is useful. The symptom cannot be dealt with until the *underlying patterns and structures* that produce it are carefully considered and addressed. If the symptom is new, with a short history, deal with it first, since its cause will likely be the easiest to diagnose and may help in uncovering the source of other, more entrenched problems.

3. *Is the problem related to some "unfinished business"?* All living systems, including individuals, families, and businesses, go through life cycles and crises. Each stage in the life cycle of a business and of a family requires certain tasks; each crisis requires increased communication and effective action plans for the family and the business to grow and move forward. All too often problems are the result of avoiding the communication and tasks that are necessary to move to the next stage. Each change in a system produces disruptions in patterns. If emotional processes aren't managed during such disruptions, the negative effects may be felt over time and over many generations. For example, in the Thomas case, it would be important to determine how much of Mort's inability to hand over the business is related to his unprocessed grief over the loss of Shirley.

4. *Where is the most energy for change?* Energy implies possibilities for change. How does the energy present itself and what does it look like? It can come in many forms—anger, excitement, frustration, enthusiasm, pain, or a combination. Where is the energy located? It can be in a person of authority, formal or informal, in a subordinate, or in an alliance among members of the family business system. Your chances for success are obviously greater if the energy for change is with a person in a position of formal authority. Often, however, with succession issues, the motivation for change is in the succeeding generation, which is highly motivated but often without much formal authority. Understanding how the whole system works and appreciating the concept of leverage can help you or your client use tools to create changes that are positive for the family and the business and get "buy in" from the key people.

5. *Does the problem serve a function? If so, what is it?* Problems often play important roles in systems. A classic example is "scapegoating" or "dumping" problems onto a person or group of people. If one person or group is frequently blamed, the first question to ask is does he or she deserve this. If the answer is "yes," then the work is with that person. If the answer is "no," then the work is with the system. Then ask: "What would happen if the scapegoat were fired or cut off from the family? Would the problems remain?" There are many reasons for scapegoating, but the most common in family business systems are unresolved conflicts, work avoidance, and denial of important business decisions to be made. In short, the question becomes "Who can we blame?" rather than "How can we fix this?" Problems are powerful forces in systems and can play a useful, if sometimes destructive, role. Do your homework. Be prepared for the fallout if the problem is removed without repairing the underlying structure.

In sum, problems often don't receive the respect they deserve. They usually play important roles in families and in the workplace and are windows into solutions. Ask these critical questions before you rush in to fix things.

Are We There Yet?

As we thought about our work with our various clients, Jane was reminded of traveling with her husband, who often takes along his GPS (global positioning system) in the car. A marvel in modern technology, the GPS is able to tell them what direction they're heading, how fast they're going, and their estimated time of arrival. The limitation is, however, that the estimated time of arrival is based on the miles per hour (MPH) they are going at the moment of any given reading. So if their destination is 325 miles away and they are traveling at sixty-five miles per hour the trip will take five hours. However, if they take a reading while they're approaching a tollbooth and going ten miles per hour they will be told that the trip will take thirty-two and one half hours. In addition to this limitation, GPS readings are often of questionable value because the readings don't account for detours, bad weather, traffic, or other unpredictable events.

In the same way, some 75 percent of change efforts do not yield promised results (Olson & Eoyang, 2001, p. 3), often because the consultant is not prepared for the twists and turns in the relationship with his or her clients. Never is this more important than with family businesses, which are powerful emotional systems as well as work systems. Collaboration with the client and the iterative feedback process are key elements throughout the consulting journey (Burke, 1994). While our consulting framework is orderly, the client system is not, and change often occurs not in tidy sequential steps but in sudden and unpredictable ways. In the initial phases of the consultation, we must make predictions as to length of consulting process and scope of work. However, the clients we work with are often unpredictable because they're using outdated role concepts and are more likely to make irrational, involuntary choices and decisions. Given these uncertainties, it is important as we engage each new client to tailor our work to each family and to respond to events as they unfold. We have found that flexibility is often the key to success.

Now that we have discussed how to contract with a family firm client and assess the health of the firm's three systems, we will move to the next phase of the consulting process. In Chapter 4 we discuss how to feed back the data from the assessment to the client and how to engage the client in planning for change.

4

Feedback
and Planning

"The art of progress is to preserve order amid change and to preserve change amid order."

Alfred North Whitehead

▶ CASE 4.1

The phone call came from Louise Church, fifty-six, president of East-South Holdings, who said she wanted help negotiating a buyout from her brother, Gerald, fifty-eight, and sister, Judy, sixty. Louise obtained Jane's name from a fellow family business executive who had used her as a consultant. The siblings owned and had developed several commercial office buildings and other real estate holdings, including a retail shopping mall in a large metropolitan area in the Northeast. The total revenues of the company were approximately $25 million annually. The idea of a family business consultant sounded like a good idea, but Louise emphasized that she didn't need a therapist—this was just a restructuring of the business. She also said that her husband, Sam, was involved in the business and would have to be included in the negotiations. "Sam is better thinking on his feet than I am," Louise said. Louise also said that she was always anxious about negotiating with her brother and sister, who were both "fast thinkers and talkers" and often still treated her like the "baby of the family." Having Sam involved in the talks was important to her. A chemistry meeting was held with Louise, Gerald, and Judy. The agenda included introductions and ground rules for the meeting, discussion of the problems and goals, a description of the consulting process, an agreement to work together, and the next steps.

After the engagement letter was signed and returned, the assessment phase was completed in a series of three meetings: Louise and Sam together, then Gerald and his wife, and, finally, Judy and her husband Carl. Gerald stressed that he wanted to get this deal completed as soon as possible. During the initial meeting with Louise and Sam, we learned that the business was founded twenty years ago by Gerald ("It was his idea.") but that Louise, now president of the company, joined him during the first year and provided most of the initial funding, $55,000. Ownership was as follows: Gerald 40 percent, Judy 20 percent, and Louise 40 percent, although Louise originally had wanted to own 50 percent with the remaining 50 percent split between Judy and Gerald. At the time, Louise gave up a successful career to join Gerald, who had been moving from job to job. Judy was persuaded to leave her real estate business to join the company in the second year. Louise and Sam spent most of this first meeting criticizing Gerald, whom they described as an "idea man" but a terrible manager; he "delegates but doesn't follow through." But they also said that outside the business they and their three kids were close to him, his wife, and their five children.

During a serious financial crisis eight years previous, Sam was brought in to "help out." But during that time, he was kept out of "knowing anything" and treated very badly by Gerald. Thus Sam doesn't trust Gerald and worries that there will be lawsuits later on for things that were handled badly on "Gerald's watch." Gerald stepped down as president six months ago. Sam is now COO. Both Louise and Sam say there has been a history of mistakes and mishandled management under Gerald's presidency. A recurring theme is Gerald's poor treatment of Louise and Sam, who are hurt and angered by this. They both agree that it's a good time to buy out Gerald and Judy. Husband and wife are adamant that Sam should be part of the negotiations.

Both Judy, who is vice president of sales and marketing, and Carl, who is the business accountant, want out of the business; they are reaching retirement age and would like to see their children and grandchildren more often. They are very tired of the arguments and worried about the potential for lawsuits. They also said that they were concerned about Sam's ability to continue because he "has a drinking problem" and that Louise wanted to keep him involved only because she felt that would keep him from drinking. Carl said that the business was beginning to slip and he felt it was a direct result of Sam's drinking and Louise's denial of the problem. Both acknowledged the family's closeness and their real concern for Sam and Louise.

Gerald's wife politely refused to be part of any of the meetings. The meeting with Gerald confirmed the hard feelings between him and Sam, whom he said was difficult to deal with: "Working with him is very, very tough." He also acknowledged Sam's drinking problems, which, he said, "were getting worse." Gerald wanted only to deal with Louise and Judy in the negotiations and he wanted to move as quickly as possible. I have "created something fabulous, but it has been a tremendous sacrifice and I have to get out." ◄

Questions for the Consultant

- Where would you start?
- How do you explain the multiple realities?
- How would you handle the issue of Sam's drinking?
- How would you design a feedback session for this family business?
- How do you predict the family will react?

Feedback and Action Planning

"You can observe a lot by just watching."

Yogi Berra

In this chapter we will cover the feedback and planning stages; we will discuss how to organize the data that we have collected (described in Chapter 3) and the best ways to present it and use it in planning with the family. There are actually three interconnected steps in what we call feedback and action planning. First, the consultant must organize and feed back the data in a meaningful way to the client. The basis for this is that information can promote change (Poza, Johnson, & Alfred, 1998, p. 313). Second, the consultant may make some suggestions to resolve the problems facing the client, but the client must own any solutions; therefore, the consultant and client must jointly problem solve to come up with solutions that can be implemented with commitment. Finally, the consultant works out a detailed action plan with the client in order to implement the solutions that have been agreed on. The goals, questions, desired outcomes, and risks of this phase of the engagement are listed in Table 4.1.

Table 4.1. Feedback Phase of the Action Research Model

Phase	Goal	Questions	Desired Outcome	Risks
Feedback/ Action Planning	To organize the data collected in the previous phases. To provide a forum for discussion, consensus, prioritizing, and planning.	What environment is best for this feedback? Who should be present? What is the best format for the data to be given? How does the family react to the report? How does the consultant react to their reactions? How does the action move from passive listening to active planning?	To reach a consensus for action steps to be taken.	Over or under simplifying the report. Not being prepared for family's response. Not being able to reach a consensus on the goals. Not introducing the information in a manner that the family can handle and move to an action plan. Not to act effectively to the family's reaction of acceptance, denial, resistance, rejection, or a combination thereof.

Giving feedback based on the assessment consists of both organizing and presenting the report. If done correctly, it can simultaneously (1) teach; (2) establish new norms; and (3) challenge old ways of defining and trying to solve the problems. Whether or not this succeeds depends on several variables:

- Chemistry between the family and the consultant;
- Competencies of the consultant;
- Quality of the report; and
- Functionality/ability of family to process the information.

In Table 4.2, we have outlined the positive attributes, desired outcomes, and risks related to providing a family firm client with feedback.

Table 4.2. Attributes, Outcomes, and Risks of Providing Feedback

Factors	Positive Attributes	Desired Outcomes	Risks
Chemistry Between Family and Consultant	Trust and respect between both parties.	Mutual positive feelings create atmosphere for learning.	Lack of trust and respect create atmosphere of mistrust and report is not heard or family disengages.
Competency of the Consultant	Consultant has appropriate skills for problems and issues presented; good at both process and content of meeting; able to focus on building consensus and solutions. Is patient with the process; teaches skills, such as decision making, reaching a consensus, and prioritizing. Is knowledgeable about problem areas.	Family wants to continue the process with the consultant and is motivated to begin working on the issues.	Consultant's skills are not adequate and he or she is unable or unwilling to bring in additional team members or expertise.
Quality of Report	Report organized in sensible and insightful format, strengths and weaknesses, whole systems perspective, educates and informs, puts issues in perspective. Report clear and specific, with suggestions for solutions.	Family's perception of problems is validated and enlarged, with solutions that fit the family's style and abilities.	Report misses the mark or focuses on the problems, with no possible solutions. Overestimates family's capability to comprehend the report. Report is not tailored to family's problems and abilities.
Ability of Family	High degree of functionality, nondefensive; motivated to solve the problem and deal with the issues. Can work together as a team; smart enough to understand the report.	Able to hear positives and negatives and appreciate the work to be done.	Family's level of dysfunction produces denial, defensiveness, disagreement with the consultant or with one another.

If the consultant is sensitized to the issues described in Table 4.2, then the feedback session can be designed to reach the desired outcomes.

Organizing the Feedback

The family may know what the problems are; however, the definition of the problems is often problematic. For example, Louise wanted help with the buyout and restructuring the business. She was defining the problem as one that required a *technical* solution. The real problems (that is, the history of conflict; Gerald's poor performance as president; lack of job descriptions, policies and procedures, performance reviews; Sam's drinking; and potential lawsuits) ran deeper than *technical* problems.

The consultant must bridge the gap between what the client presents and what is determined in the assessment. What Louise said she wanted was help in negotiating a buyout from her brother and sister. The bridge between the presenting problem and the underlying or "real" problems was littered with obstacles: resentments, Louise's denial, opposing ideas about who should participate in the negotiations, and possible desire for retribution. Within this family business, however, as with most, there were strong positive feelings; Gerald and Judy both were motivated to get out and remain close. There was also a potential threat of lawsuits, which always encourages a settlement. This "carrot and stick" combination of wanting to preserve family ties and the threat of lawsuits was a powerful bridge to the settlement.

While simultaneously respecting what the client describes and what the consultant uncovers, the consultant must present the data in a way that the family can hear and accept. The adage that "It's the difference that makes the difference" applies here. If the information is too different from the family's reality, they will not believe it. If the data is too similar to the family's views, they will be unimpressed and wonder what they needed a consultant for!

Format for Organizing the Feedback

One suggested format for organizing the feedback is the SWOT analysis (strengths, weaknesses, opportunities, and threats). We have found that a PowerPoint® bullet-type presentation is more effective than merely presenting the data orally. With the information summarized in bullet form, the consultant can use the bullets as starters for the discussion. The following is an example of how the data was presented in the case of East-South Holdings.

SWOT Analysis for East-South Holdings

Strengths

- Successful business
- Good resources
- Concern for one another
- Shared family values
- Willingness to see each other succeed
- Each has "pitched in" to help out with business

Weaknesses

- Informal entry policies; no accountability
- Contracts between family members are not clear
- Family roles and business roles are blurred
- Communications are deteriorating
- Conflict is increasing

Opportunities

- Resources for expansion and restructuring
- Expanding market for development
- Good reputation in the community
- Restructuring offers possibilities for future

Threats

- Increasing level of conflict
- Potential lawsuits
- Not taking time for a sound plan and restructuring
- Lack of decision-making processes
- Sam's drinking; Louise's denial of the problem

Another example is the SWOT analysis prepared for a family business owned and managed by the Smith family, which was a relatively healthy family and had asked for help with succession planning. The succeeding generation were in their twenties and the parents in their fifties. They were not yet ready for transition but were planning ahead. They had attended family business seminars and knew what they needed to do and needed some help getting started. Their SWOT analysis follows.

SWOT Analysis for Smith Family Business

Strengths

- Successful business
- Stable/long-term marriage
- Close-knit family
- Have used advisors effectively
- Life stages "in synch"; ideal time for succession planning
- Good resources
- Shared core values
- Shared identity of business
- Mutual respect
- Sense of stewardship

Weaknesses

- Lack of planning: structure of holdings
- Lack of planning: business strategy
- Development of management team stalled
- Career decisions of second generation on hold
- Articulation of individuals' goals postponed
- Roles for outsiders in the transition not clarified
- Conflict-management strategies unclear
- Need improved clarification of boundaries: between work and family; areas of responsibility; accountability
- What's business? What's family?

Opportunities

- Increasing value of real estate
- Opening up of foreign markets

- Expansion into suburban areas
- Succession planning creates sibling team development
- Resources enough for growth

Threats

- Difficulty in managing differences
- Lack of training for management team
- No outside board of directors
- Succeeding generation has not made career decisions yet
- No succession plan
- Aging of executive team without replacement plan
- Information systems in company are outdated

Another approach to organizing the data is to do a "Force-Field Analysis," a method developed by Kurt Lewin (1951). This approach requires the consultant to establish the "base line" for the performance of the firm and family. In other words, how they are functioning now in relationship to how they should ideally be functioning. The consultant outlines the forces that are driving the performance of the firm and family to a certain level and then describes those forces that are restraining or undermining effective performance. The family can then begin to discover ways to eliminate restraining forces or add driving forces to improve performance. An example of this approach can be seen with the Jones family business example that follows.

Jones Family Business

Current Level of Performance. The business is reasonably profitable but less than the family's expectations. On the other hand, the Jones family is conflict-ridden. The parents are in their seventies, the succeeding generation in their fifties, and no planning has yet been done. The three "kids" work in the business, as do the mother and father. They have had two previous consultants who provided notebooks of technical suggestions, which sat on the father's bookshelf, and the conflicts have only grown worse.

Ideal Level of Performance. The business has a clear mission and strategy, with increasing revenues and profitability. Family and nonfamily employees understand their roles. Conflicts are managed effectively; there is a high level of collaboration for effective decision making.

Driving Forces

- Share pride in business' history and legacy
- Hard-working family members
- Shared core values
- Sense of stewardship

Restraining Forces

- Chronic recycled conflicts
- Lack of planning: business strategy
- Lack of decision-making processes of the family
- Clarity of communications: distinguishing between secrecy and privacy. How is information used?
- Blurred boundaries: between work and family; areas of responsibility; accountability; roles. What's business? What's family?
- Have not used advisors effectively; have had two previous consultants
- Lack of appreciation of one another's roles in the family business
- Business issues are negatively affecting family relationships and individual goals

Presenting the Feedback

You can't predict what the consequences of the data feedback session will be, but you should have a good idea and be prepared. Also, you need to calculate how much work the family can do without a lot of coaching and relearning. Ask yourself the following questions while preparing to present the feedback:

- How healthy is this family?
- What will the impact of the feedback be?
- How much can they accomplish in the first meeting?
- Will the data mobilize the family to action or denial and defensiveness?
- What will be the next steps?

The feedback session may be new to families who don't regularly meet together. In fact, well-run family meetings do become "the basis for positive outcomes in the family business" (Habbershon & Astrachan, 1997). Each exercise should teach a skill related to a weakness, for example, the Smith family needs to work on conflict-management skills and better clarification of boundaries.

We often feed data back at what we call "family business retreats." For example, with the Smith family, the retreat was planned for feedback, education, personal sharing, and strategic planning. It is a combination of decision making, team building, education, and having fun together. Usually the first retreat includes more teaching and process attention; the future retreats focus more on planning and decision making. A lot was packed into the three-day Smith family retreat, but they were ready to work. The agenda for this retreat is shown in Exhibit 4.1.

Exhibit 4.1. Agenda for Smith Family Retreat

First Day

4 p.m.–7 p.m.
Introductions, Ground Rules, 3'' × 5'' Cards*
Report on the Feedback SWOT
Mini Lecturette on the Healthy Family Business

Set Agenda for Next Two Days*

7:30 p.m.–9:00 p.m.
Dinner

9:00 p.m.–9:30 p.m.
"Inside Out" Meditation*

Second Day

8:30 a.m.–10:30 a.m.

Check In
Introduce Strategic Planning Process*
(Agenda items are based on "Weaknesses" in the SWOT)
Introduce Brainstorming*

10:30–10:45 a.m.
Break

Exhibit 4.1. Agenda for Smith Family Retreat, Cont'd

10:45 a.m.–12 noon
Communication and Conflict Management Exercise
Mini Lecturette on Healthy Conflict Management/Simple-Complex Conflicts
Discussion of Samples of Each Type in the Family
Introduce Assertive Communication*

12 noon–1:00 p.m.
Fishbowl Exercise*
From the list the family has created earlier in the morning

1:00 p.m.–2:00 p.m.
Lunch

2:00 p.m.–3:00 p.m.
The Wheel*

3:00 p.m.–3:30 p.m.
Finish Agenda Items from Morning

3:30 p.m.–3:45 p.m.
Break

3:45 p.m.–5:00 p.m.
Mind Mapping*

Third Day
8:30 a.m.–9:00 a.m.
Check In: How Is Everyone?
9:00 a.m.–10:30 a.m.
Planning/Agenda Items

10:30 a.m.–10:45 a.m.
Break

10:45 a.m.–12:30 p.m.
Create Action Plan

12:30 p.m.–1:00 p.m.
Debriefing

*Instructions for these activities can be found in Exhibit 4.3.

As noted earlier, the Jones family's level of conflict was so high that with a meeting longer than a half-day there would have been high risk for a "meltdown." The retreat was designed to address the problems and to provide a safe place to discuss the undiscussables, to institute a democratic process, and to see whether there was any realistic hope for change. Process work was required, and it was carefully planned for the half-day retreat. In the consultant's opinion, this time was all the togetherness time the family could take at that point. The agenda for the Jones family retreat appears in Exhibit 4.2.

Exhibit 4.2. Agenda for Jones Family Retreat

4 p.m.–8 p.m.
Introductions

Ground Rules*

Reasons for the Consultation

Attempted Solutions

Goals and Responsibilities of Each
Family Member for Individual, Family, Business
("How *I* have contributed to the problems. . . .")

Q & A

Next Steps

*Instructions for this activity can be found in Exhibit 4.3.

Creating New Solutions

"A Japanese coastal village was once threatened by a tidal wave, but the wave was sighted in advance, far out on the horizon, by a lone farmer, in the rice fields on the hillside above the village. There was no time to warn the villagers. At once he set fire to the fields, and the villagers who came swarming up to save their crops were saved from the flood." (De Shazer, 1991, p. 104)

We have the same challenge that the lone farmer does—looking at the problems in a new way, with new solutions and helping the families to do the same. It is important to find out what the family has already tried to solve their problems. "More of the same" will likely not work, so we must (1) try something new; (2) change the environment in which the old attempts at resolution were tried; or (3) intervene at a different level in the system. Problems cannot be solved at the same level of awareness or thinking that created them. This is especially true in family businesses in which the problems are multi-layered and multi-determined. The family needs help with untangling the issues and then weaving them together in a tapestry that makes sense and offers solutions. In preparing the feedback, we must approach the problems from a new angle. This is sometimes called "lateral thinking" (Sloane, 1994) and can be developed by challenging our assumptions and being open-minded.

For example, the issues in East-South Holdings included the following:

- Restructuring ownership
- Business lacks accountability
- Siblings disagreements
- Potential lawsuits
- Sam's drinking
- Absence of decision-making processes

To solve their problems, Jane helped them reframe these issues with a different level of logic:

- Restructuring ownership—*siblings need to sever business ties to preserve family relationships*
- Siblings' disagreements—*lack of processes; lack of clarity of roles and responsibilities; no consistent decision-making procedures*
- Sam's drinking—*enabled by the system; provides distraction for the other larger systemic problems*

Instead of lecturing, teaching, threatening, or pleading with an aging founder to step down, why not redefine the problem as his needing to give himself more time to create the life he wants and encourage him to articulate his interests and goals for the remainder of his life? He may even need the encouragement or permission from his family and himself to have fun, enjoy his free time, pursue interests that he always wanted to, or join a group of retired executives. One client, a seventy-six-year-old company president who should have stepped down to let his son take over, finally concluded that he really needed a companion. He wanted to know if there was a "nice widow" that he could be introduced to. While consultants generally don't run dating services, he was encouraged to join in activities that would help him meet new friends, male and female, develop a new passion in life, or participate in a new hobby, a new venture, or some volunteer work.

Tips for Generating Solutions

- Articulate the problem to be solved;

- Find out what's been tried;

- Don't suggest old solutions, but instead help clients generate their own solutions to their problems;

- Stay focused on the *common ground, the future,* not the past and the differences;

- Help them to find a new way of looking at the issue so they can find their own new solutions;

- Do something different. This is the consultant's equivalent of lighting the fire on the hill, making a seemingly unsolvable problem solvable, by thinking outside the parameters that the client has established. (For example, Louise emphasized that the problem was simply a matter of business restructuring and did not mention Sam's drinking. *Lighting the fire on the hill* in order to save the family business meant that several problems had to be solved in order to restructure the business, for example, business and family goals, as well as Sam's drinking. It involves challenging the basic assumptions of the family business);

- Settle the ground rules for the negotiations. (For East-South Holdings, this included *who* would be in the negotiations, the length and frequency of the meetings, and the role of the spouses and the lawyers. By starting this way, the issues of Sam's drinking, buy-in to the negotiations, and the potential for lawsuits were addressed even *before* the negotiations began. The three siblings decided that they alone would be part of the negotiations; they could discuss the details only with their spouses and their lawyers. The goal was to draw up a "memorandum of understanding" that would be drafted by the attorneys after it was agreed on. In these pre-negotiation negotiation meetings, all of the tricky issues were raised and dealt with. The consultant was able to make the appropriate referrals for Sam, after a separate meeting with Louise and Sam together, to deal directly with the drinking problem. Gerald and Judy confronted Louise at the pre-negotiation meetings with support and help from the consultant. Louise was able to hear her siblings' issues in the safety of the meetings and begin to deal with them and confront Sam in a direct and supportive way); and

- Identify what's needed to close the gap between what is the present reality and the ideal future state.

Planning Ahead: After the Feedback Session

During and after the feedback session, it is important to gauge the family's reaction to the feedback and to potential solutions that have been generated. We have found that clients may openly accept the feedback and the proposed solutions, or they may deny the data, resist it, or completely reject it. How the consultant reacts to the client's reactions is critical for a successful consultation. Ways of responding to these different reactions are listed in Table 4.3.

Table 4.3. Clients' Reactions to Feedback and the Consultant's Responses

Family's Reaction	How You React	What You Do
Acceptance	Cautious optimism; commend them for taking this step.	Refer to the contract and plan next steps; be sure not to get caught up in the enthusiasm and speed up the work.
Denial	Understand position and reframe denial as system's old way of coping; clarify difference between denying problems and actions to be taken.	Have family members tell you what they actually heard from the report. Change contract steps to most effectively work through the denial; start with those who have less denial of problems to mobilize energy for change. Attacking denial "head on" does not remove it, but only makes it stronger.
Resistance	Reframe resistance as family's way of protecting itself from too much change too quickly, a normal reaction.	Refer to contract and readjust time frame to a slower one. Most of us take in information in fragments, bit by bit, with some giant leaps.

**Table 4.3. Clients' Reactions to Feedback
and the Consultant's Responses, Cont'd**

Family's Reaction	How You React	What You Do
Rejection	Respect family's position; clarify whether all in family reject the feedback or only some. If all, find out if this is temporary and they need more time to decide. If only some, is it the ones in formal or informal power? Who makes the decision? Have they rejected your report or you?	If only a few reject your feedback, see how the contract can be modified to reflect your mutual goals. If all reject, find out why and schedule a follow-up meeting to review this.

By anticipating various client reactions to the feedback, the consultant can be prepared to respond in appropriate ways and continue to make progress. Without such preparation, we have found that inappropriate responses by the consultant can spell disaster and undermine the entire consultation.

Additional Tips for a Feedback Meeting

In addition to what we have already suggested for giving feedback and generating solutions, we have found the following tips to be extremely helpful in creating a fruitful feedback session.

Tip 1. The more dysfunctional the family, the less they can hear the feedback, and the more they need the help. Slow down; pay close attention to the process. For example, in the conflict-ridden Jones family, as they were challenged in the change process, each of the individuals would pull aside the consultant at the beginning of each meeting to report on how terrible the others were, how they were not cooperating, doing anything that was suggested, and so on. This was predictable, for until they each began to take responsibility for their own roles in the problems, they would continue to blame one another. Instead of asking, "What can I do differently? How am I contributing to the problem?" they persisted in asking "How can [I/we/consultant] get [mother, father, sister, brother] to change?" One entire family meeting was spent on this issue, and the ground roles were modified to include: No talking about the others; the questions have to be framed to include *your* role and *your* responsibility in this and how *you* will change. Once this became part of the structure of the communications, each began to take more responsibility for himself or herself and stopped the blaming. The energy was refocused to possible change and solutions.

Tip 2. Continue to institute and teach new rules and norms for cultural changes. For example, one person talks at a time; make "I" statements; introduce facts and objective reality; teach compromise. (See Edgar Schein's book, *Process Consultation*, for additional help.) Seemingly simple rules like "No interruptions," "Really listen to what is being said," "Understand what your agenda is and admit it," and "Repeat back to the speaker what you heard; don't jump in with your opinion first" can create major changes in the way the family relates and go a long way in improving relationships.

Tip 3. Insight alone doesn't change behavior; behavior changes alone don't produce insight. Both are needed for change.

Tip 4. Whether or not the family actually comprehends the feedback, the feedback process can still produce a reaction. If a parent wants only to hear positive things about a son whom the parent wants to be the successor, that will definitely affect what the parent hears.

Tip 5. Although the impact of the information is enough to produce change, it may not be in the direction you want. At one meeting, the consultant suggested to the only daughter, who was criticized regularly by her brothers, that she demand respect. She took this as permission not only to demand respect but also to expect unreasonable compensation for her past poor treatment. For example, she wanted double her present salary, which was out of line with the job she was doing.

Tip 6. Invite other family advisors (such as lawyers or accountants) to attend the feedback retreat to give their recommendations only after you have discussed the feedback and the recommendations with them. This should be done early in the retreat, with the later hours saved for family only. At this point, the board of advisors, if there is one, would not be included. This is a time of risk and vulnerability for the family and the number of outsiders needs to be limited. If the consultant thinks that their input would be valuable, they should be included in the interview and assessment process.

Tip 7. You and the family are searching for common ground; conflicts during this meeting should be relegated to the background but addressed with a plan to deal with them at a later date. ("Dad and daughter will discuss this between now and the next meeting; they will report back to us what they have decided to do about this.")

Tip 8. Demonstrate a willingness to engage in conflict and demonstrate that it is not harmful, scary, or irresolvable. (We often work with conflicts "on the side" and parallel to the larger group work, for example, with siblings who are in conflict.)

Tip 9. Your reaction to your clients' reactions is critical in the change process and your survival as a consultant. Your clients may experience strong emotions; you may see anger and tears in such sessions. You must be prepared to work in an emotionally charged atmosphere and not be unnerved by emotional outbursts.

Tip 10. You should always be increasing your repertoire of skills and competencies to deal with what comes up or know where to go for help. For example, take courses or attend workshops and seminars related both to your core discipline and to the other disciplines. Join or start a multidisciplinary study group. If you're a legal consultant, take some workshops on family relationships and team building. If you're a family relationships expert or an OD consultant, attend a course on tax laws or compensation and benefits.

Tip 11. The transition from hearing the feedback to planning should occur about two-thirds of the way through the feedback session/retreat, so that the family can leave with a concrete accomplishment and plan of action. Any needed skills or techniques should have been reviewed and practiced (reaching a consensus, assertive communication, decision making) before moving to action planning. The feedback phase of the consultation should have served to (1) create a collective understanding of the problems and (2) build collective confidence in the family members to move to the next step. The family creates a list of areas to work on.

"To change and to change for the better are two different things."

German proverb

Sure Ways to Become Bogged Down in the Feedback Meeting

- Focus on the past;
- Focus on the negatives and areas of difference, rather than on positives and areas of agreement;
- Impose your values and goals on the process;
- Ignore the process; focus only on the content; be unsure of the difference;
- Ignore the undiscussables;

- Don't give everyone a chance to speak and be heard and don't use your power as a consultant to allow all an opportunity for input;

- Allow yourself to be sidetracked from the "real work" that has to be faced;

- Impose a solution rather than creating an environment that encourages safety, creativity, and risk taking;

- Confuse neutrality with giving no feedback or advice;

- Get thrown off by high emotionality of the relationships;

- Confuse noise with signals;

- Miss patterns of behavior and communications;

- Confuse disconnected events with patterns; and

- Be unclear about your role and contract with the client.

Dealing with Conflicts

As noted earlier, most of the difficulties in family businesses have to do with conflict, usually expressed as communication or behavioral problems. To save the client time, money, and energy, it is critical that the consultant know the difference between *simple* and *complex* conflicts and prepare the clients for the time, energy, and resources that may have to be spent to resolve the conflicts. *Simple conflicts* are not tangled in the family's emotional history and usually respond to commonsense remedies. *Complex conflicts* often start as simple conflicts that unfortunately have been mishandled, denied, ignored, or misunderstood and have become chronic and recycle through the family and the business. *Complex* conflicts are those in which the emotional issues obstruct the resolution of critical business decisions. The family issues and business issues are entangled in a nonproductive way. As in the East-South Holdings case, Louise and Gerald were not able to keep their negative, personal feelings out of the business. *Simple* conflicts are those in which the family issues, although ever-present, do not get in the way of business decisions, and business dilemmas are kept out of family relations.

Some complex problems must be handled by a competent counselor or family therapist rather than by someone trained as an OD consultant or in some other discipline. Most family businesses present at least one complex conflict, which can usually be quickly identified in the first phone call and explored more fully in the genogram. Table 4.4 outlines some of the differences between simple and complex conflicts.

Table 4.4. Simple and Complex Conflicts

Type of Conflict	Signs/Symptoms	Interventions
Simple	Here and now	*Linear;* common sense
	Solution-focused	Education/content-based
	No defensiveness	Insight
	Introduces solutions	Information
	Literal statement	Facts
	Able to use information	Data
	Rational thinking	Persuasion
		Suggestions
		Warn about the tidal wave
Complex	There and then	*Nonlinear;* different level of intervention
	Problem-focused	Reframe, re-label
	Defensive	Experiential/process-based
	Recycling arguments	Visioning, metaphors
	Unable to use information	Questions
	Irrational thinking	Focus on positives
		Patience and role modeling
		Light a fire!

Families need to learn not how to avoid conflicts, but how to resolve them while they're still simple. *Consultants need to know the difference.*

Family businesses are fertile ground for complex conflicts that undermine sound business decisions and practices. Paradoxically, the closer the members in the family become through work and play, the more each member may feel a pull for autonomy or independence. Conflict is a way of managing too much closeness (Lerner, 1990). Another way to manage excessive togetherness is "pseudo harmony," or "pseudo mutuality," where the family displays little overt conflict. In these cases, the goal of the consultant is to surface the issues and resolve them.

Every family who works and lives together has felt this occasionally: "How many hours in a day can you be with the same people?" This natural pull for independence is usually expressed as differences of opinion, sometimes anger, and even distancing. For example, the child who is raised in a family business may move far away, wanting nothing to do with it. (It is important to include any and all family members in the interview process and each meeting whenever possible, even if they live far away. This is especially true for the longer planning meetings, retreats, and council meetings. With technologies such as speakerphones and teleconferencing, this can and should be arranged.)

The benefits of resolving conflicts in the life of a family include the following:

- Maintaining an acceptable distance/closeness between family members and helping the family keeps a check on values and goals. For example, an adolescent's struggle with his parents serves the process of him or her becoming an adult with his or her own opinions, dreams, and goals.

- Differences of opinions are healthy and necessary in any family; when encouraged, they create a rich diversity.

- Building self-confidence, especially in the succeeding generation, which needs to feel independent from the parents, even while working with them. Differences of opinion should be encouraged and, indeed, are necessary in creative problem solving. If all agree, problem solving may be ineffective and lack creativity.

- Increasing intimacy in work and family; resolved and successfully managed conflicts create strength in the bonds between family members. A disagreement does not mean rejection or disapproval, but can lead to improved relationships in the family and planning for the business.

Simple and Complex Conflicts: Clues to Tell the Difference

Gerald and Louise's arguments invariably led to a heated discussion of the past, the *there-and-then*: how Louise had put up the money for the company in the beginning, how Gerald had not kept his eye on things, how Louise had always been difficult to get along with, even when they were kids. Each accused the other of past crimes: "You've always been careless" and "You've always been jealous of my being able to think fast on my feet." (When you hear words like "always" and "never," you're inside a complex conflict.) Simple conflicts focus on the *here and now*.

Complex conflicts concentrate on the problems and on laying blame. A single argument reminds the parties of other conflicts they never solved. Hopelessly, they can only think of their problems together. As Louise said, every time she and Gerald start a discussion, each only remembers the other times that they have felt helpless and unable to make decisions: "It always leads to a fight." (When all you can think is "This isn't going to work," you're inside a complex conflict.) By contrast, simple conflicts focus on solutions: "How can we figure out a way so that a buyout will be the best for each of us and the business?"

Louise, Judy, and Gerald were defensive with each other. We raise defenses when we perceive danger, discomfort, or difficulties or when we feel vulnerable. When complex conflicts become embedded in family members' relationships, unresolved topics trigger the defense mechanisms, which then prevent a real, honest exchange. At this point, the defense mechanisms, such as avoiding, denying, attacking, sarcasm, or "hitting below the belt" get in the way of solving the problem and making a sound decision. Louise and Gerald always put on their armor and refused to listen to one another; they would fire accusations and then retreat. (When the anger is escalating and the silence is relentless, you're inside a complex problem.) In simple conflicts, each side takes into consideration what the other is saying and the decision-making process moves forward to a conclusion.

Conflict is a normal reaction to the changes and stresses of daily work and life. The goal for the family in business together is not to eliminate conflict, but to learn techniques for solving and resolving it as it emerges in everyday experiences. By learning how to resolve conflicts early, the family business system can become more productive and can spend less time arguing and more time enjoying one another and the business.

In this chapter we've attempted to outline how to present feedback to the client, how to generate solutions, and how to develop an action plan. Inherent in this phase of the consultation are the conflicts that inevitably arise. Consultants must learn to distinguish between simple and complex conflicts and to create an atmosphere of trust and openness that allows these conflicts to be surfaced and managed. This is not easy, but is the essence of creating a successful consulting engagement. The next step is the intervention phase that will be discussed in Chapter 5. Although these steps are described as discrete stages, collaborative work with the client is never linear. The feedback stage includes interventions, and the intervention work involves as series of steps that also involve feedback and planning. Chapter 5 will build on the ideas of conflict resolution, planning, and role of the consultant in the change process.

In Exhibit 4.3, we have presented several exercises that might be useful to consultants to help families improve their communications, problem-solving skills, and conflict-management skills as they attempt to work their way through this feedback action-planning phase.

Exhibit 4.3. Retreat Exercises

These samples and exercises should be tailored to each family and made appropriate to their skills and functioning level.

Ground Rules

Each family should have ground rules tailored to fit. The consultant should make suggestions and the family then adds to or subtracts from the list. Some possible rules follow:

- What we say here remains in the room unless decided otherwise.
- Listen actively. If you are stuck, see if you can repeat what the other person has said or ask questions of him or her in order to understand what you missed.
- Keep the goals and objectives of the family and business uppermost. Continue to ask yourself, "What is best for the family and business?" This does not mean that you ignore your own feelings; in fact, you can use them as a valuable resource.
- One person talks at a time. Everyone will have an opportunity to speak.
- Keep an open mind. Remember, "Where you stand depends on where you sit."
- Make "I" statements. Don't blame or attack; talk about how *you* feel and what you think.
- Understand the boundaries. Be aware of and identify what "hat" you are wearing. Members in family businesses often wear several hats; today, acknowledge which one you're wearing at any one time. Is it brother, father, president, son, daughter, or what?

3" x 5" Card Activity

On the 3" x 5" cards in your packet, write your family role on one side and your business or ownership role on the other. As you participate, turn the card to the side that represents the role you are playing or speaking from at that moment. (Another consultant notes that he bought New Year's Eve party hats and had a card designed for each of the roles and used those during the work with the client with the instructions that they were to announce their primary role and then put on a hat when that role was changing.)

Setting the Agenda

From the SWOT report, the consultant facilitates a discussion prioritizing the work for the session. Ask the question: "What decisions or plans have to be made now that will not wait?" Make a list of "Important Issues" on a flip chart. These items are taken from the Weaknesses and Threats list. From that, usually by consensus, sometimes by vote, the agenda items are prioritized on a flip chart and this becomes a working list that is reviewed and modified on the last day for future steps and planning.

Exhibit 4.3. Retreat Exercises, Cont'd

Meditation "Inside Out"

This meditation ends the day with no discussion afterward, for a "Zeigarnick"* effect. The consultant can lead the meditation with the following instructions:

> Most successful planning and decision making starts from the inside. It is based on your own values and sense of self and what is important to you. Go inside to understand what gives you vitality and energy. What is important to you? What do you value deeply? What do you want to achieve? When was the last time in your work experience that you felt most involved, most engaged, most alive? How can you recapture that? What legacy do you want to leave? How do you want to be remembered? Now consider what you want to contribute to this weekend. What do you want to change in the ways that you are with others in the family and the businesses? What would you like to learn from others? By the end of the retreat, what do you want to say that the family has achieved? What do you want to have achieved? Now, without any further discussion, take these thoughts with you and have a good rest for the next day's work! Sleep on it!

Strategic Planning Process

- Present a lecturette on strategic planning, with several bullet points:
- Something you do, rather than have.
- Based on quality data and values (refer to meditation of previous evening)
- Ask four questions:

  Where are we?

  What is changing or staying the same in the market?

  Where are we going?

  How do we get there?

- The planning process

  Articulate mission

---

*When we end the day in the middle of a task, the need remains in us to complete unfinished business. This insight was proven by Blum Zeigarnick, a student of Kurt Lewin's at Berlin University in the 1920s. Lewin, a genius at building theory from everyday events, noticed how a waiter in his favorite coffee shop kept a running total in his head, no matter how large the group, what they ate, or how long they sat. Once the bill was paid, he promptly forgot the bill. Zeigarnick, in a series of experiments, showed that we build up a store of energy that is discharged by completing a task. By breaking in the middle of tasks on both evenings, we keep learning alive in the group and make start-up each morning easy. Hence, the term *"zeigarnicks."* (Weisbord & Janoff, 2000, p. 93). Reprinted with permission of the publisher. From *Future Search (2nd Ed.),* copyright © 2000 by Marvin R. Weisbord and Sandra Janoff, Berrett-Koehler Publishers, Inc. San Francisco, CA. All rights reserved. 1-800-929-2929.

Exhibit 4.3. Retreat Exercises, Cont'd

Identify critical issues and trends

Set goals

Identify and write down the three W's: *What* is to be done; *Who* will do it, *When* will it be finished?

Implement

Set time to evaluate

Brainstorming

This technique is introduced when creative solutions are needed, the problem is complex, and/or the participants are jumping to answers/solutions too quickly. It's also a fun break if things have become bogged down. Following are the guidelines:

· Tell participants they should suggest possible solutions to a problem.

· Allow ten minutes.

· No critical judgments are allowed.

· Quantity, not quality, is desired.

· The wilder the idea, the better, for the moment is best!

· Hitchhiking, also referred to as piggybacking, (combinations and improvements) is encouraged.

> "If at first, the idea is not absurd, then, there is no hope for it."
>
> *Albert Einstein*

Assertive Communication (Telling the Difference: Assertive, Passive, or Aggressive?)

Assertive Tone

· Opinions, feelings, and wants are directly stated without alienating others

· Speaks in a calm, clear tone of voice

· Respects differences

· Makes clear "I" statements

Passive Tone

· Opinions, feelings, and wants are withheld or expressed only partially

· Speaks softly and indirectly

· Sends message of submission

· Apologizes for stating needs and wants

Exhibit 4.3. Retreat Exercises, Cont'd

Aggressive Tone

- Opinions, feelings, and wants are honestly stated but at the expense of someone else's feelings
- Speaks loudly and directly
- Uses sarcasm, threats, negative labels, finger pointing, blaming, and so forth
- Attacks others' opinions and feelings

Fishbowl Exercise

The consultant asks for two volunteers who have a *simple* conflict that has not yet been resolved. (The consultant needs to use the information from the assessment to make certain that the two volunteers have a reasonable chance to settle their disagreement!) They are then asked to describe their conflict/disagreement. While the others observe, the volunteers try to reach a negotiated solution. They can ask for help or coaching from the others, take time to brainstorm, and try to use assertive, not passive or aggressive, statements. The consultant uses this opportunity to teach ways to reach a solution and how to handle situations that cannot be solved at the moment, for instance, more data may be needed, other opinions are necessary, or the decision is premature.

The Wheel*

This is a modification of the exercise, "Multiple Perspectives" in *The Fifth Discipline Fieldbook* (Senge, Kleiner, Roberts, Ross, & Smith, 1994, pp. 273–275). Originally designed to widen a team's point of view, it is ideal for family members to appreciate others' perspectives and their own potential role conflicts.

Step 1

Create a disk about eighteen inches in diameter (a clean pizza cardboard does the job) and draw lines across the wheel with the *names* of each person present at the meeting. On 3'' x 5'' cards, write a description of the *titles* of each person. The cards should describe not only the work titles but also the circle or circles that the person is in. For example, "President, Family, Owner, Business" or "Sister, Owner, Family." Each person sits in front of his or her name and 3'' x 5'' card description.

Step 2

The wheel is turned one "pizza slice." At each turn of the wheel, each person adds his or her perspective to the *title* in front of his or her name. Decide beforehand if you will ask for a general description ("The family's strengths are . . .") or a solution to a problem ("Harriet sees the problem this way . . ."). For example, Mort's name lands adjacent to vice president of sales (family and business) or Harriet's (owner, family,

---

*"The Wheel" from THE FIFTH DISCIPLINE FIELDBOOK by Peter M. Senge, Charlotte Roberts, et. al, copyright © 1994 by Peter M. Senge, Charlotte Roberts, Richard B. Ross, Bryan J. Smith, and Art Kleiner. Used by permission of Doubleday, a division of Random House, Inc.

Exhibit 4.3. Retreat Exercises, Cont'd

nonbusiness) and completes this sentence: "From my perspective as vice president of sales, I see the problem as. . . ." or "From Harriet's perspective, I see the solution to the problem as. . . ." All comments should be written on a flip chart as if you were the person whose card you have landed on.

Step 3

You will soon have rich descriptions of each person's perspectives. You can either have a general discussion or tackle the problem from multiple perspectives. This exercise challenges assumptions each family member has about the others and stimulates creative thinking about problems.

Mind Mapping

This exercise is an adaptation of the mind mapping technique of Future Search conferences (Weisbord & Janoff, 2000, pp. 88–92)

Step 1

Have everyone come up to a sheet of 6' x 12' butcher block paper posted on a wall, with a circle drawn in the center. Tell the participants the following: "We want to map all external and internal trends that have an impact on your family business now. This is interactive and the more ideas and connections the better."

Step 2

Everyone is then told to call out a trend, for example, "increasing demand for better and quicker service," "decreasing sales in New York," "family is getting bigger," or "increasing demand for environmental awareness." Each trend should be written on a line going out from the center circle. As lines are drawn, look for connections and draw clusters of related issues. If opposing trends are drawn (increasing conflict *and* decreasing conflict, for example), both perceptions are allowed. For each trend, ask for an example to understand what that person's perception is.

Step 3

Each person is given five to seven sticky dots, with colors determined by stakeholder group. This can be coordinated by their place in the system (all owners are blue, for example), their roles, or their place in the family (all children are green). Some people may have several different colors. Each person is told to place the dots on the trends they consider the most important. They may put all seven on one trend, four on one and three on another, or whatever they wish.

Step 4

The members discuss what they observe and make their interpretations.

Step 5

Action planning immediately follows this or begins the next morning.

5

Intervening in Family Firms

"Bloom, damn you, bloom!"

A note written by W.C. Fields to his reluctant rose bush

ON THIS CHAPTER, we will provide a framework for thinking about interventions, with suggestions/tips for you to add to your "tool box" to increase your repertoire, to be prepared for the unexpected, and to avoid cookbook cures and packaged designs. As Billie Holiday claimed, "I can't stand to sing the same song in the same way . . . it ain't music, it's close order drill, an exercise, not music." We want to make music, a "joyful noise," with our clients, and for that creativity, caring, and self-management are needed. The client system will select from those meaningful messages, designs, and information you have to offer. For this we must either know what is meaningful to them or offer enough for them to choose what they see as useful. In this chapter, we will also discuss planned, deliberate attempts to bring about changes that will also affect the unconscious processes. But often the *exact* change can be neither predicted nor designed.

To begin our discussion of how to intervene successfully in family firms, a consulting engagement conducted by Jane will help to illustrate some of the issues encountered when planning for change. While attending a breakfast meeting about family business succession, Jane was approached by a woman named Kathleen Grey, fifty, who asked her what she thought about women being able to succeed their fathers in business. This led to a lively discussion as she began to tell Jane about her family business. A few days later, Jane received a call from Kathleen. She wanted Jane to come in to meet her parents and her two brothers, to "see if you can help us out."

In the "chemistry meeting," Jane learned that approximately sixty-five years before, Kathleen's mother's father, Jim Kelly, and his brother, Bob Kelly, started the business, an automobile dealership, Kelly Cars. The uncle had died, leaving no heirs, and the business was passed on to Jim. Eventually, Kathleen's mother, Ann, and father, Joe, became involved and began to take over for Jim as he grew older. Jim died in 1970 and the business ownership and management were passed on to Ann and Joe.

Ann and Joe, both in their late seventies, still work in the business part time; they each collect $10,000 a year in salary, love to come to work, live very simply, and do not need much for expenses. Twelve years earlier, Kathleen left her job as a bank manager to "come home and help" with the business. Her father gave her the title of president and it was assumed by everyone that she was the heir apparent. Her two younger siblings are involved; Joe, Jr., forty-nine, is sales manager and Dan, forty-five, is in charge of the repair shop. Neither is interested in running the company, but each expects to share in the ownership. The brothers are married and each has two teenage children. Kathleen has no children and is "amicably separated" from her husband, Mike, who lives out of state. None of the inlaws is involved in the business, although Joe, Jr.'s older daughter, Cindy, works in the office during the summers and says she wants to work there when she graduates from college. She is presently a sophomore at a local state school.

At the initial meeting, the family cited the following problems: (1) the parents still owned all of the company, and their only estate planning has been to write a will; (2) there was confusion about who made the decisions; and (3) "We need to establish a means of communication between the business and the family." Kathleen noted, with her brothers agreeing, that Ann and Joe continued to make precipitous decisions without consulting with the family or even letting them know. They were uninformed about the problems faced by family businesses. The most recent decision was to sell a piece of real estate that Kathleen had planned to use to expand the dealership. She had done a lot of research on this and thought it was one of the ways that the business could increase its visibility and sales.

It was surprising to Jane that the business had lasted as long as it did, although there was not much competition in this small farming community. The community was growing and changing, however, and other automobile dealerships were moving close by. An e-mail from Kathleen that followed this first meeting said that "it felt like a breath of fresh air."

Jane agreed to work with the Kellys. In the individual interviews of the assessment phase, Kathleen revealed that she was a "manic-depressive, usually under control with medication." This illness runs in the family; her maternal grandmother was affected, and she thinks that Dan may also suffer from it, although he denies it. It was the reason that Kathleen had decided not to have children. The other problem that was mentioned by Ann and Joe was the fact that "sales are down." With this information and the family's permission, Jane spoke with their accountant, Phil, and lawyer, Nancy. It is important to involve, always with the family's permission and understanding, the other advisors early on in the process; they should certainly be included in the initial interview process and, at that point, a decision should be made with the family whether or not to have them attend any of the family meetings. In some cases, there should also be a contact with the therapists involved. The reasons for including them are that they have important data that the family must hear; they are part of the solution and should be kept informed; they have long-term, family-like relationships with the family members; and their presence will "sanction" the process. (See more about advisor teams in Chapter 8.) A more difficult situation arises if it becomes evident that the advisors are inadequate for the job, insufficiently experienced, or part of the problem. The consultant must be sensitive to this in the interviews and make a determination about how to deal with this issue. There are several things that can be done in this case: educate the family so that they can come to their own solutions or advise that a specialist be brought in for their situation. It has been our experience that in difficult family situations, the advisors welcome the help. Each of the situations must be handled with care and sensitivity.

In the case of Kelly Cars, both advisors were alarmed at the financial state of the business, which was "losing money"; something had to be done soon. They were very concerned that the family seemed to ignore their warnings and, except for Kathleen, wanted them to handle all the legal and financial details. When Jane asked Kathleen why she had not mentioned this at the first meeting, she said that she "didn't think things were that bad" and that she "didn't want to worry the family unnecessarily." She joked that all businesses had their "ups and downs, just like me."

Before intervening in this family business, Jane felt that she had to answer several questions:

- What should be the focus of any interventions—the business, the family, the ownership system?
- Should I start with the finances? What technical issues, such as the decrease in sales, the increasing competition, and strategic planning for the direction of the dealership do I tackle?
- What do I do about the denial of the financial problems?
- Do I need to educate the family regarding certain issues?
- Do I start by dealing with the communications problems between family members?
- Do I sit them down and let them know how bad things are?
- How "personal" do I have to get to make changes?
- How much does Kathleen's illness affect her judgment?
- What should be done (if anything) about her illness?

These are the kinds of questions that need to be answered before one takes action. In this chapter we will explore how to answer these kinds of questions in order to choose an appropriate intervention strategy.

Intervening in Family Firms

Literally, *intervention* means "to come between." It is what happens in the *Implementation Phase*. This is the "moving, changing" stage in Kurt Lewin's three phases of the "unfreeze, move/change, refreeze" model. A metaphor we use is boarding a train in the middle of the client's life journey and getting off before it reaches the end. During our trip with the client, questions about the speed, direction, and destination of the train (change process) are carefully considered. We also want to emphasize the iterative process of our change efforts. In our interactions with our clients, patterns emerge as we learn and teach new solutions. (For more on the lessons we can learn from the life sciences and organization change, see *Facilitating Organization Change*, by Olson & Eoyang, 2001.)

No matter what we as consultants do or how effective or ineffective we are, the family business will not be the same after our entry into the system. They may be better or worse off, but certainly they will be different. Our presence changes the context. As in any evolutionary process, changes in the environment, no matter how small, lead to changes in the nature of the species. For example, a colleague of ours who has developed software to analyze and manage the "tangible and intangible wealth" of family businesses has discovered, not surprisingly, that the process of completing an in-depth questionnaire is a powerful intervention. In the same way, we will not be the same after an engagement. Ask yourself: "What have I learned from each client engagement?" "How am I different after each engagement?" "If I haven't changed in my thinking or working, why not?" "How has the client changed?"

Implementation Phase of the Action Research Model

Once we understand the nature of the client's problems and are armed with good theory, we can begin to take steps to choose appropriate interventions to help the client. Table 5.1 outlines the goals, questions, desired outcomes, and risks and potential problems associated with the implementation phase of the consulting process.

In our experience, success in the implementation phase is related to (1) what the client brings; (2) what the consultant brings; and (3) the agreement that the client and the consultant have on the goals of the consulting engagement.

What the Client Brings

We have found that clients who have families that function reasonably well, who are not defensive, and who have motivation to solve their problems are more likely to succeed than those families who suffer from serious problems that are accompanied by denial, defensiveness, and disagreement with the consultant or with one another. Some clients also do not have the resources, patience, or courage to go as

Table 5.1. Implementation Phase of the Action Research Model

Goal	Questions	Desired Outcome	Risks/Potential Problems
To help the client system manage the change process effectively.	What are the most effective interventions, based on the data gathered and the reciprocal feedback between the consultant and client? What are the most likely reactions to the change process? What level of intervention is needed? What should be the focus of the change process? What type of change is needed to achieve the mutually agreed on goals? What is the most appropriate use of the multidisciplinary team with this particular family business? What will the resistance look like? What should be the consultant's response to the resistance? (Ongoing questioning of the interventions will give answers about the next steps to take.)	To achieve the mutually agreed on goals defined in the feedback meeting.	The outcome is always unpredictable. Being inflexible and approaching with a "cook book" for the family to follow. Not finding the balance between structures and allowing things to unfold creatively. The same information, process, and actions bring different results to different clients. Having a limited repertoire. Over- or under-simplifying the family's ability to achieve its goals. Not being prepared for the family's response. Not being able to achieve the goals. Not introducing the interventions in a manner that the family can accomplish. Not responding effectively to the family's acceptance, denial, resistance, or rejection or a combination. Not being prepared for the "ripple effect" or social multiplier of the changes occurring.

far as is needed to make the necessary changes. Those families who want to create a new future for themselves and their firms, who are open and optimistic, and who have the energy and resources to make needed changes are most successful. Thus, the consultant, after doing an initial assessment, may come to realize that the family is not ready for change and could end the engagement or could help the family develop the necessary commitment and skills to manage the change process.

What the Consultant Brings

Not only does the family need to be prepared for change, but the consultant does as well. As we have mentioned previously, consultants need the appropriate skill mix that fits the problems facing the clients. (See more about this in Chapter 7.) In our experience, consultants who do not have the appropriate skills for a particular client and who are not willing to bring in other professionals to help them are guilty of malpractice and do a disservice to their clients. Consultants can also miscalculate clients' readiness to change and therefore try to move them either too quickly or too slowly. Some clients also need more structure as they manage the change process, while others are willing to live with more ambiguity. Thus, the consultant must have the skills and insight to meet the unique needs and characteristics of each client. We have also found that consultants who can teach clients new skills and share with them new ways of functioning tend to be more successful. Teaching and modeling appropriate behaviors is often very important for families who have fallen into dysfunctional modes of operating. The effective consultant is also patient and recognizes the time and energy needed to help a client. The ineffective consultant often underestimates the time and energy needed and therefore doesn't develop the resources needed to make the consultation a success. In working with family businesses, we find that it is important to actually *care* about our clients as individuals and as members of families. We have found that working in family firms allows us to be party to many of the fears, hopes, and dreams of our clients. This provides us with the opportunity to develop deeper insights into our clients and develop emotional and social bonds that go beyond the typical client-consultant relationship found in the business world. Finally, consultants who have the ability to work jointly with clients to problem solve creatively are the most effective. The problems family businesses face often seem intractable at first. However, with a creative mind and collaboration on the part of the family, the consultant can often help the family come up with solutions that can solve even the most difficult problems.

Degree of Agreement on Goals of the Change Process

The final factor for a successful consultation that we will consider is the degree of agreement that is needed between the consultant and the client. There must be a high level of mutual trust and respect between both parties, and there must be agreement on the goals of the consultation. It is important to set the goals of the action plan jointly with the client. Those consultants who tend to promise too much, impose their goals and values on the client, and fail to include the client in the change process are doomed to failure. Trust between the consultant and the client is key. Thus, the consultant must follow through on his or her commitments and the client must do so as well. In many ways it is just as important for the client to pay his or her bills on time as it is for the consultant to meet the agreed-on consultation schedule. Without mutual trust and respect and a willingness to engage each other in a collaborative fashion, the consultation is likely to end in failure.

The Change System

The *change system* consists of the client and consultant (Green, 1988) and the feedback system between them, which includes processes of mutual influence and reciprocal reactions. Change does not occur in a straight line but is often disorderly. The real story is in both the consultant's and the client's reactions to the events as they unfold. Some have argued that maintaining a "steady state" or "equilibrium" should be the goal of a consultation. However, as Burke (1994) notes, consultants often "overly emphasize the client's achieving a steady state and equilibrium." The very essence of life is change and transformation. We need to shift our thinking: The real world has little to do with steady states. Family businesses with all their variables hardly hold still long enough to achieve a steady state. "Life is always poised for flight. From a distance it looks still . . . but, up close, it is flitting this way and that, as if displaying to the world at every moment its perpetual readiness to take off in any of a 1,000 directions" (Weiner, 1995). In fact, our job as change agents is (1) to challenge the status quo; (2) to teach and model behaviors that will help the client deal with life's ever-changing nature; and (3) to help our clients see change as normal and necessary to adaptation and survival.

It is at "the edge of chaos" that creativity usually occurs. Chaos in this modern sense is not the same as disorder, but a delicate balance between order and disorder, a dynamic tension. A systems framework helps us to accept the challenge of this tension between persistence and change. The Kellys are approaching this point of chaos with their finances, with Kathleen's health, and with their confused communications. But their caring and loyalty for one another, their good family name in the community, and the talent of their employees can carry them through the rough times to success. Kelly Cars had survived for sixty-five years, but now their world was changing. The sleepy farm town was becoming a bedroom community of a large metropolitan city. This external change offered both opportunities and threats. The key to their survival was in their ability to adapt and change, to reorganize and use the strengths that existed in their system.

Type of Change Required

Since change is always the goal of interventions, we need to be clear on the type of change needed and possible. There are two major types of changes, incremental and fundamental.

Incremental or First-Order Change

Beckhard, in *Changing the Essence* (Beckhard & Pritchard, 1992), described *incremental change*; family therapists refer to this as *first-order change* or a change that occurs within the system and conforming to the existing rules. First-order changes, which are evolutionary and continuous, would include the following:

- *Readjustments to the work roles and/or family involvement.* An example of this for the Kelly family would be for each to discuss what he or she could do to create more open communications.

- *Fine-tuning or adjustments to procedures that improve the business but do not change it fundamentally.* The Kellys would all work harder to increase sales and modernize the show room.

Fundamental or Second-Order Change

Fundamental or second-order change involves a change in the rules of the system and, subsequently, the system itself. Thus, this type of change, which is revolutionary and discontinuous, includes the following:

- *Essential changes in the organization's culture, vision, and strategy.* For the Kellys, this might mean opening a new store, changing the existing vision or product of the company.

- *Large changes in the way a company or family functions.* This might include building new systems for succession and management, selling the company, or dividing it into separate companies to be managed by each of the siblings.

It is important for the consultant to differentiate the kinds of changes that are going to be needed. Incremental or first-order changes require less time and effort and typically don't foster a great deal of resistance. On the other hand, second-order changes often require significant paradigm shifts on the part of the client. They are being asked to think, feel, and behave in very different ways. This type of change may take a significant amount of time and energy—and it may not even be possible given the characteristics of the client. To choose the type of intervention needed, one must know how "deep" he or she must go to achieve the change that is necessary.

Depth of Intervention

Roger Harrison (1970) describes in his article, "Choosing the Depth of Organizational Intervention," a useful framework for thinking about family business interventions. Table 5.2, an adaptation of Harrison's framework, outlines intervention possibilities for family business systems and applies this framework to Kelly Cars.

Table 5.2. Levels of Intervention

Level	Task	Intervention/Example	Kelly Cars
T-1	*Analysis and development of operations in the business, ownership:* roles and functions within the business and ownership; balance sheet; sales; legal entity; ownership structure; strategic planning	Designing roles and role relationships involved in tasks, resources, operations of the business; evaluating how company is doing, environmental pressures; assessing functioning of boards of advisors and directors	Who does what? Job descriptions; Who makes what decisions? The financial picture; strategic planning. Legal, tax, and financial picture of parents' estate plan; developing an outside board; strategic planning
T-2	*Individual performances and structures for implementation:* what an individual is able and likely to achieve; job descriptions; evaluations	Work with selection, placement, and appraisal of employees, family and nonfamily; influence performance by rewards, and punishments; compensation and benefits packages for nonfamily	Best people for jobs; compensation and benefits; training employees; hiring and firing policies; employee handbook; whom to hire for which positions

Table 5.2. Levels of Intervention, Cont'd

Level	Task	Intervention/Example	Kelly Cars
T/E-3	*Analysis of working relationships:* how an individual perceives his or her role, what he or she values and devalues; integrated succession planning	Interested in the individual as a doer of work or performer of functions, not in relationships; mentoring programs for family; comp and benefits for family; values-based strategic planning	Long-range strategic plan for family and its involvement in business; family's mentoring program; reward system for family; frank discussion of future roles. Develop outside board. Skill development for family. Facilitating family meetings
E-4	*Interpersonal relationships:* focus on feelings and attitudes, perceptions individuals have of one another; sibling relationships; parenting; family dynamics	Concerned with the quality of human relationships, acceptance, rejection, trust, and suspicion among groups and individuals; work to create openness and help individuals develop mutual understanding of one another as persons; sibling team building; sibling conflicts; family communications and history. Experiential activities; communication exercises	Sibling team building; family communications; group dynamics; role conflicts; family dynamics: triangling, scapegoating; boundaries between family and business roles. Values and mission for the family and the business
E-5	*Intrapersonal analysis:* individual's deeper attitudes, values, feelings; focus on increasing the range of experiences the individual can bring into awareness and cope with; individual perceptions; self-esteem; addictions	Interventions may include nonverbal and non-interpersonal strategies. Therapy: individual, couples, and marital; leadership and executive coaching; educational/behavior therapy; identity issues	Kathleen's ability to function in her role; Dan's denial of his illness; coaching for siblings to move into sibling executive team; parents' ability to let go and plan for next stage

T = Technical   E = Emotional

Adapted from Harrison, 1970.

The assumptions underlying this approach to choosing an appropriate intervention include the following:

Each level requires specific skills and competencies. For example, lawyers would be needed to deal with the legal restructuring of a company or the legal issues of a succession plan. An accountant would be needed for the tax and financial details of a buyout. An OD professional may be best suited to sibling team building and developing reasonable and fair compensation and benefits for family members. A trained therapist would be necessary to deal with the intrapersonal interventions.

The technical and emotional exist in a reinforcing loop. Improvements in the technical levels, such as clear roles and role relationships, development of a sound estate plan, fair compensation and benefits packages, promote healthier emotional relationships which, in turn, support good business practices and creative planning.

The lower the level, the more hidden and private are the issues and the more difficult, and sometimes more risky, to access and change. Although it is tempting to say that second-order changes only happen as a result of the lower levels of intervention, this is not always the case. Huge events can have a negligible effect and a small event can have huge effects. Input is not necessarily proportional to output, especially where there are as many variables as there are in family businesses. So we need to be sensitive and strategic about our small and large interventions. For example, in the middle of one family retreat, an accountant, not part of the advisory team but a long-time confidant to the parents, asked what appeared to be a "simple question" of the thirty-year-old middle child in the family. The question referred to his plans for the future. The son was suffering from clinical depression and, consequently, could not imagine his future. He broke into tears and fled the room. His response and his parents' reaction changed the course of the consultation, which was initially about succession planning. This simple event had a significant effect. Mistakes can lead to profound changes and chains of events and magnify small changes. (This incident also demonstrates the challenge of multidisciplinary teams, forming good partnerships, and the critical need to pay attention to who does what at the retreat.)

Assets and liabilities are on a continuum in the table from tangible (T-1) to intangible (E-5). We can only intervene in a tangible, visible, objective way; the patterns that connect, the values that direct, and the scripts that persist are not accessible to a conscious planned design, but the results of changes at any level may be both visible and invisible, tangible or intangible. For example, a change in the financial picture (Level T-1) of the Kellys may have an enormous effect on the family's sense of security. A change at Level E-5, the most private and invisible, in Kathleen or other family members may have a large impact on the running of the company and subsequently on the financial picture. Leadership coaching, although private and individual, may influence an entire company.

Family businesses have an influential and strong emotional component that requires a deeper level of intervention that will access those emotions. For example, what do Kathleen's brothers think of her being made president as soon as she entered the company? How capable are the siblings of doing their jobs? What are the parents' hopes and fears of transferring the company to the next generation? What has stalled the process? Intervening at the level of T-1 (analysis and development of operations, business, and ownership) or T-2 (evaluating individual performances and structures for implementation) will not be adequate for this. Only when the consultant has intervened at the T/E-3 (process analysis of business and family values and roles) and E-4 (interpersonal relationships) levels will he or she be able to move up to the operations level and deal with the poor performance of the company.

The deeper the level, the less the information is readily available. Getting to it requires special skills of the behaviorally trained professionals. This requires time, commitment, and the agreement that it is necessary. Although the Kellys appear to be open about their communication and decision-making problems, it will take a deeper look at what's beneath the surface to understand what's *really* keeping them from changing, although they know they need change in order to survive. It is also important to understand the level of denial, which can be either healthy or unhealthy. *Healthy denial* means continuing to hope and imagine that things will be better, while continuing to do what is necessary for improving the situation. For example, a cancer patient will believe that he or she will get better but continue to receive the necessary chemotherapy, radiation, or surgery. The Kelly Car family didn't want to accept the financial problems, but did all the things they needed to do to improve the picture. *Unhealthy denial* means continuing to believe that things will be better, against all odds, without obtaining the necessary treatment, doing the things that are necessary. For example, Kelly Cars not only denied the financial problems but did nothing to improve the situation.

The benefits at the lower levels are less transferable in nonfamily businesses but more transferable in family businesses. The emotional, personal impact is greater, especially when dealing with owners and upper-level management.

Harrison's (1970) guidelines outlined in his article apply equally as well to family firms. Thus consultants should:

- "Intervene at a level no deeper than that required to produce enduring solutions to the problems at hand." (p. 417)

- "Intervene at a level no deeper than that at which the energy and resources of the client can be committed to problem solving and to change." (p. 422)

Questions asked about the finances in the assessment phase tell only one part of the story; you also need to know who in the family has the energy, desire, and power to make the necessary changes. The Kellys may all say they want changes in how the family communicates or in how the business is run, but may not have the money, time, or energy to stick to the change process. To which we would add:

- Intervene at a level no deeper than your skills and training allow; and

- Intervene at a level no deeper than that described in the initial contract *without* getting permission from the client system.

In order to deal with the Kelly family's denial of the financial problems, Jane had to gain their agreement to put that on the agenda. Without that permission, their resistance would have overwhelmed the process.

It is important to remember that technical interventions often have reverberations at the emotional level. In adult development, mastery of tasks is critical to self-esteem. How we feel about ourselves affects not only our ability to work with others but our ability to understand and respects others' points of view. How successful a technical intervention is often depends on what happens in the emotional domain and the change system's (client + consultant) reaction to it. In our experience we have found two other ideas to be quite helpful:

1. If focusing on the technical issues doesn't get a response, then it may be appropriate and necessary to move to the emotional levels, assuming that the consultant and client are prepared. For example, in the Jones family in Chapter 4, the previous consultants concentrated only on the technical issues (Levels 1 and 2), leaving notebooks of technical solutions and plans sitting on the shelves.

2. Don't start with the emotional levels, but be ready for them. The family in business will invite the consultant into these levels as they build a relationship of trust with the consultant.

Questions to Ask Yourself About the Client

- What methods, interventions, or techniques can you think of for each level?

- What or who is the focus of change at each level?

- How would you gather data at each level and what information do you need?

- What are the problems you might face at each level?

The Intervention Grid

Figure 5.1 presents a framework that describes different types of interventions organized by where they fall along two continua. The levels of intervention on the "technical-emotional" continuum can be plotted against the "process-content" continuum. For example, an intervention that is high in technical information and content but low in process and emotions would be a tax seminar or educational program. Family retreats, on the other hand, are high both in technical information and in process. This grid suggests the skill set that will be needed by the consultant (or consultants) to work with a family firm client. If the problems are highly emotional and are related to family processes, then a consultant would likely need some skills in therapy. If the problems are just content-oriented—the family needs to know how to set up a buy-sell agreement—then technical skills may be all that are needed. In some cases, such as conducting a family retreat, a mixture of skills is needed. It is important for the consultant to recognize the scope of the skills required to be successful when intervening in a family system. Once the consultant has chosen a specific intervention (or interventions) to employ, he or she needs to understand how to plan and execute the intervention.

Figure 5.1. The Intervention Grid

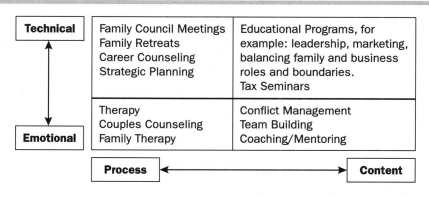

Achievements in either the technical or emotional areas can reinforce future successes. For example, if the Kellys hold regular family council meetings and plan strategically for the family and the business' future, they will have practice in dealing with conflict more effectively, which, in turn, will put them in a better position to tackle succession planning. The important thing to remember is that success at one level can produce success in the other.

Resistance

"We rather bear those ills we have than fly to others we know not of."

Shakespeare in Hamlet

Before we turn our attention to specific interventions, a discussion of resistance is fitting since it is a normal and healthy reaction to any change process. In this age of accelerating change, consultants who learn to respect resistance and use it productively discover a wonderful resource.

Resistance is *not de*nial nor is it the opposite of readiness. Resistance creates an inertia, procrastination, and avoidance of what needs to be done. It appears as missed appointments, not doing homework, avoiding the future or making plans for it, and lots of excuses. The underlying fear that leads to resistance is giving up or losing control. In contrast, denial shows up as repetition of questions, acting as if things are normal, not seeking proper advice or care for problems. Giving up hope of a better way leads to denial.

Anyone going through planned or unplanned changes must do the following to reduce resistance:

- Increase communication and interactions with others;
- Gain information specific to their roles and positions;
- Actively participate in the process;
- Recognize the past;
- Pay attention to rituals of letting go of the past and making new beginnings, as problems with change management may relate to an inability to let go of the past, poorly managed past changes, or inability to vision a new future;
- Understand why the change is necessary (Answering the "why" for ourselves helps us understand and cope with what others need from us to deal with the change; the "why" is an individual thinking and feeling process, so we must answer the question for ourselves in a way that makes sense. A son

may know that his sister was chosen over him to be the next CEO. He may hear all the reasons, such as "He is not a self-starter" or "He doesn't follow through." But until he can really grasp why, he will have a hard time accepting the decision);

- Feel in control of the process, not the outcome;
- Gain some idea of the direction and goals of the changes;
- Come up with milestones to check progress;
- Have authority equal to responsibility; and
- Acknowledge and express the feelings that accompany change.

Resistance is one of the ways that we all have of protecting ourselves from change or of dealing with fear. If we see it *not* as an enemy of the change but as a protective *"friend"* of the client, it will help us put it in perspective and deal with it productively. As change agents, we have to be acquainted with it, to learn all about it. We must ask questions about the missed appointments, the procrastination, and the avoidance of tough business decisions. The answers to the following questions can provide the key to the solution going forward:

- Is more information needed?
- Is the inability to see beyond the pain of the change process related to a deeper issue?
- Is there confusion about the future?
- Is someone in the family or business actively opposing the change?
- Is there a fear of what lies beyond?

Types of Interventions

Many of the interventions in this section have been described by Dyer (1986), Ward (1987), and others. Rather than describing all of them in detail, we will briefly discuss those we commonly use that focus on individuals, relationships, or systems and how the dynamics of these individuals, relationships, and systems play out in the family, business, or ownership/governance systems. Of course, as we have said, any intervention will affect other systems, but the initial focus of these interventions is described in Table 5.3.

Table 5.3. Types of Interventions

	Family	**Business**	**Ownership**

Individual	Goal Setting
	Career Planning
	Counseling/Coaching
		Coaching
		Skill Sets/Goals
		Mentoring
		Executive Coaching
		Performance Reviews
			Decisions to Stay
			  or Leave
			Inactive Shareholders
			Stock Ownership for
			  Nonfamily and
			  Inlaws

Interactional,
the "In-Between"
	Conflict
	Family Roles
	Family Dynamics
	Boundaries
	Retirement
	Sibling and Cousin
	  Teams
	Copreneurs
	Relationship Issues
	Interactional Dialogue
		Role Clarification
		  and Negotiation
		360-Degree Feedback
		Educational
		Organizational
		  Structure
		Team Building
			Boards of Directors
			Board of Advisors
			Ownership Council

Systemic	Family Councils
	Family Retreats
		Strategic Planning
		Leadership
		Nonfamily Managers
		Entry/Exit Policies
		Comp/Benefits
		  for Family and
		  Nonfamily
		Professionalization
		  of the Business
		Culture
		Structural Changes
		Professionalization
		  of the Firm
			Valuations
			Leadership
			Governance
			  Structures
			Boards of Directors

Adapted from Dyer (1994, p. 112).

In the rest of this chapter, we will describe the following interventions listed in the table in more depth:

- *At the individual level:* counseling and coaching;
- *At the interactional level:* interactional dialogue, team building, and creating an ownership council; and
- *At the systemic level:* family councils, strategic planning, and governance structures.

We will also explore issues related to family dynamics, such as scapegoating, triangles, communication, experiential interventions, and scenario building. Resources for further reading are included at the end of this chapter.

Individual Interventions

One of the more common roles we play as consultants to family firms is the role of counselor or coach. This role is particularly important because clients often have a difficult time obtaining good feedback and often do not have a good "sounding board" to hear their issues and concerns. Clients also often require new ways to think about their problems and to develop strategies to problem solve. They also find it helpful to have someone to monitor their progress and give them encouragement. We generally find ourselves in the counselor/coach role after having developed some rapport with the client. This typically occurs in the process of interviewing our clients during the assessment phase of the consultation or during early activities such as a family retreat. We often find ourselves not only coaching the leader of the family business, but other members of the family as well. Indeed, even nonfamily employees may need significant counseling to help them cope with the problems they encounter in working in a family business. If indeed counseling/coaching is needed, we identify who will be involved and how such coaching will take place during the contracting period. It is often enough to indicate that you, as the consultant, will be regularly meeting with key members of the client system to coach them. How one defines "regularly" depends largely on the depth of the intervention. Typically, the more the intervention focuses on deeper, emotional issues, the more time will be needed.

For example, in one family firm we have worked with, the father and the son had a great deal of difficulty understanding one another. The role of the consultant in this case was in many ways to be a "go-between" and to counsel the son and the father about how to interact more successfully with one another and, in particular, to help the son to sort out his career goals and aspirations. He was struggling with the issue of whether he should stay in the family business or look elsewhere for work. Also, both needed counseling to help in clarifying their roles as boss/subordinate and father/son. In this particular case, the father and the son felt more comfortable meeting with the consultant one-on-one, rather than meeting together with the consultant. They felt more comfortable expressing the concerns, fears, and anxieties with the consultant alone, rather than in the presence of the other. This was an effective compromise for getting the work done.

Interactional Interventions

When we enter a family business system, we land in a web of relationships. How we navigate in these relationships will help us to avoid the fate of the fly that was invited by the spider to "Come into my parlor." It helps to remember what our job is and where we want our focus to be initially.

Interactional Dialogue

While relationships and the interfaces are generally important in any consultation, they are critically important in family businesses. The interactional dialogue approach used in working through relationship issues follows the general approach outlined by Richard Walton (1987). The approach involves getting the key parties together, identifying the issues that separate them from each other, and then helping to come up with some agreements to help them solve their problems and improve their relationship. A good example of this type of intervention was conducted by Gibb as he worked with a father who had just fired his son. The firing of the son had caused all kinds of negative repercussions in the family. (The father had been kicked out of the house by his wife and he was sleeping on the sofa in his office.) In this intervention, Gibb interviewed both the father and the son and then had them meet with him. Both father and son presented their grievances and declared that they were at an impasse. In this case, however, both did agree that if they could work together it would improve their relationship and help mend the rift in the family. After listening to each tell his story, it became clear to Gibb that the major source of the problem was the fact that both the father and the son had relatively unrealistic expectations concerning the other. Moreover, these expectations were not spoken or made explicit, so they continually found themselves in a sea of violated expectations and hostile feelings. Thus, the "solution" was to have both father and son describe the expectations that they had for each other, identify which expectations were realistic and which were not, and then to draw up an explicit, written agreement describing what each expected of the other. The father wanted the son to be more accountable for his time and more cooperative in working with employees, while the son wanted a clear description of his wage schedule and to know what he could expect in terms of salary in the future. He also wanted his father to give him more autonomy to make certain decisions. As a result of this third-party peacemaking intervention, the father and son were able to go back to working together and, as their communications improved, so did their relationship.

Team Building

While improving a relationship between two people involves the type of intervention previously described, in other situations, relationships among the entire family or team (which may also include nonfamily employees) may need to be improved. In these cases, team building may be appropriate. Dyer (1997), along with many others, has described various approaches to team building, and Lane (1989) has outlined how team building can be used in family firms. One approach that we have found particularly successful for team building is what is termed "role negotiation." The steps in the role negotiation intervention are as follows:

1. *Identify the team that is the target for team building.* This team may be the family or it may include nonfamily employees. The team should be one that works together in the business; don't create an arbitrary team. The family/client should help you determine membership of the team. This approach works well when the family has reasonably good communication skills and is not highly dysfunctional. If there are serious interpersonal problems between team members, the consultant would likely be more successful by working with team members one-on-one or in pairs to work through certain issues before meeting in a team-building session.

2. *At the team-building sessions, ask each team member to describe his or her formal job description and role in the company.* Have everyone also describe what he or she actually does (if there are discrepancies between the formal role and actual behavior).

3. *After hearing the description of the person's role, ask each member of the team whether he or she agrees or disagrees with that role.* If there are disagreements, the consultant facilitates a discussion wherein the person and the team eventually agree on the role for that person.

4. *Have each team member in turn describe what he or she needs from the other team members in order to function effectively in his or her role.* The team members can either agree to help the person as requested or negotiate an arrangement for some other form of help for the person. Family issues that may make it difficult for them to perform in a particular role can be raised at this point.

5. After each person has negotiated for what he or she needs, *ask the team members whether there is anything else they, as team members, might do to help the person function more effectively in his or her job.*

6. *Write down those items that have been agreed to for future review.*

In our experience, it takes about thirty to forty minutes per person to complete this exercise. Hold periodic follow-up meetings where the agreements made in the role negotiation session are reviewed and modified if necessary.

We have found this approach to team building to be very successful, for it forces the team to look at how to improve both the individual functioning of team members and the dynamics of the team. It also allows family members to raise family dynamics and other issues in a legitimate way since the focus is on improving performance.

Ownership Councils

Managing the performance of family members in a family business is often a difficult problem, given the nature of the relationships in the family. One approach to performance management used by some consultants is to create an "ownership council." Those on the ownership council are typically senior nonfamily managers and more senior family members who have developed credibility and trust among family and among employees. The ownership council generally includes persons different from those who serve on the board of directors, but it may include board members. The ownership council meets on a regular basis and focuses on the following issues:

- Selecting the criteria that will be used to determine whether or not a family member should be allowed to work in the business;

- Determining who will conduct the performance review of family members. Questions that come up include: "Should it be the family member's supervisor?" "What if the supervisor is also a family member?" and "Should the council conduct reviews for the family members?" (This last option is frequently true in the case of family members in senior management positions.);

- Setting up guidelines for the compensation of family members;
- Setting up guidelines for the discipline or firing of family members; and
- Determining how to develop family members and improve their skills and abilities.

The consultant usually meets with the client to identify who should be on the ownership council and then meets with the ownership council to set the initial guidelines and work through the issues. Clarifying how the performance of family members is to be assessed and managed, along with creating a developmental plan for family members, may help to eliminate many of the conflicts that are inherent in dealing with such sensitive topics. Nonfamily employees who serve on this committee can help to bring a third-party perspective in dealing with the thorny problem of performance review and relieve some of the pressure that the family leaders may feel as they work through these issues.

Systemic Interventions

Governance Structures

Often family firms do not have an effective board of directors. Ward (1997) has suggested that the most effective boards in family firms have some outsiders and that they play an active role in advising and critiquing management. Too often, family firms have boards that only exist on paper or are a rubber stamp for the founder and family's decisions (Dyer, 1986). If this is indeed the case, the consultant can work with the family to create a board of directors to help provide the needed direction. The consultant works with the family:

- *To identify potential board members.* The most effective board members generally have the following characteristics: (1) they are independent; (2) they have knowledge and experience related to the problems facing the business; (3) they have good business sense; and (4) they understand financial data. Board members can be found through industry trade associations, the chamber of commerce, or a local college. You should also consider retired executives who have worked in a similar environment.
- *To interview prospective board members to ascertain their interests, experience, and skills.*
- *To select the board.* We have found that a board works well when not too small or too large—generally five to seven members.

- *To help the board manage its internal processes.* Often the consultant will meet several times with the board initially to serve as a "process consultant" to help the board develop a collaborative style of decision making and to ensure healthy group process. Often the consultant provides some training on group dynamics and process as he or she works with the board.

Strategic Planning

Strategic planning is often an important intervention to help a family business' success. While Carlock and Ward (2001) have written much on this topic, the basic approach is for the consultant to do the following:

- Have the family develop a family mission statement as well as a mission statement for the business;

- Make sure the two mission statements are compatible, for example, if the family wants to increase its wealth, but is unwilling to grow the business by bringing in outside professional managers to help the company grow, they will not likely meet their goals. The consultant should help the family sort through the tradeoffs that are often inherent when trying to meet the firm's and family's objectives;

- Help the family develop a strategic plan that allows them to achieve their mission and goals. This involves using a strategic planning framework, such as the one suggested by Ward (1987) or more recently by Carlock and Ward (2001); and

- Monitor the progress of the family business in regard to mission and strategy. This can be done by having the consultant attend board of director meetings or executive management meetings where the performance of the firm is discussed.

To illustrate how strategic planning might work with a family business, we will discuss the case of the Price family (described briefly in Case 1.1 in Chapter 1), who asked to have an assessment done of their family business. In the assessment phase it was discovered that the family had four businesses—three of which were quite successful, but one was not. The failing business was run by one of the founder's daughters; the founder was using the profits of the other businesses (which were run by her other two daughters and herself) to subsidize the poorly performing retail operation. This business was started to give the daughter employment (she had had difficulty finding steady employment), but the company had become a "money pit," devouring the profits of all the businesses.

After the assessment phase, the family was brought together in a family retreat and the findings of the consultant were shared with the family—the founder, her husband, and the three daughters. In particular, the problems related to the retail operation were shared. The family and the consultant then began to look at alternatives related to the current operations. While the family had not written a formal mission statement, they believed that it was important for the family business to employ family members. What they needed to discuss, however, was what to do when one of the businesses employing family members was failing. Should the family indefinitely support a family member in a failing business? This was a difficult discussion, but eventually the family came to the conclusion that the retail business should be shut down and that the daughter running that enterprise should look for a job within the other businesses or leave the business altogether. This was a difficult decision to make, and it did lead to the daughter leaving the family business completely. But the decision did serve to protect the assets (and the jobs) of the other family members. It also helped to protect the inheritance of the daughter who left the business.

Family Business Council Meetings

The family business council meeting serves many purposes and is high both on the technical aspects and on process. This forum is different from the "ownership council" inasmuch as it is typically composed of family members both in and out of the business. It is also different from the family forum, which usually meets once a year with a primary focus on information, education, and relationship building. Family council meetings occur more frequently and have a greater focus on decision making. (A note on the terminology: Some authors and consultants use the terms family council and forum interchangeably, meaning the family's "board," providing a governance structure.) In smaller, earlier stage companies or those with high conflict, more frequent, highly structured meetings of the family are necessary.

The Kelly family needed to hold regular family council meetings to provide a more formal and structured setting for them to discuss the issues of the family and their relationship to the business. The family council meeting serves as the organizational and planning branch for the family, which requires data about the financial and technical aspects of the business. It also provides a forum for discussion of values, policies, and direction for the future. Additionally, regular family meetings serve to develop family identity, themes, rules, and roles. A system of shared beliefs (who we are and what we do) creates bonds that hold the family together in crises, conflicts, and times of change. Both the forums and the council meetings enhance these family bonds.

An agenda for a regularly held family council of the Kelly family meeting might look like the one in Exhibit 5.1.

Exhibit 5.1. Council Meeting Agenda

8:00–8:30	Follow-up to action plan from last meeting and updates on sales
8:30–9:00	Presentation by president on new store development
9:00–9:30	Discussion of other options for the family
9:30–10:00	Plan for actions to be taken between now and next meeting (in two weeks)

Exhibit 5.2 illustrates an action planning worksheet, one method for approaching the task of action planning. The consultant illustrates the interrelatedness of the issues and weaves them together to help the family think and plan systemically. As you begin action planning, it is important to ensure that all of those involved understand exactly what is to happen. At each action planning session, the group should complete the worksheet with the following information: (1) the key tasks to be accomplished, (2) who will carry out each task, (3) when they are to do it, and (4) how the task is to be accomplished (what resources, people, and so forth might be needed to carry out the task). This worksheet should be copied and shared with all participants in the change efforts because it serves as the roadmap for change.

Exhibit 5.2. Action Planning Worksheet

Task	Who	By When	How
Sales initiatives	Joe, Jr.	November 30	Will meet with sales staff and create plan based on today's priorities.
Finalize building plan agreements	Kathleen	October 30	Meet with architect, banker, and lawyer.
Finalize building plans	Dan and Kathleen	October 15	Will meet together with architect.
Arrange for a presentation on succession planning by accountant and attorney	Joe, Sr., and Ann	Next meeting	Will contact attorney and accountant to arrange their coming to next meeting. Will inform them of family's questions and concerns to be covered at meeting.

The council meetings can help the family build consensus, improve and maintain open, direct communication, and address other issues of concern. An effective process for these meetings requires ground rules and procedures for interacting and solving problems as well as a clarification of roles. This is an evolving structure that the family can use to meet the ever-changing and complex needs of the individuals, family, and business. As with any family business infrastructure, it is important to have a process to decide who attends, the purpose and goals, frequency of meetings, and the agenda. Some suggest that council meetings be held quarterly or annually. It is our experience that more frequent meetings are needed when the family is going through a transition or is highly conflicted. Any work with family businesses involves building and developing structures, mechanisms, and processes that encourage healthy family and business practices. The family council provides a structured, regular meeting time, with ground rules for communication and decision making that give everyone a voice. It provides an opportunity for all to be informed by having presentations and allows them to plan for the future. The consultant must attend to the process and take responsibility for doing his or her homework on the content issues as well.

In facilitating the first family council meeting, we usually have a short teaching module on what a council meeting is (see Exhibit 5.3) and what it should accomplish. After that, the family sets the agenda for the afternoon (see Exhibit 5.4 for an example) and chooses people to do the jobs of timekeeper, scribe, and process cop. We take the responsibility for facilitating the first two or three meetings, becoming less and less directive as the family takes over.

Exhibit 5.3. Guidelines for a Family Council Meeting

- Set timetable—beginning and ending times—and stick to it.
- Agree on ground rules (phone calls, interruptions, breaks, and so on).
- Create an agenda that includes the purpose of meeting, the topics, and the lead person for each topic.
- For complex topics, desired outcomes can be noted.
- Allow time for "brainstorming." (See Exhibit 4.3 on page 86.)
- Save ten to fifteen minutes at the end to evaluate.
- Create an action plan with follow-up for each topic.
- Decide, either by consensus, vote, or other agreed-on manner, who will take the following roles:

    Meeting leader

    Timekeeper

    Note taker

    Process cop (the person who sees that the process keeps on track and that timelines and ground rules are respected)

Exhibit 5.4. Kelly Family Council Meeting Agenda

Morning

Family Councils: What they are and what they do

Preparations for afternoon Family Council meeting

Review guidelines and set agenda

Establish roles and ground rules

Afternoon

First Family Council meeting

One helpful early exercise is to have each family member state his or her goals as well as goals for the family and the business. Each family member takes ten to fifteen minutes to think about goals for himself or herself, the family, and the business and a time line. Each person completes a chart like the one in Exhibit 5.5. When the group reconvenes, each individual shares his or her goals with the group. A discussion follows and should include comments about any conflicting goals or surprises as well as observations. This becomes a touchstone for checking in. (As you can see, the family had some very different ideas for the future!) Some families may never be able to run the meetings themselves, and others can take over after just a few meetings.

Exhibit 5.5. Sample Goal-Setting Chart

By 2010	Individual	Family	Business
Kathleen	I hope to be retired by then and back with Mike, living in a sunny climate! I also hope that Joe, Jr., will take over the company or we can sell it by then.	I hope that each of us in the family has been able to choose his or her own path, especially the next generation, and they will only work here if they choose it's best for them.	I hope that the business is successful, either with Joe as president or having been sold and run by others.
Joe, Sr.	I will be 89 and hope to be still here and healthy!	I hope my grandchildren are in the business by then—at least some of them—and that Kathleen, Joe, and Dan are happy working together.	I hope the business has doubled in size and tripled in sales. I hope we can also triple what we give to the community in time and money.
Joe, Jr.	I hope to be doing just what I'm doing; I love sales and I'm good at it, even though the numbers don't show it right now.	I hope that both my daughters go on to college; I hope my wife and I have more time for vacations and traveling. I hope the family continues to stay in this town and work together.	I hope Cindy comes into the business full time after college and we're all working together, just like now.

Another useful tool is the multidisciplinary matrix shown in Exhibit 5.6. The tasks that need to be accomplished are listed on the vertical axis; the emotional issues are on the horizontal axis. The family completes the matrix and builds its understanding of the complexity of the interplay between the task/technical and the emotional concerns. The family should then create a plan for both the tasks and the emotional issues involved.

Exhibit 5.6. Interdisciplinary Matrix

Emotional → Factors Tasks/ Technical ↓	Parents Letting Go	Sense of Loss/Closure	Relationship with One Another After	Kathleen's Personal Issues and Decisions	Our Own Lives After the Succession Is Complete
Succession Planning	Joe, Sr., and Ann are having a hard time "letting go"; this has been their life.			How able is Kathleen to take over the reins of the business?	
Increasing Sales			Joe, Jr., is worried that he will not have the flexibility of time when/if sales increase		
Long-Range Strategic Planning for Business	Can we/should we separate the ownership plan from the management plan?				What will our relationship be like after the job roles change and mom and dad are no longer in the business?
Other?					

Developed by Jane Hilburt-Davis and Jack Wofford in preparation for a family business retreat.

Some guidelines and tips for the family to get through the rough spots follow:

- Encourage brainstorming—try to see things in new ways;
- Strive for common ground and actions to be taken;
- Decide on a conflict-management plan and stick to it;
- Continue to plan for the future: groups are energized by contemplating the future and often depressed by focusing on problems;
- Clarify goals;
- Clearly define roles and ground rules;
- Establish well-defined decision-making procedures;
- Enforce clear rules of behavior;
- Teach awareness of group process; and
- Make sure that adequate resources are provided.

The most effective activities operate on the individual, interactional, and systems levels simultaneously. As in any living system, one change has ripple effects throughout the entire system. Seemingly small changes, such as the establishment of performance reviews for family members, can stimulate improved job performance. Improved communication in the family meetings will have spillover into the executive management meetings. Strategic planning based on family values makes family members feel better not only about the company direction but about themselves as well.

Family Dynamics Issues

Before describing some of the interventions that focus on family dynamics, let us briefly review some of the common problems that we find during the assessment phase of a consultation.

Scapegoating

The term scapegoat or "one bearing the blame for others" comes from the biblical ceremony in which the sins of the people are placed on the goat's head and it is sent into the wilderness. The term refers to the person or object that is blamed. In family therapy, it is a term that often refers to the child unconsciously chosen by the parents to blame for the problems of the family. It is also often used to refer to the one in the work or family situation who "carries the symptoms" and the one most obviously affected by the conflicts and problems. The scapegoat often serves as a focal point for the anger in the family and the business. If the family or business is a closed system, and the scapegoat is removed without changes in the interactional patterns, another scapegoat will be chosen. In family businesses, often the family is the scapegoat for all of the business problems, and we professionals often accept that without challenging these assumptions.

Triangling

This concept comes from the work of intergenerational family therapist Murray Bowen (1976). Triangling is a tendency of two people who are unable to resolve a conflict, or who are experiencing distress in their relationship, to involve a third person. Triangling is a normal reaction and transient triangles exist in every family. They only become dysfunctional when the same people repeat the process for the same reasons over time.

Bringing in a third person is a way of avoiding problems and of temporarily lowering the intensity of the conflict. Over time, however, families who have longstanding triangles or a longstanding process of triangling instead of dealing with problems will not succeed in business or complete family tasks. Most conflicts have as their foundations a triangle. Another important lesson of longstanding triangles is that consultants can be drawn into triangles, especially in highly conflicted families. When the family members are trying to put us into a triangle, it may deflect the intensity of the change process, as we will have a difficult time being creative and gaining perspective on the situation. An example of this would be two siblings who have a long-term conflicted relationship with each other and one tries to convince the consultant how right he or she is and just how wrong the other is. The best move the consultant can make is to address the triangling process and facilitate a dialogue between the family members that can help them work together more productively.

Genograms are a way of identifying and teaching about triangles. (McGoldrick, Gerson, & Shellenberger, 1999). Genograms are useful for understanding triangles, as they repeat themselves over generations and help families to understand how this process can affect the functioning of the family and of the business.

Communications

Ideas about communication from family systems theory include how information is delivered and processed and how accurately individuals express themselves. Healthy systems (1) send congruent messages in which the verbal and nonverbal messages are the same, (2) provide an environment in which individuals feel free to be open about their plans, feelings, and problems, and (3) allow conflicts to be discussed in a way that they can be resolved and managed. Communications include all ways we have of conveying messages: words, gestures, and body language.

Here's what to look out for when examining communications:

- *Double-bind messages.* These occur when people are given conflicting or opposing verbal or nonverbal messages. The receiver is given no way out. This joke contains a classic double bind: Dad has given Charles two ties for his birthday, a green one and a blue one. Charles wears the green one and dad says, "Oh how nice, you're wearing your new tie. What's the matter? You don't like the blue one?" Sarcasm can also contain double-bind messages, as in, "You're not coming to the family meeting? Well, I guess *you* need some time off";

- *Signs of resistance;*

- *Blaming;* and

- *"Four Horsemen of the Apocalypse"* (Gottman, 1994a), which are predictors of serious breakdowns in relationships: complaining and criticizing, contempt, defensiveness, and stonewalling (refusing to discuss).

Experiential Interventions Focusing on Family Dynamics

To deal with these types of problems, consultants may need to intervene using what has been called "action therapy," which applies to a variety of exercises from role playing to psychodrama, sculpting, scenario building, or "What if?" rituals. They include actions, with or without talking. We use these techniques (1) with "stuck" situations, (2) when the individuals talk too much or not enough, and (3) sometimes just to have fun. These activities are used to interrupt old patterns; to teach new behaviors; to externalize ideas, stories, dreams, and fears; and to challenge mental models, views that individuals have of themselves and others. Some are direct interventions, such as role playing and role reversals, in which each person takes the role and position of the other. They are especially effective in conflict situations and improve understanding of the other's position. Others, such as sculpting, are *symbolic* (representative of something else) or *metaphoric* (linking one image to another). For example, in a role play, Judy, Gerald, and Louise each played another's role in a discussion of what got in the way of the negotiations. The debriefing of this short exercise revealed that they had each made inaccurate assumptions about the others. These activities bypass our defenses and shake our old stories and beliefs about self and others, all of which is needed for change. As Bunny Duhl (1983, 1993), a family therapist who was one of the early developers of sculpting, states, "The body in action does not lie."

On the next few pages, we will describe several experiential activities: sculpting, boundary sculpting, and scenario building.

Sculpting

"Sculpting" was developed by family therapists David Kantor, Fred and Bunny Duhl, and others. In Jane's early training and teaching at Boston Family Institute, she used sculpting for assessment and treatment. She also used it in team building, large change activities, and families in business together. Basically, sculpting, a metaphor in space, explores family and work relationships through spatial arrangements. Individuals are asked to describe their family or work setting in a sculpture, giving each individual a gesture or stance that shows the way he or she experiences the problem, situation, or focus of change. The consultant assists by asking questions aimed at the systemic and transactional patterns. Choreographing sculptures avoids vagueness of language, compares individuals' perceptions of the issues, captures the patterns, and illustrates multiple perceptions. For example, Mort, Harriet, Mark, and Steve were asked to describe, with movements only, what it was like for each of them to experience the conflict in the family. After this was played out for a few minutes in silence, the following questions were asked: "Mort, what happened when you moved in to intervene between Mark and Steve?" "Harriet, what was it like for you to watch this?" "Mark, what did Steve do when you approached him?" Participants are asked not to interpret but just to describe their physical reactions to the exercise. Mort was able to observe how his sons moved away as he approached them and how, when he backed away, they approached him. Harriet described how helpless she felt. Each was able to understand more clearly the patterns of their interactions.

Boundary Sculpting

This type of sculpting is made for members of family businesses who struggle with boundary issues. This explores personal, interpersonal, and systemic boundaries. Bunny Duhl (1993) notes that she started to use boundary sculpture with couples as a key diagnostic process. Jane began to use it with family businesses and found that the results were sometimes amazing. She started with individuals, asking each one to think of an image that would describe his or her own personal space and the boundary that surrounds it. We then expand this to have the family define the boundaries of the family and test those boundaries with the business boundaries. In this exercise, the family is asked to define a space in the room for the family and a space for the business. They are to place themselves in the spaces and describe how and when they move from one space to the other. Questions include: "When do you move from one to the other?" "How do you make that decision?" "How do you keep the spaces separate or don't you?" "Where do you spend most of your time?" "What pulls you from one space to the other?" In this discussion, the family gains important insights about the boundaries between their family and the business.

Scenario Building

This technique is useful for planning purposes. It is usually constructed around the question, "What if?" For example, you might have a family business answer one of the following the questions: "What would you do if dad died this afternoon?" "What would you do if your sales dropped suddenly?" "What would you do if none of the next generation wanted to own or work in the business?" "What would you do if your daughter, who is also the vice president, divorced?" These *what if* questions stimulate the family to plan for the unexpected. To be effective, the scenario planning must be realistic, specific, and encourage the players to create an action plan for the event.

Guidelines for Interventions

In summary, we have a few suggestions or guidelines for a consultant who begins to intervene in a family firm:

- Clarify goals and your agreement about them with the client;
- Focus on both the technical and emotional learnings;
- Look for champions of change and reward them;
- Focus on results as you tend carefully to the process;
- Build competencies;
- Be flexible;

- Consider the larger context; then divide goals into small, achievable, and familiar steps;

- Always ask yourself: "How well am I listening?" "Am I assuming too much?" "Am I careful to challenge my assumptions as well as my client's?" In postmodern language, this is about letting our clients' stories become the dominant ones in the narrative; ours take a back seat;

- Always ask: "Am I asking the right questions?" Problems may persist if you ask the wrong questions or even the right questions in the wrong way. For example, if succession is stalled, are you asking what is keeping the owner/founder from letting go or are you asking what does he or she have to look forward to outside of work?

- Never work harder than your clients; never do your client's work; and avoid consulting engagements that assume the consultants will do the work;

- Have a good time; do what you need to enjoy your work (If you are bored with a family meeting, you probably aren't the only one);

- Know when to call in help;

- Be alert for positive changes while managing the negative ones;

- Although change doesn't always or often start at the top, leadership must be the champion of the project. Too often in family businesses we see a "command and control" approach to leadership. We should help to improve the capabilities for collaborative decision making and high functioning teams in families. The more simple, clear, and understandable the thinking of the owners and managers is, the more efficient and effective the thinking of the younger generation and other employees will be;

- Collaborations with clear parameters increase speed, flexibility, creativity, and resilience. For example, for a cousin team of third-generation owners to function well, there must be clear expectations, job descriptions, titles, performance standards, and fair compensation for the individuals. This must be supported by team norms, such as how frequently the team meets, what the responsibilities are, and to whom the team and its members report; and

- Avoid "interminable" consultations. Know when to declare victory and get out! This includes both real victories in which you and the client have reached the agreed-on goals and near victories in which each of you has gone as far as you can for now.

In this chapter we have discussed some of the important issues and strategies related to intervening in family businesses. In the next chapter we will discuss how to intervene and help family firms deal with normal developmental changes, crises, and what is considered their most serious problem—the problem of succession.

Additional Resources

Conflict Management

Kaye, K. (1994) *Workplace wars and how to end them.* New York: American Management Association.

Developing Boards

Ward, J.L. (1997) *Creating effective boards for private enterprises.* Marietta, GA: Business Owner Resources.

Relationships

Hoover, E., & Hoover, C. (1999) *Getting along in family business.* New York: Routledge.

Selling the Business: Deciding

Cohn, M. (2001) *Keep or sell your business.* Chicago, IL: Dearborn Financial Publishing.

Strategic Planning

Carlock, R., & Ward, J. (2001) *Strategic planning for the family business.* New York: Palgrave.

Other Useful Resources

The Family Firm Institute website has a search engine for articles, cases, and books on family business topics. (www.ffi.org)

The *Family Business Magazine* website also offers a search for specific topics to subscribers. (www.familybusinessmagazine.com)

6

Helping Family Firms Make Developmental Transitions

INTERACTIONS **BETWEEN LIFECYCLE EVENTS** cut across organizational, family, and individual development. While there is concurrent development of the family and the individuals in that family, there is also a developmental progression of the family business itself. Articulating these intersecting developmental patterns in individuals, the family, and the firm increases the complexity of the models we use when diagnosing problems in family firms. Yet it is essential to understand how they evolve over time. (A good summary of this developmental approach can be found in Neubauer & Lank's *The Family Business: Its Governance for Sustainability*, 1998.) Our role as family business consultants is to help our clients through these relatively predictable developmental transitions.

The Greeks saw the future as something that came upon them from their backs, with the past receding away before their eyes (Pirsig, 1984). We can help our clients learn from the past as it recedes and prepare for the future as it comes up behind them. What we add to the discussion in this chapter are the interplay, the risks, and the tasks of each developmental stage and the importance of the transitional dynamics when planning any intervention.

There have been a variety of developmental models posited by family business consultants and scholars. For example, Leon Danco (1982), one of the early family business consultants, concludes that there are four stages, which he calls (1) the *wonder* period (filled with excitement and energy); (2) the *blunder* period (as the company grows and risks are taken, missteps are inevitable); (3) the *thunder* period (strong growth); and (4) the *sunder or plunder* period (companies either grow and diversify, are taken over, or go out of business). Others have discussed the organizational lifecycle in terms of managerial roles that are required for managing the succession process (McGivern, 1989). Gersick, Davis, Hampton, and Lansberg (1997), in *Generation to Generation*, propose a developmental model that includes three overlapping systems modeled on the three systems of family, business, and ownership. Carlock and Ward (2001), in the most complex model to date, maintain that ownership is not a lifecycle, but "rather an ownership configuration influenced by lifecycle forces and family decisions" (p. 26). They propose a model in which family businesses can be structured with six ownership configurations that result from lifecycle forces and family decisions: *entrepreneurship* (first generation); *owner-managed* (first generation); *family partnership*; *sibling partnership* (second generation); *cousins' collaboration* (third generation); and *family syndicate* (later generations). We will draw on this and other previous works to present the following developmental stages that occur in the lives of individuals, families, and organizations.

Sometimes referred to as the "benevolent framework" because it considers systems as "stuck" or "unstuck" rather than pathological, the developmental approach adds a time dimension that contextualizes human behavior and organizations and puts their attendant problems in a natural progression through time. It is a framework that is flexible and holistic. It serves as an assessment, predictive, and treatment tool to help consultants determine what issues those in family firms may be facing currently and helps to predict those issues that they will likely encounter in the future. Indeed, the complexity of family businesses is found in the paradox of their changing and staying the same simultaneously. (As consultants, we can think, metaphorically, of viewing the family and business with a video camera rather than a Polaroid; that is, we want to capture a complete ongoing picture, rather than a moment in time.)

At times the interactions of the family, the business, the individuals, the ownership, and the market environment enhance each other's development and at other times they undermine it. Chapter 5 was about planned change. In this chapter we will describe the changes, some anticipated, others unanticipated, that happen during the journey through time and the tasks and the risks of the transition phases. Being aware of these challenges, including managing the various perspectives, competing interests, and often "out of synch" stages, is essential for the advisors who help family firms.

Developmental Stages and Tasks

"Most of us are about as eager to be changed as we were to be born, and go through our changes in a similar state of shock."

Baldwin, 1977

This quote from James Baldwin suggests the trauma, excitement, and possibilities associated with transitions in our lives. The following models that we will present suggest the "typical" developmental patterns we find in the client systems we work with. It is important to note that these models for families and individuals follow their progress in a traditional pattern of marriage and child rearing. They are appropriate for many families and individuals, but we want to note that there have been many variations on these patterns recently. With this in mind, we'll now explore how individuals, families, and firms develop.

Individual Developmental Stages

The models of individual development incorporated in Table 6.1 are from Erickson's (1976) development studies and were further popularized in the 1970s by Gail Sheehy's (1977) *Passages,* Levinson's (1978) *The Seasons of a Man's Life,* Gilligan's (1982) *In a Different Voice,* and Miller's (1976) *Toward a New Psychology of Women.* Each individual lives in an ever-changing context within the family constellation. The child born first to young parents has characteristics different from the child born into a family of three or four children. Birth order and gender effects on personality and behavior are described by Toman (1976) in *Family Constellation* and should be taken into consideration when studying human development and behavior.

Table 6.1. The Individual Lifecycle

Stage	Stage Critical Tasks	Risks	Family Business Participation
Childhood (0–11)	Becoming increasingly independent; developing physical skills; learning problem-solving skills; building relationships; developing sense of responsibility; balancing self-identity with intimacy; expanding social world	Physical, social, and emotional skills are not developed; responsibility does not emerge; overly dependent; poor skills; poor ability to build relationships; social world does not expand; not prepared for adolescence	May join family retreats when appropriate
Adolescence (12–19)	Social world continues to expand; skills continue to develop; increasingly independent; emotional struggles with self and family; bodily changes leading to sexual maturity; balancing individuation with intimacy	Individuation process is stalled; skills aren't developed; sense of responsibility is undeveloped; social isolation; over-dependency on or estranged from parents; shows symptoms of maladjustment (depression, acting out, eating disorders); poor ego development	May work part-time in the business with specific age-appropriate jobs for fair compensation
Young Adulthood (20–40)	World is expanding; developing life as adult in both love and work; prime time of life; full of possibilities and responsibilities	Inability to balance independence and relationships with parents; developing ability to leave home and stay connected; skills are not developed; identity not clear; not satisfied or able to form love and work relationships; not able to cope with adult responsibilities and relationships	Encouraged to work outside the family business early in this stage, gain other experiences; later in this stage, if interested in working in the business, is interviewed; hired by objective criteria for clearly spelled out position, fair compensation, and performance reviews. Title appropriate to work, mentored by senior nonfamily managers

Table 6.1. The Individual Lifecycle, Cont'd

Stage	Stage Critical Tasks	Risks	Family Business Participation
Middle Adulthood (41–55)	Expanding responsibilities of own family and work; productive period; balancing relationships and self; often juggling responsibilities of parents and children; "generativity"; refocus on mid-life career and marital issues; moving from authoritative to consultative with "children"	Inability to find fulfillment in love or work; "stagnation"; inability to juggle multiple roles; isolated	Continuing to take on more responsibilities and rewards commensurate with those responsibilities; moving into more senior position, if competent; rewards increases with responsibilities
Late Adulthood (56–65)	Children leaving home; more responsibilities at work; preparing for "retirement"; some physical decline; enriched relationships; taking on roles of personal and social value	Inability to prepare to "let go" of children or productivity of middle age; inability to do meaningful work, make contributions, find value; keep busy to avoid facing aging process	Most senior and productive time; leader in the business; planning for retirement and creating a succession plan in discussion with family and advisors
Old Age (66 +)	Letting go of work; personal relationships continue to develop and deepen; faced with physical decline, death of others; dealing with "ego integrity"; sense of self and values; contribute to society or family; reflective; active; closing or adapting family home	Depressed; sense of regrets; inability to face aging and losses; keeps busy to avoid dealing with own aging process, "stagnation"	Letting go of the business and pursing other interests

Developmental Stages of the Family

Table 6.2 incorporates the models of Carter and McGoldrick (1989) in *The Changing Family Life Cycle* and of the Becvars' (1996) *Family Therapy: A Systemic Integration*. These stages describe critical tasks and issues families face at different stages in their development and outline the risks and potential problems associated with each stage.

Table 6.2. Developmental Stages of the Family

Stage	Stage Critical Tasks	Risks	Participation in Family Business
Leaving home; single young adults	Differentiation of self from family of origin; development of peer relationships; establishment of self in relation to work and financial independence; accepting emotional and financial responsibility for self	Inability to form mature relationships, find meaningful work, be responsible; move to interdependency; have not established roles, responsibilities, open and honest communication	Good time to work outside the business, establish self as independent and prepare to "go back home"
The new couple; joining of families	Formation of marital, couple relationship; realignment of relationships with extended families and friends; commitment to new system, family; adjusting career demands	New couple fails to establish healthy relationship; boundaries are closed to new relationships; inability to adjust to new extended family; inability to balance career and family roles and responsibilities	Age-appropriate time to join family business; new financial responsibilities; some stress balancing job and family demands
Families with young children	Adjusting to children; joining in child rearing, financial, household tasks; realignment of relationships with extended family to include parent and grandparent roles; accepting new	Inability to handle multiple roles of career and family; difficulties with extended families; difficulties adjusting to children; closed relationships; children are not encouraged to	Increasing responsibilities at home and at work as well as increasing financial demands; age appropriate time to develop career in the family business

Table 6.2. Developmental Stages of the Family, Cont'd

Stage	Stage Critical Tasks	Risks	Participation in Family Business
	members into system; allowing children to establish relationships outside family; teaching responsibility; increasing responsibilities	become responsible, independent; couple is not flexible; cannot deal with changes in roles, growing family, and work	
Families with adolescents	Shifting of parent-child relationships to permit adolescents to move in and out of system; refocus on mid-life marital and career issues; beginning shift toward joint caring for older generation; increasing flexibility of family boundaries to include children's independence and grandparents' frailties	Difficulty encouraging adolescents to move in and out of the system; inability to adjust to lessening dependence of children; career and work are not satisfying	Continued family and financial responsibilities; children may be working part-time in the business; taking on more senior roles
Launching children	Renegotiation of couple system as dyad; development of adult-to-adult relationships; realignment to include children's in-laws and grandchildren; dealing with disabilities and death of grandparents; accepting a multitude of exits from and entries into family system; maintaining supportive home base; letting go and rebuilding marriage	Cannot renegotiate couple system as children are launched; difficulty letting go of children; limited resources, financial and emotional, to deal with aging parents; difficulty dealing with exits and entries into family system	With children leaving, more energy to invest in work; responsibilities and rewards are increasing; developing succession plan

Table 6.2. Developmental Stages of the Family, Cont'd

Stage	Stage Critical Tasks	Risks	Participation in Family Business
Families in later life	Maintaining health and independence in face of aging; support a more central role of middle generation; accepting the shift of generational roles, making room for wisdom of elderly; supporting older generation without over-functioning for them; dealing with losses and preparation for death; life review and integration	Physical and emotional functioning declines; depression of couple system; lack of financial and emotional resources to deal with addition of third generation; difficulty letting go and letting next generation take over; inability to deal with losses; inability to prepare for illness and death; refusal to accept the inevitability of end-of-life passage	Letting go of work demands; stepping down; mentoring children to take over; developing other interests

From Dorothy Stroh Becvar & Raphael J. Becvar, *Family Therapy: A Systemic Integration (3rd ed.),* copyright © 1996, and B. Carter & M. McGoldrick (Eds.) (1989), *The Changing Family Life Cycle: A Framework for Family Therapy (2nd ed.),* copyright © 1989. Reprinted/adapted by permission by Allyn & Bacon.

Stages in an Organization's Lifecycle

Table 6.3 incorporates Greiner's (1972) five phases from "Evolution and Revolution as Organizations Grow" (*size* is the vertical axis and *age* the horizontal); Flamholtz's (2000) seven stages of organizational growth in *Growing Pains;* and Adizes' (1979) ten phases in "Organizational Passages: Diagnosing and Treating Lifecycle Problems of Organizations," in which the *behavior focus* (production, administration, entrepreneurial, integration) is the vertical axis and *age* (mental age, market share, functionality of the organizational structure) is the horizontal axis. From this previous work, we have identified five stages of development that are common to most organizations.

Table 6.3. Lifecycles of Organizations

Stage	Critical Stage Tasks	Risks	Challenges of the Family Business
New Venture; Start-Up	Develop products and services; identify and define market; survival	Poor planning; failure to develop market niche or develop products; lack of human and financial resources; poor leadership; lack of vision	Finances stretched; family often pitches in to help, members play many roles, children often helping out; demands of family and business combine to create stress; excitement for the possibilities; occasional resentment about the time and energy taken from family life; boundaries often blurred
Expansion; Growth	Develop operational systems and infrastructure; acquire resources; growth	Lack resources for growth; communication within organization faulty; drop in quality of products; time and space limitations; technical resources are limited; personnel needs may cause turnover; personnel stretched to limits; poor strategic planning; crisis based, day-to-day rather than long-term problem solving	With expansion, finances may be better; infrastructures created, operational systems developed, additional staff, family less involved, a relief but can incur sense of loss; may be less time together

Table 6.3. Lifecycles of Organizations, Cont'd

Stage	Critical Stage Tasks	Risks	Challenges of the Family Business
Professionalization; Early Bureaucracy	Develop management systems; "professionalize" transition to different type organization; transformation; balancing entrepreneurial, family-like spirit with formal systems required for growth; delegation and co-ordination needed	Unable or unwilling to make transformation from entrepreneurship to professionally managed firm; lack of formality required for planning, performance appraisal, and communication systems	Family sees more financial benefits from the business; the business takes more time and energy; a need to create more effective boundaries between business and family; develop outside boards
Consolidation; Mature	Develop the corporate culture; reinforce professional management; attention to values, beliefs, history; lose the entrepreneurial or family-like atmosphere norms; growth through collaboration	Failure to transmit culture throughout growing and expanding company; still counting on informal socialization; failure to stay creative and nimble; bureaucracy weighs organization down; lack of diversification	Succession planning should be underway; family values are inherent in the business; some family members are working in the business; some share ownership
Decline or Revitalization	Make decision actively (rather than reactively) to diversify; create new products; identify new markets; integrate new business units; revitalize company; new units may start as entrepreneurial ventures	Inability or reluctance to revitalize; failure to beat competition; recognize market saturation early enough; financial or human resource limitations; poor planning; little vision	Make-or-break stage; lack of succession planning, conflict, poor leadership or lack of financial or human resources to expand, diversify

Our approach in consulting with family firms is to identify, during the assessment phase, the stage of development for (1) the key individuals—particularly the family leader/founder and potential successors; (2) the family itself; and (3) the organization. Identifying where the individuals, the family, and the organization are in terms of their development alerts us to potential issues and concerns that need to be addressed during the consultation. For example, if during an assessment we find that the founder of the family is aging and has not been able to work through "letting go," the family has not encouraged the children to be responsible and independent, and the organization is in a state of decline, such a pattern has distinct implications for how we might help this client. In this case, the optimal solution may be to sell the business or bring in someone other than the family to help turn it around, since it is unlikely that the next generation will be prepared to take over in the short run and the founder is unlikely to be willing to relinquish power. Another approach might be to help the founder and his or her children work through issues they are facing to keep ownership and management of the firm in the family. However, this is likely to be a difficult proposition and may require "deep" interventions. Given that the firm is in a state of decline, the consultant may feel that there is not time to attempt this.

We also look to see whether the various developmental stages are "in synch" with each other at the lifecycle intersects (Davis & Tagiuri, 1989). For example:

- The life stages of the individuals may be in or out of synch with the changes that are needed. The best times for formal succession planning would be with the founder in his or her fifties and the successors in their early thirties. The appropriate developmental task for the "fifty something" is preparing to let go and for the "thirty something," who is in his or her most productive time of life, to take over.

- Avoid the Queen Elizabeth/Prince Charles syndrome in which the elder hangs on until the potential successor has almost reached retirement. Interestingly, in Davis and Tagiuri's (1989) study of eighty-nine father-son pairs, harmonious, respectful relationships were found between fathers in their fifties and sons in their mid-to-late twenties or early thirties. The relatively problematic relationships were between fathers in their sixties and sons in their mid-thirties to mid-forties. This study reaffirms the need for careful attention to the ever-changing goals, tasks, and struggles of men and women throughout the lifecycle. It also reminds us that there are better and worse times for succession planning and other plans that require cooperation between generations.

Transitional Dynamics

The transitional phases in between the life stages can be considered discontinuities in life space that result in stress and strain. Greiner (1972) describes these crisis periods in between growth periods as "revolution stages." How the management handles each crisis stage directly influences its ability to move to the next phase. This also applies to families and individuals. Bridges (1980) labels this as a period of confusion between the ending and new beginning. Flamholtz (2000) says that growing pains occur in the gap between the organization's size and necessary infrastructures, what he calls the "organizational development gap." It is during this period that stress is high and problems are more likely to show up.

Symptoms of organizational growing pains (Flamholtz, 2000, pp. 47–48) include the following:*

- People feel that there are not enough hours in the day;
- People spend too much time "putting out fires";
- People are not aware of what other people are doing;
- People lack understanding about where the firm is headed;
- There are too few good managers;
- People feel that they have to do everything themselves if they "want it done correctly";
- Most people feel that meetings are a waste of time;
- When plans are made, there is very little follow-up, so things just don't get done;
- Some people feel insecure about their place in the firm; and
- The firm continues to grow in sales but not in profits.

---

*From E.G. Flamholtz, *Growing Pains: Transitioning from an Enrepreneurship to a Professionally Managed Firm.* Copyright © 2000 John Wiley & Sons. Reprinted by permission of John Wiley & Sons, Inc.

Each change includes *restraining* forces, for example, not being able to think ahead, not keeping up with new advances, and a CEO who can't let go of the "good old days," and *driving* forces, such as shared core values, infrastructures in place, and mutual respect between the generations. These opposing forces do battle in the in-between phase. These are often obvious in the succession process, with the older generation hanging on to the past and the younger generation pushing for change.

The significance for the family business consultant is that it is an *at-risk* time in which there is confusion and uncertainty. Crisis theory teaches that, at this time, a minimal force can have a maximum effect. It is a time of dangerous opportunity: The ordinary defenses are weakened and infrastructures are stretched to the limit. But just because the client has an increased capacity and motivation for change, we should not assume that the change would necessarily be in the right direction. It is a time for very sharp assessment skills to evaluate the client's ability to change, available resources, restraining forces, and resistance. *Remember that the client's definition of and reaction to the event is a bigger story than the event itself.* This idea is captured nicely in Ella Wheeler Wilcox's (1936) poem, *The Winds of Fate:*

> **The Winds of Fate**
> *One ship drives east and another drives west*
> *With the selfsame winds that blow.*
> *'Tis the set of the sails*
> *And not the gales*
> *Which tells us the way to go.*
> *Like the winds of the sea are the ways of fate,*
> *As we voyage along through life:*
> *'Tis the set of a soul*
> *That decides its goal,*
> *And not the calm or the strife.*

You need to find out how the client defines the problem and its dimensions from his or her perspective. Don't assume that you know the effects of the crisis on the client system. What you assume might cause a huge impact may only result in a small disturbance and vice versa. From others' perspective, Kathleen Grey's mental illness implies a life-long challenge; from her perspective, this may not seem like a problem. Values and mental models affect our sense of loss; what matters most to one may not matter at all to another. Ask your clients: "How has this affected you?" "What is the most difficult thing to deal with right now?" "How have you coped with loses or crises in the past?" and "What helps? What hurts?"

Assessing the Client's Abilities to Work Through Developmental Stages

To help clients set their sails in the right direction and coach them through these developmental stages, it is important to assess the factors associated with positive and negative outcomes for the client. Factors that tend to influence the outcome include the following:

- Current adaptive capabilities of the client (Does the client have effective problem solving, communication, and negotiating skills?);

- The resources of the client (Does the client have social, emotional, and financial resources and other support systems to help manage the transition?);

- Prior success in managing other transitions;

- Ability to let go of the past;

- Ability to conduct the necessary planning work and follow through on the necessary steps to the next phase; and

- Self-awareness by the client (Can the client recognize tension, anxiety, denial, and so forth and be able to manage them with the help of the consultant?).

Guidelines for Consultants

As we have worked with clients through these developmental transitions, we have found the following guidelines to be helpful:

- Respond to the perception of emergency or crisis on the part of the client (While we as consultants may not see the current situation as a crisis, it's the client's perception that is important);

- Reassure the client that feelings of guilt, anger, and extremes of optimism and/or pessimism are not unusual;

- Offer a realistic perception of the situation after doing the assessment;

- Provide a forum for discussion of feelings and differences;

- Know when to push and when to slow down;

- Present opportunities for new thinking and learning, not just immediate relief from frustration or escape from discomfort of the moment; and

- Understand how the client has coped with similar problems in the past (Ask clients about their perceptions of the present situation and what they have done, if anything, to help manage the transitional crisis they now face. Then ask them to describe how they will deal with this going forward. What have they learned and what will they do in the future?).

Implications for Practice

We will now turn our attention to the ways in which the theories about lifecycles affect our clients' lives and our work with them. We have incorporated concepts from family systems, crisis intervention, developmental psychology, organization development, and whole systems change in order to understand the challenges presented by crises, unresolved issues, and uncompleted tasks. We need to think beyond simple cause and effect and try to understand that the past does not simply determine the future. Many variables in constant motion can create changes at any time. But the developmental framework can shine a light into the dark corners of the past and point to what is needed for future successes. For example, Mort Thomas in Chapter 3 continues to grieve for the death of his wife Shirley; he has also not been able to let go and allow the next generation to take over. He is not able to accomplish the "anticipatory grief" necessary in preparation for letting go. It is widely accepted among family systems therapists that unresolved losses and grieving are related to ongoing conflict in succeeding generations (Paul & Paul, 1974). Internal and external forces combine in each stage to determine the success of the next stage in this *epigenetic* process in which each stage builds upon what has been accomplished in the preceding stage. The present state is a sum of the changes and transitions of the past. For example, Jane was working with a business owner who wanted to divide his assets so that his son would receive an insurance business and an office rental property. The other third of his assets was comprised of real estate that his son didn't want and he could no longer manage. All outside advisors agreed that the timing was right to sell the real estate. He postponed and avoided what he knew rationally to be the best decision. He finally acknowledged that his fear of selling was based on something that his grandfather and mother repeated always:

"Never sell land or property; it's the only real thing there is." He hadn't forgotten this and, in selling, believed that he was, at the age of seventy-nine, "disobeying" his grandfather and mother! After discussing this issue with Jane, he could see that this was a different era and that he needed to make his own decisions based on today's reality. He was then able to get on with the sale.

We often find that to help clients move forward we have to help them move through "unfinished business" and identify those issues that have stalled the development of the individual, the family, or the firm. Unfinished business presents itself in several ways: tasks not completed, unresolved issues, or stalled or slowed development. We will discuss each of these and how the consultant can help the family business move on.

Tasks Not Completed

In the case of the White family in Chapter 1, in which the children became prematurely wealthy when the business was sold, the following questions should have been asked: "What were the children taught in the early stages of their lives?" and "What did they learn about money and responsibility?" An external force, the volatility of the firm's industry, influenced the sale of their business, which they later questioned because of the immaturity of the children. This was related to the failure of the parents to teach responsibility and foster maturity in the children in earlier stages, a task not completed. To affect change, the consultant must retrace the steps and, with the family, decide what needs to be done in the present to prepare for the future and compensate for the past. If the children are going to handle their wealth wisely, then they must be held responsible and accountable.

Another common example is in second-stage family businesses that require infrastructures, accountability, performance reviews, and clear communications. In families that bring emotionality into the business and have poor communications and little accountability, moving to and beyond the expansion stage in the business is very difficult.

The *informal* succession process takes place in the years before the *formal* succession process. The long-term *informal* process includes all of the tasks of rearing children to become responsible and independent adults who may or may not want to take over the business. If the *informal* succession process has not been successful, then the *formal* process, which takes place over a relatively short period of time when documents are being signed, is less likely to be successful.

Unresolved Issues

"The first half of our life is ruined by our parents, and the second half by our children."

Charles Darrow

Another example of unfinished business is "baggage," the unresolved issues that are carried from one generation to the next. It is not unusual to see third-generation cousins re-enacting the old battles of their parents. For example, three cousins who owned and managed a fourth-generation restaurant continued to argue about how large the restaurant should be and whether they should include a small, upscale delicatessen next door. Their fathers, who were brothers, had argued about this before they turned over the business to their sons. The argument continued. It took a strategic planning meeting of fathers and sons and their daughters, as well as a downturn in business, to motivate them to make the decision. They decided it was time to diversify and open the adjoining deli. Pittman (1987) calls this inability to make the necessary changes the "snag point" or the core inflexibility. The consultant must ask: "What is impeding the family's ability to make those changes?" This must also be asked about the business. Three generations' thinking (at least) should always be considered in making an assessment. A genogram of the individual, family, or organizational subsystems can be a useful tool for reviewing the past and identifying key events or issues.

Stalled Development

In Case 1.3 from Chapter 1, the skills, talents, and work ethic of the family members fit the start-up phase of the business, but not the next stage, which required more specialized technical and managerial skills. Progressive evolution requires developmental changes in the people, the functions, and the structures. At this point, new varieties of behaviors and management will have the edge over those that stay the same and will become the dominant form. In this case, the consultant should ask questions such as: "Is it realistic to retrain the family members?" "If not, what is needed to make the transition?" "What is the best way to deal with the loyal family members?" and "Can the family survive this second-order change?"

Accidental Shifts/Discontinuous Changes

Divorce, disability, and death cause detours—some temporary, some permanent—in the developmental cycle of a family. For example, after the untimely death of her husband, Katherine Graham dealt with her grief and low self-esteem and took over the *Washington Post*, the family business. She died recently after a respected, successful career that she had not planned or prepared for before her husband's suicide. She told her story in her memoir, *Personal History* (Graham, 1998).

On the other hand, when tragedy struck the Binghams (the Louisville newspaper family) twice, with the sudden, accidental deaths of two sons, the family was not as resilient. *The Patriarch* (Tifft & Jones, 1991) details the history of the family, which was destroyed by bickering, bitterness, and jealousy of the succeeding generation. Eventually, the father, Barry, Sr., sold the business. The deaths did not cause the family's collapse, but the reader can learn a lot about the family's reactions to the deaths of two members and predict that when things became tough and emotional, they would not have the skills or the practice in processing, negotiating, and resolving crises. As Brown (1993) notes, "The timing of loss in the family's lifecycle involves issues and dilemmas that affect the family's risk for difficulties. . . . Early widowhood, early parental loss, and the death of a child are all examples of losses that are experienced as out of synch with normal family development" (p. 122).

The consultant must always look below the surface of the events to the patterns and underlying currents. Some decisions are not based in the here and now but in the past. Be aware of these; ask the questions that can shine light on the past as it affects the present and threatens the future: "So why do you think you're having such a hard time making this decision?" "What messages did you get that suggested this course of action?"

Crises: Opportunities and Risks

Crisis is simply the state of things at the time of impending change (Pittman, 1987). Sometimes crises catch us by surprise, such as a death or a sudden downturn in the economy, and other times they are of our own doing. For example, if we don't plan for developmental transition points during which the system moves from one stage to another, these normal events will become crises. Examples of transition points that affect family businesses are succession, retirement, and individual development. Much has been written about the dynamics of the transition points and, as consultants, we should familiarize ourselves with the risks and the opportunities they present. Levinson (1978), Greiner (1972), Pittman (1987), and Bridges (1980) all emphasize the risks associated with this period. In fact, the term "mid-life" crisis was used by Levinson to describe the potentially tumultuous time in which man "begins to realize that the summer of his life is ending and the autumn is fast approaching" (1978, p. 21). It is during this period that second-order changes are necessary.

Concepts of crisis intervention have largely been developed in studies of groups or communities confronted with disaster and then applied to family, organization, and individual functioning. There is usually a reaction of disbelief, followed by stages of denial, anger, questioning (Why us?), and, finally, acceptance and moving on. The source of the crisis can be internal, such as addiction or death, or external, for example, violence in the workplace or community disasters. The family, individual, or organization is faced with a problem for which novel patterns of problem solving are needed. New solutions must be developed. Two types of crises have been described: (1) *developmental*, which occur in the normal development of a system and (2) *accidental*, which are precipitated by unanticipated, unplanned events, usually associated with a loss, such as a war, economic recession, or illness, but sometimes associated with a gain, such as winning the lottery, the birth of triplets, or an unanticipated change in the market that greatly increases sales. A third type, a hybrid, has also been described, for example, the birth of a special needs child.

If succession is not planned for during the *informal* succession process, over time, the *formal* succession process will come to resemble an accidental or hybrid crisis, rather than being the developmental change that it should be. If this happens, the process has less chance of being successfully managed. The consultant should be able to tell what events have been planned for, what needs to plan for, and how to help family businesses deal with those accidental crises that could never have been planned for.

Helping Clients Manage Stress

Many entrepreneurs start companies in their thirties, an age when they are also starting families. They often work long hours that leave little time for the family. These hours and commitment put strains on the marriage, the business, and family members. Often spouses feel that "if you can't beat them you might as well join them" and enter the business, too. Many second-generation adults describe spending many hours doing homework or waiting for their parents at the family business. The developmental transitions can strain the clients' physical, emotional, and financial resources, generating a great deal of stress in their lives.

During the past fifty years, researchers have been looking at the relationship between stress and disease. We know that stress creates anxiety (and vice versa) and can lead to physical, mental, emotional, and behavioral problems. It is wear and tear on our souls; it stimulates many of the conditions that cause early aging

(Roizen, 1999). In fact, stress can become so high that the system can decompensate or exist in a dissipative state, a point of flux in which the customary rules do not hold. Before any real teaching or learnings can happen, the stress and anxiety must be dealt with. It has been suggested by some that family businesses are states of chronic anxiety and stress. Symptoms may develop as a solution to stress. For example, a reluctant successor may become depressed or exhibit other physical maladies to avoid becoming the future leader of the business. Such a response may be easier for parents to accept than his or her reluctance to take charge.

Stressors and their effects are highly personalized phenomena. What may be stressful for one family or business or individual may be brushed off as "no big deal" by another. A family retreat may precipitate a crisis, while a downturn in sales may be taken in stride. It is important for consultants not to make assumptions about the level of stress that the family or individuals are experiencing. It is also important to realize that it is not the event itself that is key, but the reaction to it. It is important to ascertain why this particular change, planned or unplanned, is difficult or impossible for *this* family business.

Signs of Increased Stress in a Family Business System

- Difficulty dealing with even small frustrations;
- Blowing up easily or showing increased impatience with others and the work;
- Disrupted sleeping, eating, exercise patterns;
- Difficulties with solving even the simplest problems;
- Physical problems, such as high blood pressure, an increase in colds, or other illnesses;
- Increased absences, lateness;
- Inability to finish jobs;
- Neglecting other social, community networks; and
- Difficulty taking and using advice.

Our bodies typically react to stress with a fight/flight response. Our heart rates, muscle tension, and breathing rates increase; the stomach tightens and produces more acid; and we are in a continuous state of siege. Stress-hardy individuals and families have the ability to stop this reaction and, instead, produce a relaxation response in a variety of ways, including:

- Seeing the big picture;
- Reacting to whatever happens as a challenge, not an overwhelming threat;
- Believing that they have control over what happens to them and their company;
- Approaching life with courage and humor;
- Embracing a spiritual perspective and seeing self as part of a larger whole;
- Making a commitment to work, others, and life;
- Maintaining good physical health habits of sleeping regularly, eating right, and exercising;
- Developing and nurturing social networks;
- Living within their means; and
- Regularly practicing the relaxation response (the opposite of flight/fight) through meditation, physical exercise, and recreation.

Consultants must, in collaboration with their clients, decide which is dealt with first—the stress response or the problem. Additionally, because consultants work in the boundaries, it is critical that we manage our stress responses to our clients and our work.

Succession

Although much has been written about succession in family firms, managing succession is still a significant challenge to families and consultants. It is important to recognize that succession typically involves transitions in terms of ownership or management or both. The following describes one approach that we have used in working with families who are attempting to manage succession.

If, after the assessment phase, succession is the key problem to be managed, then we typically try to create the conditions that are associated with successful transitions. These conditions have been outlined previously by Dyer (1986) and describe the "ideal" situation to be found in the family, in the firm, and in the ownership/governance system. These conditions are as follows:

Conditions in the Family System

- The family shares a common view of what is fair and equitable;
- The family has plans for unexpected emergencies (deaths, illness of key family managers) and therefore has created buy-sell agreements and so forth;

- The family is able to manage conflict successfully;

- The family has superordinate goals and a clear vision of the future and they agree on whether the business should continue to be run by the family, turned over to professional management, or even be sold; and

- High trust exists within the family.

Conditions in the Business System

- The transition occurs when the firm is relatively "healthy";

- The founder/family leader moves gradually away from active involvement in the firm's operations;

- There is a well-developed training and socialization plan for successors in which mentoring of successors is critical; and

- There is an interdependent relationship between the founder/family leader and the successor.

Governance/Ownership Conditions

- Power relationships are clear so there is little ambiguity and

- The board has the necessary expertise to manage the succession issues with the family.

The goal of the consultation is to create these conditions in the three systems and thereby improve the chances of a successful transition. This generally involves the following interventions:

- Assessing the current ownership structure and developing a picture of what ownership should look like after succession;

- Assessing the current state of the family's will(s) or other contingency plans, such as buy-sell agreements, and making sure those documents/plans are consistent with the succession plan (In spite of the challenge posed by succession, in most cases little work will have been done in these areas and the consultant must help the family put the proper safeguards into various legal documents);

- Developing a process for selecting, training, and mentoring future successors;

- Conducting family team-building activities to improve trust, solve conflicts, develop common goals and values, and improve relationships within the family;

- Providing coaching and career development planning for the founder/ family leader and potential successors so they can prepare for the transition;

- Creating an effective board of directors (or other types of boards, such as an asset management board or family council) to provide a forum to discuss some of the important business and family issues and to help oversee the transition process; and

- Determining the managerial or organizational weaknesses that need to be improved for the organization to grow (This often involves changes in the organization's basics structure, systems, and processes).

A good example of a consultation that dealt with succession is the Jones family. The Jones family enlisted Gibb as a consultant when the four brothers, who were asked by their parents to take over the business, were suspicious of the parents' motives. While the parents were willing to turn over the running of the business to their boys, they wanted to continue to own all of the assets. Thus, the sons didn't know whether their parents trusted them or not. This information was discovered during the assessment phase of the consultation. To help remedy the situation, Gibb did the following:

- Held family team-building sessions to resolve conflicts, clear the air, and build trust (During these sessions many of the misconceptions held by family members were cleared up, as they were able to openly express their feelings in a safe atmosphere);

- Helped the family to identify a successor (Fortunately, in this case, one brother was the clear leader. He had recently received his MBA degree and was well-prepared to take over the business. Both his parents and his brothers looked to him for leadership. The brothers agreed that all should be paid the same, regardless of their position in the firm hierarchy, to symbolically represent the fact that each brother was valued equally. This helped to reduce some of the jealousies that often occur when one family member is given a more important position in the organization); and

- Gathered data from nonfamily employees to ascertain the organizational issues that needed to be addressed (As a result, the company was reorganized to reduce the span of control [everyone before had reported to the founder] and to set up systems to improve information sharing and accountability).

The family and the consultant together took the following steps:

- Restructured the board of directors to include outsiders and to function like a board on a regular basis (Previously, the board rarely met and when it did it was typically an informal meeting of family members); and

- Restructured the ownership to leave the firm to those actively in the business and assets to family members not in the business (Those family members outside the business preferred not to have their inheritance contingent on the brothers' and the firm's performance).

Through these interventions, the family relationships and unity was enhanced, the organization was prepared for change, the ownership transition was clarified, and the founder and his successor developed a successful working relationship. As a result, the transition went smoothly and the firm has continued to grow and prosper under new leadership.

Resistance to Succession Planning

Handler (1994) has written about the problem of resistance and in her model of resistance to succession in the family business lists factors that both promote and reduce resistance (see Table 6.4). In this model, Handler categorizes factors that can help or hinder the succession process on four levels: individual, interpersonal, organizational, and environmental. This inventory provides a systemic perspective for both assessment and planning.

Table 6.4. Handler's Model of Resistance to Succession

Factors Promoting Resistance	Factors Reducing Resistance
Individual Level	Individual Level
Good health	Health problems
Lack of other interests	Other interests
Identity with business	Delegation of responsibilities to others
Retention of control over time	Opportunity for new life and career planning
Fear of aging, retirement, and death	Capacity for self-reflection
Avoidance of self-learning	Pursuit of technical advice and consultation
Avoidance of technical advice and consultation	

Table 6.4. Handler's Model of Resistance to Succession, Cont'd

Factors Promoting Resistance	Factors Reducing Resistance
Interpersonal Level Lack of open communication Minimal trust Heir(s) are or appear disinterested, inexperienced, or inappropriate Minimal training Power imbalances Family conflicts or issues permeate the business Nuclear and extended family members as potential heirs	**Interpersonal Level** Honest, informed communication is encouraged High level of trust Heir(s) are actively and capably involved in the business Mentoring is encouraged and practiced Shared power Family dynamics are separate from business interests One child as potential heir
Organizational Level Culture threatens organization development Stability of organizational growth Maintenance of structures promoting unilateral control	**Organizational Level** Culture reinforces organizational continuity Impending organizational crisis Organizational structure promotes functional delegation
Environmental Level Non-problematic environment Many industry requirements Specialized professional prerequisites	**Environmental Level** Problematic environment Few industry requirements Minimal professional prerequisites

Handler, 1994, p. 146. Reprinted with permission from The Family Firm Institute, Inc. All rights reserved.

Lansberg (1988) has also written of the "succession conspiracy" of the family and business to resist the change. He notes that the "founder, family, owners, senior managers, and other stakeholders typically experience poignantly ambivalent feelings toward succession planning. . . . These feelings cause the constituents to procrastinate in developing a plan" (Lansberg, 1988, p. 133). As consultants to family firms, we have often thought about trying to find an ethical way to give our clients a near-death experience to motivate them to think about succession.

Because founders may feel that succession planning is like planning their own funeral, feelings of denial, anger, and depression are not uncommon as they work through succession issues. We have found that holding one-on-one counseling with these individuals and allowing them to share their feelings in family meetings to be very helpful. Such experiences allow them to work through these difficult issues. Also, having the founder or family leaders talk to other family firm leaders who have successfully gone through the succession process can also be helpful and can create social support for the changes they will need to make.

Importance of Rituals

The function of rituals in families and businesses is to punctuate and celebrate transitions and they can create a new reality. Rituals are both symbolic and real events that provide meaning to events of transition and rites of passage. They are bounded by certain times and places with as little interruption as possible. They are important to maintaining and nurturing family identity, building the family culture, and bonding. Family council meetings are rituals; family retreats serve this purpose also. Rituals are also critical for transitions in families, to mark passages of time and identity, to honor the past, and to plan for the future. When a couple starts a life together, they choose their rituals, some from their families of origin and some created anew. These rites of passage are the way in which traditional societies structured life transitions and give us occasions to celebrate.

Consultants can help families create rituals to deal with the passages of life, to mark changes, and to reinforce the family's identity. They may be large, like family councils, or small, like a mother and daughter-in-law "burying" old hurts. Rituals fit into three groupings (Bennett, Wolin, & McAvity, 1988): (1) celebrations such as weddings, funerals, or baptisms; (2) family traditions, such as vacations, anniversaries, reunions, and special meals; and (3) patterned events or routines, such as regular dinner times, everyday greetings and good byes, or leisure activities.

In helping the family firm through an important transition, the consultant might find it helpful to use a ritual or create new ones to help in managing the process. For example, the consultant might find helping the family develop a ritual—such as an annual family retreat or celebration where they recognize individual growth and organizational success or assess where the family business is going and how to plan for the future—is critical to helping the family anticipate and manage these developmental transitions. Also, certain family rituals may be used to make announcements about key decisions, share information, or even gather information to help the client work though various transitions.

In conclusion, helping a family business through developmental transitions is often the role of the family firm consultant. To succeed, the consultant must (1) understand where the individuals, the family, and the firm are in their developmental cycles; (2) diagnose the problems associated with the various cycles being "out of synch" or determine whether there is "unfinished business" that needs to be addressed; and (3) develop and carry out interventions that help the client move through these developmental transitions and deal with the resistance that often accompanies them. In particular, since succession is generally the key developmental transition for most family businesses, the consultant needs to help the client create the conditions that will foster a successful transition.

In Part 2, we have discussed the feedback, planning, and intervention stages of the action research framework in working with family businesses; we have also included a description of the challenges and opportunities of the transitions involved in the intersecting lifecycles of the individual, family, and business in these special entities. In Part 3, we will describe the special skills required, the ethics issues, and special situations that may arise in family business consulting. We will also present interviews with seasoned consultants who find this work rewarding and challenging.

Part 3
The Family Business Consultant

7

Skills and Ethics of the Family Business Consultant

AS WE BEGIN OUR DISCUSSION of what it takes to be a successful family business consultant, we present the following two cases and related questions. The questions suggest the kind of insight, knowledge, and skills that are needed to help each client.

► CASE 7.1

Judith, the human resource director of a mid-size company, calls you, an organization development consultant, to do some team development with the company's employees. You contract with her to do an assessment first. In the process, you discover that this company is family owned and operated, started by the eighty-one-year-old father, Paul, who still comes to his office every morning to oversee "what's going on." Two sons run the company: David is vice president of sales, and Tom is vice president of operations. You speak with both sons, and it is soon clear that they are frustrated with their father's inability to let go. The father and the sons also have constant conflicts about everything. Their father is not impressed with having a consultant come into the business; he has run everything well and the company is prospering. He gives you only twenty minutes, and you know that he's not interested in your ideas. Judith is at her wit's end. She has tried to establish executive management meetings, but the sons usually end up fighting and the father walks out.

What should you understand about ownership issues, that is, who owns how much; are there plans for ownership transfer?

What do you need to know about how the father feels about his age, succession, and letting go?

What do you need to understand about how the family deals with conflict?

What do you think the succession plan is and how does it affect the conflicts? ◄

► CASE 7.2

You, as an attorney, have been called in to design an estate plan for a couple who have two daughters and two sons. The parents are the founders of a large automobile dealership that has expanded into other locations of the metropolitan area. The parents, Shirley and Bob, are in their late sixties; the "children" are in their mid-thirties to mid-forties. Only one son, Herb, and one daughter, Joan, are in the business. The other two siblings, Dick and Martha, and the parents receive regular "dividend" checks from the business. Martha, who is divorced, depends on her income from the business to support herself and one child. The parents do not need the checks at this point; they have invested wisely and live a rather modest lifestyle. You have worked with the parents to design what you consider to be a great estate plan. Shirley and Bob want to make sure that they treat the four children equally and fairly. All the documents have been drawn up and given to the parents. You have just received an irate phone call from Joan, who insists on knowing why you divided ownership of the company into four equal parts. She cannot believe that you recommended that her siblings who do not work in the company would share ownership! She says her parents just couldn't talk with her about this; they had never been able to discuss money issues with the children directly, but always had advisors do "the dirty work."

Who is the client?

What do you need to know about family decision making?

What is your role in consultation?

What is the best advice to give the family about ownership and management? ◄

Self-Assessment

To assess what you need to know to advise family businesses in these case examples, take the self-assessment test in Exhibit 7.1, which is a part of the Family Firm Institute's certificate program for family business consultants. (To find out more about the program, go to www.ffi.org.)

Exhibit 7.1. Self-Assessment for Family Business Consultants

Instructions: The following is a list of topics that family business advisors frequently use in their practices. Take some time to evaluate your current and desired levels of knowledge. See the key for meaning of the letters.

KNOWLEDGE AREAS Behavioral Science	Current Level of Knowledge				Desired Level of Knowledge			
	N	A	U	P	N	A	U	P
Human Development								
Personality Theory								
Lifecycle of the Family								
Conflict Management								
Systems Theory								
Family Therapy								
Gender Issues								

KEY:

N = None—don't even know what the term means

A = Awareness—have heard of it and know that it is used by one of the four disciplines in working with family businesses

U = Understanding—have a working knowledge as to how the area is applied in work with family businesses

P = Proficiency—have both a thorough working knowledge of the area and the ability/credentials to apply and implement the content of the area in working with family businesses

Exhibit 7.1. Self-Assessment for Family Business Consultants, Cont'd

KNOWLEDGE AREAS	Current Level of Knowledge				Desired Level of Knowledge			
	N	A	U	P	N	A	U	P
Birth Order Issues								
Family Dynamics								
Interpersonal Communications								
Treatment of Addictions								
Diagnosis and Treatment of Family Dysfunction								
Diagnosis and Treatment of Individual Psychopathology								
Assessment of Family Functioning								
Financial								
Financial Statement Analysis								
Business Valuation								
Financial Planning								
Principles of Accounting								
ESOP								
Insurance Types and Uses								
Wealth Management and Investment Return								
Types of Financial Advisors								
Sources of Financing								
Capital Structures								
Estate and Income Tax								
Legal								
Types of Ownership Entities								
Ownership Transfer Methods								
Rights of Shareholders								
Types of Corporations								

Exhibit 7.1. Self-Assessment for Family Business Consultants, Cont'd

KNOWLEDGE AREAS	Current Level of Knowledge				Desired Level of Knowledge			
	N	A	U	P	N	A	U	P
Structure and Use of Trusts								
Partnerships								
Laws for Corporate Directors								
Employment Law								
Estate Planning Techniques								
Management Science								
Business and Strategic Planning								
Organization Design								
Organization Development								
Work and Job Design								
Management Theory								
Leadership Theory								
Organizational Culture								
Work-Flow Design								
Change Management								
Team Building								
Performance Appraisals								
Coaching and Counseling								
Management Succession								
Compensation Systems								
Production and Operations Management								
Organizational Assessment								
Systems Theory								

Reprinted with permission from The Family Firm Institute, Inc. All rights reserved.

After you have finished completing the matrix, answer the following questions:

- In which areas do you feel you need to increase your learning?
- In which areas do you feel competent in both skills and knowledge?
- How will you go about learning more?
- Are there other areas you would add to this matrix?
- List specific learning goals for yourself in the next twelve months.

Knowledge and Skills Required

Until the mid-1990s there had not been a unified, multidisciplinary paradigm for consulting in family business situations. Too many well-meaning consultants had been claiming to be family business consultants without having the necessary skills and training. And without this integration of knowledge and training, the conventional methods had been insufficient to handle both the emotional and the business complexities. This situation still exists for there has been no evidence to date of a reduction in the high number of family business failures. However, the good news is that training programs are being developed that will add to the professionalization of the field. In the near future, family businesses will expect their advisors to have the proper training and experience in order to call themselves "family business consultants."

As previously mentioned, the Body of Knowledge committee of FFI that began its work in 1995 has identified basic knowledge for the "core professions": *behavioral science, management science (which includes organization development), law,* and *finance.* It is not required that family business consultants become experts in the four fields, but they are expected (1) to be experts in their core profession; (2) to have an understanding of the critical issues in the other professions that are relevant to family businesses; (3) to have the knowledge, training, and experience to know when to refer a client to others; and (4) to become knowledgeable in the areas that intersect all professions. To this list we add the competency of "self-awareness" as a key to being effective in this field.

Self-Awareness: Management and Use of Self

"We do not see things as they are; we see things as we are."

Talmud

Many family business consultants come from family businesses; their own experiences affect the work they do. If they have not worked through these experiences, whether negative or positive, their own agendas may take over. Consultants who come from OD and therapy fields have been trained to consider the effect of their past experiences; this is much less so for attorneys and accountants. Our experience is, however, that the level of intensity in family businesses can be so high that old, automatic patterns of responding may be triggered. As Quade and Brown state in *The Conscious Consultant*, "If we are unconscious of important aspects of ourselves, we will impact our clients in unknown ways, and reactive change is likely. If we are aware of our capabilities and limitations, we can include that knowledge in our planning, all the while actively changing our self. In this way we can continue to grow in excellence, utilize our strengths, and compensate for our weaknesses" (2001, p. 20).

For example, one consultant played the role of "peacemaker" in her family of origin, the family she grew up in. Her automatic response to a conflict was to try to settle it quickly. This is not always the best response, so she has to be conscious about deciding to use peace-making attempts. Sometimes the family is not ready for resolution and the intervention is premature. For example, another colleague was the problem solver in his family; his first response in a challenging situation was to solve the problem quickly. He has to remember not to rush to judgment or solutions but to ask questions and start a dialogue. These automatic behaviors can be powerful skills, but they must not be used reactively.

A first step is to understand what situations might be most threatening, for it is when we feel threatened, vulnerable, or not up to the challenge that we revert to our "automatic" protective behaviors. Is it silence? Is it conflict? Is it ambiguity? The second step is to understand how we're most likely to react. And the third step is to manage those responses so we can be effective, deliberate, and strategic—not automatic—with the client. For example, one consultant who grew up in a family business with "a dad who was a dictator and a mom who was a doormat" has a very difficult time with tough, take-charge male owners. When he can manage his reactions, he can be very effective because he learned from a master. If he loses it, he becomes the young son who can't speak up.

If we can see our own triggers, we are less susceptible to the family's pull on us, which is very strong in any family in crisis, especially in family businesses. The end result of doing our own emotional work is that:

- We don't confuse our own reactions with those of others;
- We can stay mentally alert;
- We can jump into tough situations with courage; and
- We can use our feelings as data, as keys to solutions, rather than acting them out.

The way we use and manage our own feelings in a highly emotional system is defined in different ways by different disciplines. Therapists refer to these feelings in a session with a client as counter-transference, or the effect of a client's personality or the material presented that produces or represents something from the consultant's past. For example, working with family businesses of great wealth can lead to feelings of envy or anger in those who grew up in a family where money was tight; these consultants also might object to "kids" having been spoiled. Consultants need to understand the money messages they received from their own parents and how these affect their work with clients of wealth. Goleman (1995), in *Emotional Intelligence,* refers to the "The Master Aptitude" as the ability to keep emotions from overwhelming our ability to think and plan. Argyris (1991) describes "defensive reasoning" that can block learning. Murray Bowen (1976) uses the term "differentiated self" to describe the ability of a person "whose intellect could function separately from the emotional system." Coming from different perspectives, these writers all mean the same thing: *To be effective, we need to keep our feelings, thoughts, and actions separate.* One of the best things we can do to improve our work is to manage ourselves, monitor our own reactions, and be aware of our personal agendas.

Whatever it is called, self-awareness identifies our strengths, weakness, allergies (situations or people that we have a strong negative reaction to, usually the result of past influences that have not been acknowledged or managed), personal agendas, and emotional triggers. This does not mean that we are detached or neutral, but that we identify what we are experiencing in a client situation and know how to use those feeling appropriately *in the client's best interest.* The adage that "we can't take clients farther than we've gone" applies here. If we haven't dealt with our own family ghosts, then we can't help our clients who are dealing with similar issues. We can't lead the way if we haven't been down that trail before. What we know about clients and ourselves and how we manage the boundary between our clients and ourselves can make the difference between a successful consultation and a failure.

But before we put feelings aside, we should examine them and ask whether they are useful. If we feel muddled, or upset, most likely others do also. For example, a president of a company has begun to understand that his "automatic" reaction to interfere comes from his early experience of being the oldest son who had to go to work early to support the family, who *had* to interfere to save the family. Peter Drucker (1999) suggested that, in order to manage oneself, certain questions should be asked on a regular basis, because success in the knowledge economy "comes to those who know themselves—their strengths, their values, and how they best perform . . . and the need to manage oneself is therefore creating a revolution in human affairs." We have adapted and expanded his list to include the following:

- What are my strengths?
- How do I perform?
- How do I learn? How do I pay attention to triggers?
- What are my values? How do I judge the values of my client systems?
- What messages did I receive about gender issues from my family?
- What was my emotional role in my family? Was I the peacemaker? The troublemaker? The clown? The realist?
- What were my responsibilities in my family?
- What issues did we not discuss in my family? How do I handle these now?
- What types of situations or people do I feel "allergic" to?
- What difficult situations have I had quite a bit of personal experience with?
- When do I feel most vulnerable?
- When I feel vulnerable, what is my automatic reaction (without thinking first)?
- What is my reaction to authority figures?
- What do I do when I see conflict?
- What messages did I hear about money when growing up?
- What was my family's experience dealing with change or crises?

Our conclusions or reactions may dramatically affect the change management process.

Consultant's Genogram

Using Figure 3.2 on page 45 as a model, draw your own genogram, including at least three generations. Take time to look at the patterns, the main issues that you carry from your family into your present life and work. Particularly relevant to our work with family businesses are the areas of power, money, gender, work, addictions, siblings, intergenerational relationships, conflicts, and roles. Notice whether you were a part of any triangles. Next, think of a client failure you have had and see whether you can see any connections between your genogram and what contributed to that failure.

How Can I Get Help to Improve My Skills?

"Experience is the name everyone gives to their mistakes."

Oscar Wilde

None of us can go it alone when working with family businesses. We need the help, advice, and challenge of others in our work. There are several ways to find this support and, in your practice, you should arrange for at least one of the methods outlined in Table 7.1.

Table 7.1. Types of Support and Advice

Support Methods	Relationship	Advantages	Disadvantages
Shadow Consultant/ Coach	One-on-one; "behind the scenes," in the shadow consultation from one who is more experienced; value of advice depends on experience and skills of the "shadow"	Relationship can provide support and valuable insights into self and work with client	Cost: quality of advice depends on several variables; may need "trial and error" to find right match in terms of skills and personality
Supervisor	One-on-one; superior/ subordinate relationship; usually in a work or educational context; accountability and authority must be clearly spelled out	Supervisor has more experience and is "senior"; fee often is covered in educational or job context	Depending on situation, supervisor may be "assigned"; employee must follow supervisor's suggestions/advice; employee is accountable to the supervisor
Mentor	One-on-one; superior/ subordinate relationship; combination coaching and personal development	Both personal and professional guidance and support; helpful in navigating client's territory; often longer, deeper relationship than coaching	Fee depends on contract; personal guidance may not be welcomed by all

Table 7.1. Types of Support and Advice, Cont'd

Support Methods	Relationship	Advantages	Disadvantages
Study Group	Group learning and support; ideal is six to twelve members; level of advice depends on trust and length of time group has been meeting; sometimes evolves out of other meetings; decision should be made if this will be a multidisciplinary team or not	Cost is in time only; networking; getting to know others' work; useful in building a "multidisciplinary" team; many opinions can add to creativity of solutions	Usually meets less than once a month; chance to present depends on group numbers and meeting; finding the right "mix" is difficult; building commitment takes time

With each approach to gaining support from various sources, such as other consultants or a study group, it is imperative that the contract between you and the other "support systems" be clearly spelled out in terms of accountability, fees, length, frequency of contact, scope of work to be done, and how it will happen (by phone, fax, e-mail, or in person). Generally, intense counseling and mentoring only happens in one-on-one situations. However, how the mentoring takes place also depends on the relationship and trust built up in the parties.

Jane has belonged to a study group for over fifteen years, and the level of trust in her study group is very high. Typically, the advice given and received in Jane's study group is at both a technical and an emotional level. This has evolved over the years and is mutually agreed on by all in the group. Other study groups may deal only in technical issues.

As a suggested format for case discussion, the consultant typically describes the client he or she is working with. The consultant outlines the referral source, nature of the problems, the dynamics in the various systems, and so forth. The consultant then discusses the challenges he or she has been experiencing during the consultation. After presenting the case, the consultant then may ask questions such as, "Am I on the right track?" "What should I do next?" or "Do you know anyone who could help me solve this problem?" It is important for the consultant to prepare to hear the suggestions that are given. To illustrate this preparation to listen, we will turn to the example of the Zen master:

> "A Japanese master received a professor who came to understand more about Zen. The Master served tea and continued pouring the tea even as it was overflowing the cup. The professor cried out, 'Stop; it is full and over-flowing! No more will go in!' The Master responded, 'Like this cup, you are full of your own opinions and speculations. How can I teach you Zen unless you first empty your cup?'" (Reps & Senzaki, 1994, p. 7)

As consultants, we often learn more by emptying our cups first, rather than retaining cups full of our own ideas.

Another skill we need as family business consultants is the ability to work in a team. We will now turn our attention to the various ways we can team up with the family firm's other advisors or create our own teams.

Multidisciplinary Teams

Multidisciplinary work is not unique to family business advising. Hospitals, schools, and organizations of all sizes appreciate the value of developing teams of individuals with accountability to separate departments and an allegiance to the larger company or organization, sometimes referred to as cross-functional teams. However, professionals advising family businesses are beginning to appreciate that working together in a team benefits the client; increasing numbers of groups are forming to offer multidisciplinary services. The complexity of the client's problems have challenged those who have wanted to work independently and have previously been threatened by sharing their work. Family businesses increasingly are demanding that their advisors work as a team.

Since family business advisors come to this field from a variety of backgrounds, the challenge is to identify the body of knowledge that comprises the family business profession, as well as the knowledge specific to each of the professions of origin, that is, law, finance, behavioral science, family systems, management science, or organization development. In order to gain the potential benefits of a team approach, the professions must understand what each can contribute and then work together. There are several models of teams (Hoover & Hoover, 1999). Teams function on a continuum in terms of how often they work together, the level of coordination and organization of the team, and the members' commitment to one another. Teams may be categorized as follows:

1. *Consulting (interdisciplinary)*: a pre-existing team that is hired by the client;

2. *Collaborative (multidisciplinary)*: advisors from different disciplines meet in a study group forum, get to know one another's work, and bring one another into client situations on an as-needed basis or in a shadow consulting function;

3. *Strategically allied:* advisors from two or more disciplines work with one another on a frequent basis; they may also have their own individual practices;

4. *Accidental:* advisors meet and connect through the client only, with little to no coordination; and

5. *Dysfunctional:* advisors unknown to one another, even if working with the same client, and with no coordination.

Despite their growing acceptance in the field, and the recognition that teams of advisors leads to better and more cost-effective advice, the multidisciplinary team still poses several challenges. (Whether apocryphal or not, it is accepted among therapists who work in teams that the client will not improve if the therapy team has problems of coordination, competition, or conflict.) It may not be as McClure (2000) notes in his article, "Leading a Team of Advisors," that advisors "are as difficult to herd as alley cats." His advice for advisory teams follows:

- Have a truly integrative problem to solve (Most family firm problems are "integrative," that is, they affect both the family and the business, although some, like succession, have the potential to have a profound impact on both.);

- Have specific goals; and

- Have a leader who can keep the group focused on the client goals and communicate well with the owner, the family, executives, and other advisors.

The following are questions that must be resolved by any team before beginning the work:

- Who will be the quarterback? Who will see that work is coordinated?

- How will the billing be handled?

- How will differences be managed?

- Who will be the liaison to the client?

- How will the client be sold on the multidisciplinary team?

- How will competition for the best idea, suggestions, and recommendations be dealt with?

- How will everyone find the time necessary to plan and best meet the client's needs?

Krasnow and Wolkoff (1998), both lawyers, make the case for a multidisciplinary approach to three often-presented "integrated" problems: prenuptial agreements, estate planning, and liquidity agreements for dissatisfied minority shareholders. They suggest that too often lawyers act "as dutiful scriveners without questioning the wisdom of some of the client's goals" in these cases. The authors raise questions for study, such as: Do prenuptial agreements have any real-world value in the family business situations in which they arise? Do alternatives work just as well? Are lawyers, accountants, and insurance salespeople aware of the shortsightedness of making tax savings a priority? And, if they are aware, why do they think that clients reject these ideas? Do traditional minority shareholder buyout agreements achieve the expected benefits?

Vinton (1998) examines nepotism (the practice of hiring relatives) from an interdisciplinary point of view using five perspectives: environmental, managerial, behavioral, legal, and financial/economic. She emphasizes the importance of considering how these areas interact and affect each other over time. This broader approach encourages us to look at each case, each client, with an openness to understand the situation from all perspectives to be more effective as advisors. Table 7.2 is an adaptation of Vinton's chart.

Table 7.2. Multidisiplinary Study Sheet for Family Business Issues

	Legal	Financial	Relationship	OD/Management
Prenuptial Agreements	Is this the most effective legal solution? Will it prevent protracted court battles? Is it enforceable? What are some more effective methods for accomplishing the same goals?	Will this prevent an unfair alimony award? Will this keep the business in the family? What are the financial implications in not having a pre-nup?	What impact will the pre-nup have on the couple and the family? What are the ways to make this productive and emotionally fulfilling?	Will the pre-nup agreement have any effect on the management or the organization of the business? Will there be any fallout?

Table 7.2. Multidisiplinary Study Sheet for Family Business Issues, Cont'd

	Legal	Financial	Relationship	OD/Management
Succession	What are the legal options for ownership structure? What are the legal implications of succession planning in this family?	Will the older generation have its financial needs met? How can this be accomplished and what do they need? What should the compensation and benefits be of the next generation leadership? Can business compete in the next generation?	What will the emotional impact be on the choice of the successor? How strong and adaptable are the relationship and family bonds to deal with the succession effectively? Does the family have the capabilities to own and run the business into the next generation?	How will the transfer of ownership affect the executive team? How can the choice of the new leadership structure be assessed? How do we pick the best leader? How is the communication within the company?
Minority Shareholders	Have the minority shareholders asked or been asked to sell back their stock? What has been the reaction and what are the legal implications? What are the long-range legal issues with the presence of minority shareholders?	Are the minority shareholders not involved in the business receiving dividends? What is the effect of financial arrangements with these shareholders? Is there a minority discount?	What are the feelings of the minority shareholders who are involved in the business and those who are not? What is the effect of the minority discount on the family relationships? What is the effect of the minority shareholders receiving dividends and not working in the business?	How are the minority shareholders who work in the business treated? What, if any, is the impact on the business? Are there any long-term strategies for dealing with the minority shareholders involved in the business?

Adapted from Vinton (1998), p. 302, and Krasnow and Wolkoff (1998). Reprinted with permission from The Family Firm Institute, Inc. All rights reserved.

Guidelines for Using Table 7.2

- If you can't generate informed planning questions and answers for each "professional block," then call in other professionals on your team.

- The questions can become the blueprint for assessing the family business problem from a multidisciplinary perspective.

- Be as specific as you can be with each of the questions, continuing to "fine tune" as you learn more about the situation.

The next practice management topic that will be discussed is billing for your services.

Fees

Billing is a subject that is not often written about, but which is discussed frequently, for a combination of reasons, including our own vulnerabilities, competition, and criticisms of fee setting. Because the field of family business consulting is comprised of professionals from several professions, there are differences in the way they charge for services. You will have to decide what works best for you and/or your team. Several methods of charging for services are described in Table 7.3.

Table 7.3. Billing Practices

	Method	Advantages	Risks
Per Hour	You are paid for each hour you work. Adopted from the legal, accounting, and therapy professions.	Clear; simple; amount of time can be re-negotiated; your work for the client, either face-to-face or on your own, is recorded and paid for.	Some clients feel limited in their contacts, especially if money is concern, that is, the clock is running.
Per Day	For each day you work, you are paid a day's pay	Clear; simple; you are paid for the days you work for and with your client.	Same as above; the amount of the initial contract often has to be renegotiated since family businesses are rarely simple to fix.

Table 7.3. Billing Practices, Cont'd

	Method	Advantages	Risks
Per Project	The client pays for you to do a certain project or amount of work, that is, a family retreat, a family business assessment, or building an outside board.	Based on your experience, an educated "guesstimate" of the amount it will take to do a certain piece of work for the client. Client knows up front what the project will cost.	You are paid the same amount no matter how many hours you work to finish the project. With family businesses, with unique and complex systems, this is often more hours, rather than fewer.
Retainer	You are paid a given amount for a certain period of time to be available, whether or not the client uses your services during this time; for example, agreement could specify a certain number of months.	Gives client access to you and your services; usually happens after the consultant has a proven track record of effectiveness; good if you are involved in several projects or client voices concern over consulting fees or client wants priority time with you; meter is not running.	Consultant can be overused without built-in agreements about the best use of his or her time and talents; should specify "subject to mutually convenient schedules" and should be understood that client gives as much notice as possible.
Per Product	The client pays for a product (workbook, report, and so forth).	Simple, clear, provides additional income from a product that is separate from the work and time spent with the client.	Under- or over-priced; appropriate training or explanation of product is not heeded or given.
Results-Based	Based on output, rather than amount of time worked with and for the client. Measurable results agreed to at time of contracting. Results can be in sales, profit, or cultural, that is, number of new ideas from teams, promotions from within.	You participate in the improvements or gains in the organization; meter is not running. Cost to client is fixed at the beginning; output or improvement is arrived at collaboratively with client; builds the relationship; defines the goals clearly. It is a great exercise for the family, as well as the business, to objectify results.	Results may be a moving target in the family business, with so many variables and emotional components; sometimes difficult to define output; results may change as the consultation progresses; results have to be objective, not subjective. (An interesting discussion of "value-based fees" can be found in Alan Weiss' *The Ultimate Consultant,* 2001.)

Guidelines for Choosing a Fee Schedule

"Nowadays, people know the price of everything and the value of nothing."

Oscar Wilde

We have found the following guidelines to be helpful in setting a fee schedule with our clients.

- Choose the method that fits your values, skills, bookkeeping, and comfort level;

- Be clear with your client exactly what they are paying for and stick to it;

- Renegotiate around the work and not the fees, if necessary;

- Be consistent in your charges; know what the "going rate" is in your area and, if you travel, what the "going rate" is elsewhere;

- Charge for travel time, as well as for expenses;

- Remember that one size does not fit all, so decide in advance what fees you will charge for different size companies, the geographic area, and your level of skill and experience;

- Choose cases that you want to work with;

- If money is a concern, discuss it with the client and come up with a mutually agreed-on list of priorities;

- Remember that it is about the value you bring, as well as pricing;

- Pro bono work has its own rewards; is you accept the work, be clear about your contributions and why you are agreeing to do the work, for example, is challenging, adds to society or community, or eventually will lead to more work and/or bigger contracts; and

- When working in a team, decide beforehand whether you will bill as individuals or as a team (This is usually a function of how the team works together. Teams composed of consultants from the same discipline generally will submit one bill; often the individuals on multidisciplinary teams submit bills separately).

Although being paid is obviously of great importance to consultants, money cannot be the only consideration. Among the other issues to consider is ethics, which should be a foundation of our work. The following section details many of the ethical questions that arise in family businesses and family business consulting.

Ethical Issues

"Art, like morality, consists of drawing the line somewhere."

G.K. Chesterton

The word ethics has the same root as ethnic and ethos: *one's own, traits of one's own* (Watkins, 1985). The origins suggest that "ethics" really is about character, how we think of ourselves, who we are in relation to others, how we treat one another, principles that govern our conduct, and a definition of good and bad. Ethics involves our personal and professional sense of right and wrong.

Ethics in Our Clients

Until recently, there has been little research on ethics in family businesses, although pop literature is filled with gothic tales of jealousy, greed, and unethical behavior among families who work together. Out of seventeen inductees into the most recent "Hall of Shame" of *Family Business* magazine (Editors, 2001), we present four as examples of unethical behavior:*

1. Herbert Haft, the founder and CEO of the discount retailer, Dart, fired his oldest son, Robert, as president in 1993; he thought Robert was trying to displace him. The controlling Haft family split into two camps. Four years and once divorce later, the Hafts lost control and wound up filing Chapter 11.

2. The controlling Singer family of the Cooper Companies manipulated prices of high-yield bonds by fraudulently trading bonds between the company's account and accounts set up in the names of Chairman Gary Singer's wife and aunt. The schemes produced about $3M in illicit profits for entities controlled by the Singer family before Gary Singer's conviction on twenty-one counts of fraud in 1994.

3. Rite Aid founder Alex Grass built a retailing giant; then older son Martin pushed him out in a boardroom coup in 1995 and stripped the offices of his father's memorabilia. Martin was ousted by Rite Aid's board in 1999 for improperly pledging corporate assets to secure a bank loan for the company, then falsifying board minutes concerning the pledge. The company admitted myriad accounting violations under Martin.

---

*Reprinted by permission of the publisher from Summer 2001, *Family Business*, Philadelphia, www.familybusinessmagazine.com.

4. The $80 billion Korean industrial conglomerate, the Hyundai Group, founded by the autocratic Chung Ju Yung, broke up amid huge debts and infighting by factions led by two of his sons. Two of the largest units are near bankruptcy; another son, Chung Mung Woo, killed himself in 1990.

In a 1996 *Family Business Review* article, Adams, Taschian, and Shore report on ethics in family and nonfamily owned firms. The authors found that there were few, but important, difference between family and nonfamily firms. The differences were found in the methods used to teach and enforce moral codes. The authors concluded, "Nonfamily owned businesses appear to rely primarily on formal means such as an ethics code, ethics training, and sanctions. In contrast, family businesses rely on modeling of appropriate behavior and behavioral norms transmitted informally among members."

Gallo (1998) studied ethics in successful Spanish businesses. Describing the responses of 253 employees, he noted that the most frequently perceived ethics violations were in delaying succession processes, avoiding complex strategic planning, and building an organization based on the buying of loyalties.

Building on family business historian, William O'Hara's (2000) research, the editors of *Family Business* magazine, in the Spring 2001 issue, described the traits that America's oldest family businesses share: good genes, luck, rural or small-town location, a genuine interest in serving the needs of a larger cause beyond the company's stockholders, a *moral imperative that remains a sustaining force long after the passion for profits has worn off.* In other words, doing well *is* linked to doing good.

Our goal, as consultants, should be to help our clients maintain their ethical bearings. This often involves confronting our clients regarding their choices and helping them develop an "ethical framework" from which to view their behavior and make appropriate choices.

Our Own Ethics

With advisors coming from a variety of disciplines and professions to create a new model of practice, here are some questions for each profession making the transition:

- *Lawyers* will ask: Who is my client?
- *Therapists* will ask: What are the issues of confidentiality? What are the boundaries; for example, can I have lunch with these clients?

- *Accountants* may ask: What are the financial priorities and how do they fit into the family priorities and values? How are the intangible assets of the family included in the valuation?

- *Organization development consultants* struggle with the depth of the level of intervention: What do I do with the conflict in the family that is causing the unfair treatment of the employees?

In a thought-provoking practice paper available online, "One Social Worker's Reality Check with Her Board of Professional Responsibility," Marty Carter, a family legacy advisor in Birmingham, Alabama, describes her censorship by her state's board of social work for violation of confidentiality. The board refused to recognize that her work "was a part of a totally new field." They even refused to consider creating guidelines and requirements within the existing practice of social work. The author concludes, "Consultants to family owned businesses are in the process of creating a new model of practice that has marked differences from traditional roles. Changes in practice have come before changes in guidelines established by governing boards."

In an attempt to establish a statement of ethical behavior for consultants, FFI has written the only existing ethical code for family business advisors. It is shown in Exhibit 7.2.

Exhibit 7.2. FFI Code of Professional Ethics

Adopted April 2001

Purpose

Members of the Family Firm Institute are obligated to maintain the highest standards of professionalism. Members of FFI come from a variety of professions of origin, many with their own codes of ethics. Membership in the Family Firm Institute, however, represents a willingness to adhere to the standards of professional conduct outlined below. When a member's specific professional discipline's code of ethics calls for a standard of conduct different from the following, whichever code or guideline is the more stringent or more extensive or demands the higher standard and sensitivity will apply.

Clients

- At the outset of an engagement, the family business advisor will state in writing whose interests he or she is representing during the course of the engagement. Should the need arise to revise the definition of "client" during the engagement, this need will be communicated to and negotiated with all appropriate parties and confirmed in writing.

Exhibit 7.2. FFI Code of Professional Ethics, Cont'd

- Members, their organizations, and professional associates will keep client information and the identity of the client confidential and will not disclose it without the written consent of the client.

Professional Conduct

- Members will not represent their education, training, experience, professional credentials, and competence, or areas of skill and expertise in a deceptive or misleading manner.
- When a member refers a client to another party, the member will disclose to the client the nature of any business relationship between them or their organization and whether there will be any referral fee or other fee sharing.
- Members agree not to misrepresent their affiliation with the Family Firm Institute, nor to imply that being a member of FFI holding a "Certificate in Family Business Advising" implies either credentialing or endorsement by FFI.
- Members will avoid real or perceived conflicts of interest whenever possible and will disclose them to all affected parties.
- Members have an obligation to provide a client with all information obtained in the course of conducting their engagement which is pertinent to the decisions the client is contemplating.
- Members have a duty to keep current in their professional practices through self-study and regular attendance at family business-related conferences and courses.
- Members, in their professional activities, will treat all persons fairly regardless of their race, creed, color, national origin, religion, gender, age, marital status, sexual preference, physical condition, and/or appearance.
- Members will recognize and respect intellectual property rights, including providing specific acknowledgment of the original authorship and source when publishing or publicly representing another person's work.
- Members will assist other members in their professional development, where possible and appropriate, and support them in complying with this Code of Professional Ethics.
- Members will respect the development and growth of the field of family business and will take positive steps to promote the field.

Fees

- Members will disclose in writing and at the outset of every engagement the basis of their fees and expenses and provide an estimate of the total cost of the service whenever possible.

Exhibit 7.2. FFI Code of Professional Ethics, Cont'd

Research

- Members who do research will carry out the research with respect and concern for the dignity and welfare of the people who participate. It is the members' responsibility to be adequately informed, and abide by, relevant laws and regulations regarding the conduct of research with human participants. Individuals entering into research must do so voluntarily and with adequate information.

Reprinted with permission from The Family Firm Institute, Inc. All rights reserved.

Additional Resource

The Cambridge Center for Creative Enterprise, a nonprofit training institute in Cambridge, Massachusetts, has offered multidisciplinary training workshops for family business consultants for almost a decade. For schedule and seminar content, see www.camcenter.org.

8

Special Situations and Challenges

ON THIS CHAPTER WE WILL DISCUSS the following special situations and challenges presented by the family business client:

- Copreneurs,

- Emotions,

- Addictions,

- Gender issues,

- Nonfamily managers,

- Family offices/family foundations, and

- Ethnicity.

While we cannot provide an in-depth look at each of these topics, we will point out those elements most important for family business consultants. For further information, we provide suggested readings and resources at the end of each section.

Copreneurs

"We have only one person to blame, and that's each other."
Barry Beck, New York Rangers hockey player, when asked who started
a brawl during the National Hockey League's Stanley Cup playoffs

Copreneurs, dual-career couples who also share an entrepreneurial business enter-prise, have only become a focus of study and writing in the past fifteen years. Among the earliest authors were Sharon Nelton (1986) and Frank and Sharan Barnett (1998) who first used the term "copreneurs." The 1990s saw a growing interest in couples who owned a business together. In 1990, Dennis Jaffee presented a lecture, "Married to the Business and Each Other," in which he emphasized the unique qualities of the copreneurial relationship. In a good review article in *Family Business Review*, Mar-shack (1993) noted that the literature to that point had focused either on the business or on the relationship and that family business literature could contribute to the trend toward the integrated systems perspective. If family businesses are the graduate school of relationships, copreneurs are the post-graduate!

The number of copreneurships is increasing and, along with women-owned businesses, is the fastest growing segment of the business population. The growth has been attributed to the boom in franchises; the shift from corporate to entrepre-neurial values; technological advances that make it easier to work out of the home; and a need to have more control over the economic and emotional health of the family (Ponthieu & Caudill, 1993).

There have been generations of mom-and-pop businesses, from the local store and dry cleaners to big businesses such as the Estee Lauder cosmetic empire, founded by Lauder with her husband Joseph in 1946. Donna Karan and her hus-band run her fashion company. Lucille Ball and Desi Arnaz were married in 1940 and for years before their divorce in 1960 ran Desilu Productions. Often the wife starts the business and her husband, retired, laid off, or disenchanted with corpo-rate life, joins her.

Tasks of the Couple

There are several critical tasks for couples who want to work together successfully. These include:

- Balancing the individuals' and the couple's development and growth;
- Managing the boundaries of the couple, individual, family, and work;

- Sharing power, especially if the business has been started by one and joined later by the other; and

- Challenging gender stereotyping.

Cultural traditions seem to continue to play a role in the copreneurial relationship. Marshack (1994), in a study of copreneurs, found that the adherence to traditional sex-role orientations is limiting in both defining work assignments and in succession planning. Ponthieu and Caudill (1993) concluded in their study of 184 copreneurships that gender predominates in decision making at work and at home; the husband tended to be dominant at work, while they disagreed about who was the predominant decision maker at home. Both husband and wife denied that they were the predominant decision maker at home.

There are numerous rewards awaiting couples who work successfully together. First, we generally find that successful pairs accomplish more together than apart. Paul Edwards, co-author of "Teaming Up: The Small Business Guide to Collaborating with Others to Boost Your Earnings and Expand Your Horizons," notes, "Like that famous novel says, it can be the best of times or the worst of times." In the same article, his wife, Sarah, claims, "If you can have your spouse as part of your life for twenty-four hours a day, that's the closest thing to heaven I can think of" (Trollinger, 1998). Second, couples report that the thing they enjoy most is the ability to work together, spend time with one another, travel together, and create something together. As one client said, "Some days we could kill each other, but most of the time we know there's nothing better than this." Third, customers and clients can have confidence that either partner can speak for the team, the company, the service, and the products. Fourth, working together allows the couple to share childcare responsibilities. Finally, it often allows the couple more control of their schedules.

The Couple's Dance

In a groundbreaking 1968 book, *The Miracles of Marriage,* Lederer and Jackson, influenced by the application of mathematics and cybernetics to social problems, human communications, and family relationships, describe marriage as a system in which the ways in which the partners interact are "mysterious." The "mystery" is the *paradox* of a couple's relationship—the closer the pair, the stronger the pull for autonomy.

The "couple's dance" refers to the repetitive sequence of interactions or vicious cycles between partners (Lerner, 1985). Typical in a copreneurial couple is their focusing on work instead of a disagreement that they have; she works harder and longer hours, and, in response, he works harder also. This reinforcing loop does not solve the basic problem they have and exhausts both of them.

All couples have "dances" or patterns of interactions. Some may be simply a result of the interaction of the two partners' characteristic styles of relating learned from cultural and familial influences (Middleberg, 2001). These patterns become destructive under the following circumstances:

1. When they become the couple's predominant way of dealing with each other *and their only way to regulate anxiety and maintain a balance between separateness and intimacy.*

2. When the "problem maintenance structure" acts as a constraint to making the necessary changes in the patterns of interaction. The "structure" usually takes the form of a "default conversation" in which the couple argues about the same things—money, employees, vision of the company, childcare—no matter what the problem. In this way, the real issue is never dealt with.

Most couples can learn to change these patterns without first resolving the deeper internal issues that require their defensive dance (Middleberg, 2001). The consultant should be aware of the patterns of the dances and know what to try to break these patterns. If the interventions don't work or the symptoms grow worse, the couple should be referred to a therapist for the deeper level of work that is required. Couples' issues can ripple through the family firm, setting the tone and the culture. Most couples' dances include two or more of the processes listed in Table 8.1.

Table 8.1. Couples' Dances and Associated Business Risks

Dance Pattern	Interaction	Risks to Business
Conflict	Blame and attack; escalating cycle of attack and counterattack	Inability to create a shared reality or vision for the business; conflicts create tension among employees; anger seeps into business culture
Distancing	Mutual withdrawal; avoidance and cutoff (no contact)	Problems are not solved; duplication of work; contradictory messages to customers, suppliers, staff; ineffective indirect communications; avoiding tough business questions

Table 8.1. Couples' Dances and Associated Business Risks, Cont'd

Dance Pattern	Interaction	Risks to Business
Pursuer/Avoider	To-and-fro: one moves in with feelings; one moves out with intellectualizations (factual arguments or opinions)	Increased difficulties giving authority to employees and work teams; unstable infrastructure; rigidity of roles; difficult time with crises
Over-functioner/ Under-functioner	Polarized positions of over-responsible caretaker/parent and under-responsible patient/child	One partner gets burned out by taking on too many of the re-sponsibilities; the other is left out, not involved in critical plan-ning or communications and is ignored by customers, employees, suppliers
Triangulation	Focus on a third party as scapegoat, ally, hero, avenger, or patient	Business is an easy target for negative or positive projections: the hero or the enemy; too much or too little time spent on work issues; scapegoating employees or projects; couple never feels like a team; culture reflects this; fertile ground for others, such as FBC, to be triangled into this dance

Early Warning Signs

- There is a history of unresolved issues (When interviewing these couples, each question sets off "land mines" related to unsettled work and home issues: "How do you divide the work roles?" "Who takes care of the sales-people?" "How do you, or do you, divide childcare?");

- Each wants to blame the other for problems, rather than accepting responsibility;

- Often they pull you aside to report on the failures and shortcomings of the other;

- Employees are dragged into the couple's arguments;

- The couple disagrees on vision, future of company; and

- There are secrets between them and communication is not open and easy.

When the marriage deteriorates, it happens in stages that are repeated over time and become a part of the relationship.

One couple that Jane worked with included a wife who had started two businesses. Sara was competent and a highly energetic entrepreneur. She started a temp agency and pleaded with her husband, Jeff, to join her. He agreed to do so and took charge of information services. For a few weeks, things went well. Sara then began to ask him to do other tasks unrelated to his job. By the end of two months, Jeff was exhausted, but when he tried to say no to her, she would become angry and stay that way for several days, both at home and at work. Jeff finally left and returned to his own job. Sara found someone to replace him and the problems ended. After Sara sold this business, she started a second one and the same thing happened. Jeff had initially refused to help her, but then gave in and the cycle started all over. When Jane first met with the couple, they said that this happened at home, too, and it was nothing new, except now the stakes were higher. Sara had been able to get her way as a young girl by becoming angry and pouting. She continued this behavior as an adult. The angrier she became, the more Jeff gave in to her. The more he gave in, the angrier she grew. Jeff would then pull away and leave. This reinforcing cycle was destroying their relationship. Once they were able to "map" the cycle and see how destructive it was, they were able to stop the cycle more and more frequently.

Another couple who ran a successful food service business decided to bring a third person into the partnership to share the rewards and the responsibilities. After months of interviewing, they hired an experienced man who was close to their own age, had recently sold his restaurant, and was looking for a new challenge. Things went well for about three months, but the couple began to realize how difficult it was to let the third person in. As the wife said, "This is how it felt when we had our first child!" They were also aware that they would often not confront each other with complaints or problems but go instead to the partner. To avoid the triangle that was developing, they established regular weekly meetings to air complaints and to plan.

Implications of Copreneurial Divorce

Two interaction patterns are associated with divorce:

1. Attacks and defensiveness predict early divorce and

2. Suppression, avoidance, stonewalling, and emotional disengagement predict later divorce (Roberts, 2000).

Couples are often reluctant to create contingency plans in the event of divorce or disability, but it is critical to build these into the process. If couples do not have a signed agreement, the consequences can be financially and emotional disastrous. Our experience has been that if the marriage has been "hot" and stormy, then the divorce will be difficult; if the marriage has gone cold, things are likely to work out more easily. Our experience has also been that the longer the divorce negotiations go on, the more acrimonious they become. Preventive measures include prenuptial agreements and buy/sell agreements.

For example, one couple that Jane worked with did not have a legal agreement describing how the business would be divided if they divorced. The company was put up for sale as a result of the divorce proceedings. And the stakes can be large. When Susie and Doug Tompkins divorced in 1989, the company's earnings had peaked that year at worldwide revenues of $1 billion (Hofman,1989).

What Works?

The following myths about what it takes to build a successful business partnership and marriage have been shown to be unfounded by researchers:

- The more compatible the couple, the more successful the marriage;
- Personality flaws are the underlying cause of distress;
- Problems early in the marriage get better over time;
- If there is enough love, the marriage will last;
- Avoiding conflicts will lead to disaster; and
- Frequent fighting is not good for a marriage.

Findings by Notarius and Markman (1993) and Gottman (1994a), who have studied happy and unhappy couples over a fifteen-year period, suggest that the marriages most likely to dissolve are those in which the following behaviors take over: criticism, contempt, defensiveness, and withdrawal. These four behaviors, also referred to as the "four horsemen of the apocalypse," are predictive over time of separation and divorce.

Gottman (1994b) has also found that conflict must be regulated rather than resolved; in fact, he claims that 69 percent of all marital conflicts are never resolved. In other words, the deeper issues that maintain the destructive dances are managed, although not resolved. Regulation or management of these unresolved issues thus may be the goal—to agree to disagree and move on. The key to business success is not to let the conflicts get in the way of creating and implementing action plans. He also found the following patterns connected to longevity in marriages:

- A ratio of 5:1 of positive to negative interactions;
- Liberal use of humor;
- Expression of positive affection;
- Consistent turning to and responsiveness to one another;
- Seeing one another as allies even when in conflict; and
- Effective, quick repair after conflict.

Gottman concludes: "A lasting marriage results from a couple's ability to resolve the conflicts that are inevitable in any relationship" (1994b, p. 28).

If couples ask for advice in beginning a business together, the best advice you can give is for them to choose a business partner based on objective criteria, regardless of whether their prospective partner is a spouse or not: compatibility of personalities, complementary business skills and expertise, compatible money goals, compatible vision for the business, commitment to the business and family, and ability to maintain appropriate boundaries between business and family.

If the couple is suffering problems in their business relationship, the good news is that the problematic patterns, if not fed by deeper issues, can be changed once the partners recognize the patterns and learn to communicate more effectively. Consultants can start with what Gottman (1994a) terms "minimal marital therapy." He recommends teaching the following, *until they become automatic*:

- Self-soothing, self-care, and stress-management techniques;
- Time-management techniques;
- A decrease in distress-maintaining cognitions;
- Nondefensive listening;
- Giving of validation;
- Recognition and censorship of hot thoughts; and
- Practice in "better talk."

In addition, we recommend the following:

- If things are really hot, have the partners communicate through you at first and

- Establish decision making and conflict management procedures, by helping the partners decide:

  How the business will be structured in terms of ownership, that is, how the stock will be split;

  Who the boss is and in what situations;

  What the titles are;

  What to do if one person wants to leave the business but stay in the marriage or *vice versa*;

  What will happen in case of divorce, disability, or death;

  How the home and work tasks/roles will be divided, that is, who specializes in what, who's good at what, and who will do what.

Finally, it's important that the couple (1) put things in writing; (2) develop negotiation skills and establish "fair fighting" rules; (3) build resiliency and offer hope; (4) search and encourage new and different responses/solutions to stressful events; (5) have gender sensitivity, that is, the minimal skills may be different for men (who tend to withdraw) and women (who tend to engage) during conflict or stressful situations; (6) clarify vision, values, and goals; and (7) have time alone and time together, in the business and as a couple.

Working with older couples in later stages of the family businesses can be rewarding. The genogram can be used as a life review to help them rediscover and retell their story; it also helps build a legacy for them and their heirs.

Pitfalls for Consultants

There are several pitfalls to be avoided by consultants when working with couples. These are as follows:

- Looking for a quick fix;
- Working harder than your client (If you find that you are putting more effort and energy into the engagement than your client, find out why);
- Not being clear about who has the power in the system and confusing power and control (Consultants are often called in by the person in the most pain, who is often the person with the least power);
- Failing to distinguish simple from complex conflicts (see Chapter 4);

- Becoming triangulated in the couple's process (Getting out of this requires practice, practice, practice on self-management and insight into triggers; see the genogram exercise for consultants, page 167);

- Not appreciating the investment the couple has in keeping the conflict going (secondary gains) or taking sides; and

- Not working with the couple to formalize the agreements or to develop structure and processes (These will be difficult to formalize when working with problematic couples, but go a long way toward improving both the business and the relationship).

Suggested Readings

Jaffe, A. (1996). *Honey, I want to start my own business.* New York: Harper Business. This planning guide offers practical suggestions for couples who want to work together. Jaffe includes the rewards (greater intimacy, quicker resolution of issues, improved sex life, complementary skills, child and elder care flexibility) and the challenges, both relationship and business. An eighteen-question "Assessment Test for Joint Partners" is included.

Jaffee, D. (1990). Married to the business . . . and each other: The two worlds of entrepreneurial couples. In *The best of the Family Firm Institute conference proceedings, volume III: The best of behavioral science*, pp. 20–26.

Kaye, K. (1991, Spring). Penetrating the cycle of sustained conflict. *Family Business Review, IV*(1), 21–44.

Lerner, H.G. (1985). *The dance of anger.* New York: Perennial Library, Harper & Row.

Lerner, H.G. (1989). *The dance of intimacy.* New York: Perennial Library, Harper & Row.

Emotions

"It's not easy to find happiness in ourselves, and it is not possible to find it elsewhere."

Agnes Repplier, The Treasure Chest

Historically, the emotions of the family members have been blamed for the problems of succession, strategic planning, team building, and everything else. There is no doubt that family businesses are emotional systems and that their level of emotional intensity can approach and sometimes surpass that of a "normal" family.

The prejudice consultants have against dealing with emotions and feelings has hindered their effective work with family businesses. But there is mounting evidence that emotions and feelings play an important role in successful, rational decision making and planning. Here are some myths we have noted. The last is from Whiteside and Brown (1991).

Myths About Emotions/Feelings

- Emotions are about being "touchy feely";
- Emotions hinder good business sense;
- Emotions are about letting it all hang out;
- Emotions are messy;
- Emotions are just for clients and consultants should remain neutral;
- Emotions are roadblocks or barriers to progress;
- The family is the emotional arena and the business is the logical arena;
- Women are the individuals in charge of the family and the domain of relationships, emotion, and process; and men are better at rational, logical, work systems.

The Role of Emotions in the Decision-Making Process

Emotions play an important role in rational thought and can either expand or contract intelligence. There is increasing evidence that individuals who cannot identify their emotions are at a disadvantage. In "When Robots Weep: Emotional Memories and Decision-Making," Juan Velasquez (1998) of the MIT Artificial Intelligence Laboratory states that the "traditional view on the nature of rationality has proposed that emotions and reason do not mix at all. . . . Research in neuroscience, however, has provided evidence indicating quite the contrary, showing that emotions play a fundamental role in perception, learning, attention, memory, and other abilities and mechanisms we tend to associate with basic rational and intelligent behaviors." In tests Velasquez conducted, patients with lesions in the prefrontal cortex of the brain (the feeling brain) performed well on a variety of intelligence and memory tests, but when faced with real-life situations, they seemed to be unable to make "good" decisions.

Sensory signals from hearing and sight travel from the thalamus to both the neocortex (thinking) and the amygdala (emotions); the amygdala processes information faster and creates physiological responses. People feel before they think and act. Abusive, reactive individuals have no pause or thought between their feelings and their actions.

Making decisions without the use of our emotions is like making a budget without the numbers. Several times in the life of a family business, the ability to make a reasoned decision is especially critical. During the succession process in family-owned businesses, our experience has been that those who make better decisions about their future and the future of the business are those who know what they feel and who use those feelings to make the hard choices. The key is in how emotions are identified, managed, and used as data for the determination. One exercise that is useful is the Left-Hand Column (see Exhibit 8.1) developed by Chris Argyris and Donald Schön and first presented in their 1974 book, *Theory in Practice.*

Exhibit 8.1. The Left-Hand Column

Purpose: To become aware of the tacit assumptions which govern our conversations and contribute to blocking solutions; to develop a way of talking about assumptions safely and more effectively.

Step 1. *Selecting a Problem:* Select a problem in the family business you've been involved with during the last month or so, the kind of tough, interpersonal difficulty that many of us try to ignore. Write a brief paragraph describing the situation. What are you trying to accomplish? Who or what is blocking you? What might happen?

Step 2. *The Right-Hand Column (What Was Said):* Recall a frustrating conversation that you had over this situation—or imagine the conversation that you would have if you brought up the problem. Take several pieces of paper and draw a line down the center: In the right-hand column, write out the dialogue that actually occurred. Or write the dialogue you're pretty sure would occur if you were to raise the issue. Leave the left-hand column blank until you're finished.

Step 3. *The Left-Hand Column:* Now in the left-hand column, write out what you were thinking and feeling, but not saying.

Step 4. *Reflection: Using Your Left-Hand Column as a Resource:* Participants can learn a lot just from writing out the scenario. Ask yourself the following:

· What has led me to think and feel this way?

· What are my assumptions?

Exhibit 8.1. The Left-Hand Column, Cont'd

- What were my goals?
- Did I achieve the results I wanted/intended?
- Why didn't I say what was in the left-hand column?
- What are the costs to me, the family, and the business of operating this way?
- What are the payoffs?
- How can I use my left-hand column as a resource to improve communications and problem solving?

Further uses of this exercise:

- Rewrite the previous conversation, as you would like it to be.
- Check out the assumptions that have been made about the other person or situation.
- Show selected parts of the exercise to the other person to begin a dialogue about misunderstandings and assumptions.
- Consider what should not be said, when our internal censors are most useful, especially in family businesses and when they are destructive.

Adapted from P. Senge, A. Kleiner, C. Roberts, R. Ross, & B. Smith, 1994, pp. 246–252.

In the same way, the most effective advisors know how to use their own feelings strategically with clients ("I'm confused by what you are saying right now. Could you be more explicit?" "I understand your reasoning but think you need to try to understand others' points of view." or "That last sentence sounded like you were very angry with your dad's position. Could you explain?"). We do family businesses a disservice if we try to repress, contain, and ignore our own feelings or theirs. The key to competency is the management of emotions.

Emotional Intelligence

Daniel Goleman provides more evidence of the significance of emotions in his books, *Emotional Intelligence* (1995) and *Working with Emotional Intelligence* (1998). Goleman gave the name to the skill that predicts not how well someone will do in school but how well they will do at work and at life. Emotional intelligence (EI) combines thought and feeling, a competency that involves some degree of skill.

Goleman stresses that emotional intelligence skills are synergistic with cognitive ones and that top performers have both. According to Goleman, IQ accounts for perhaps 25 percent of success. Expertise and luck are also factors, but what may carry greater weight is a set of capacities that make up emotional intelligence, which includes elements of both personal and social competence (Goleman, 1998, pp. 226–227):

- Personal competence (knowing and managing ourselves)
  - Self-awareness (know our internal states, preferences, and intuitions);
  - Self-regulation (managing our internal states, impulses, and resources); and
  - Motivation (using emotional states to motivate ourselves in spite of setbacks)
- Social competence (awareness of and response to others)
  - Empathy (awareness of others' feelings, needs, and concerns) and
  - Social skills (adeptness at inducing desirable responses in others).

This means that we get in touch with what we are feeling, manage our own feelings, recognize what others are feeling, and work with people in helpful ways. This is about the heart and the mind, the facts and the feelings. It is a critical competency for family businesses and their advisors who struggle with the management of emotions.

According to an article in *Family Business* (Stone, 1998), Enterprise Rent-A-Car is the largest car rental company in the United States—and growing. How did it grow so fast? Partly from a new strategy of delivering cars directly to customers, but much of the credit goes to the practices of the founder, Jack Taylor, and his son, Andrew, the CEO. Enterprise scouts campuses looking for outgoing, upbeat students whose EI is higher than their GPA. They are usually described as having "good people skills."

Simply being high in EI "does not guarantee a person will have learned the emotional competencies that matter for work; it means only that they have excellent potential to learn them" (Goleman, 1998, p. 24). A consultant might be empathic, for example, and not have learned the skills to translate that into effective work with a client. Emotional intelligence can be taught and practiced in families. Some people are poor at reading emotional cues, not because they lack the basic wiring for empathy but because, lacking emotional tutors, they have never learned to pay attention to messages and practice this skill. They make poor team players, leaders, and planners (Goleman, 1998).

As consultants, we need to help family businesses develop their emotional competencies. For this, we should develop our own. Emotional intelligence ideas, tests, and teaching have a special appeal and use in a family business, "an emotional institution" (LeVan, 1990). It gives a name to what the family members often are experiencing and gives hope for changes and coaching, especially if emotional intelligence is connected to success on the job.

Tips for Working with Feelings

- Remember that if feelings are not given voice, they will be acted out;

- Provide space and time for feelings to be accessed and processed;

- Know when to move on to the decision making;

- Be aware of and strategic with your own feelings;

- The more ambiguous the choices, the more important role the feelings play at the beginning of the decision-making process;

- Know when expressions of feelings should be ignored or delayed;

- Fear of feelings can lead to symptoms or problems, such as addictions, which serve as buffers between our feelings and ourselves; and

- Clues to EI and empathy are not only, as Goodman (1998) notes, "using the word love naturally in conversation, having a box of Kleenex in the conference room, asking about kids with genuine interest," but are about using our feelings *strategically* in the best interests of the clients ("I wonder if you could share with the rest of the family the reason for your tears?" "I know that there's a lot of caring in your family; how do you show this during times of stress? How do you know or how have you learned what each of you needs during crises?" "You are naturally very proud of your kids; what are your hopes for them in the family business?").

Suggested Readings

Goleman, D. (1995). *Emotional intelligence.* New York: Bantam Books.

Goleman, D. (1998). *Working with emotional intelligence.* New York: Bantam Books.

Quade, C., & Brown, R. (2001). *The conscious consultant.* San Francisco, CA: Jossey-Bass/Pfeiffer.

Addictions

"Every form of addiction is bad, no matter whether the narcotic be alcohol,
or morphine, or idealism."

Carl Jung in Memories, Dreams, Reflections

Addiction is a leading public health problem. It often results in family conflict and violence, decreased family cohesion, and loss of health, money, and effectiveness. The most recent estimate of the overall economic cost of alcohol abuse alone was $276 billion for 1995 and growing (National Institute on Alcohol Abuse and Alcoholism, www.niaaa.nih.gov/press/1998/economic.htm). Nearly fourteen million people in the United States—one in every thirteen adults—abuse alcohol or are alcoholic. The cost of drug abuse was $97.7 billion. (This estimate includes substance abuse treatment and prevention costs, as well as other healthcare costs, costs associated with reduced job productivity or lost earnings, and other costs to society such as crime and social welfare.)

Addictions are grouped into two forms: *substance* addictions, which include alcohol, drugs—both legal and illegal—caffeine, and food and *process* addictions, which are related to activities or interaction, such as work, money, sex, gambling, relationships, and some eating disorders (Schaef & Fassel, 1988). In our experience, 90 percent of the family business clients we have worked with have one or more addictive members. Factors contributing to a higher risk of addictions going undetected in family businesses include the following:

- Family members are often not subjected to company physicals;
- It's hard to fire a brother, sister, or father, if he or she has an addiction, refuses treatment, or has relapses;
- Often the individual or the business has funds available to pay for the addiction; and
- Denial in the family keeps the problem from coming out.

Signs of Addiction

The following are the *signs of addiction* that the consultant should look for (Bepko & Krestan, 1985; Kaye, 1996; Schaef & Fassel, 1988):

1. Increasing tolerance (the addict has to take more and more of the substance or process to achieve the same level of response);

2. Increased cravings (a strong need for or compulsion toward the substance or process);

3. Denial, lying, defensiveness, low self-esteem;

4. Physical dependence;

5. Loss of control; erratic behavior and actions;

6. Over- and under-functioning or over- and under-responsibility in the system;

7. Oscillations in sense of self, whether under the influence or not, from self-loathing to grandiosity, from depression to euphoria;

8. Tension and stress in the system and individuals;

9. Abusive behavior;

10. Missed meetings;

11. Erratic behavioral or emotional states; and/or

12. Financial questions or losses not easily explained.

Addictions: Cause or Effect?

The causes of addictions have been debated in great depth and at many levels. At the heart of the debate is whether or not addiction is a cause or an effect. In other words, do alcoholics, for example, cause the family or work system to become dysfunctional or does the system create the alcoholic? A more useful process is to see the addiction as *both* a cause and an effect of the dysfunctional changes affecting everyone involved. This helps us in understanding the severity of the problem and seeing what or who might reinforce it. For example, who makes excuses for the addict's chronic lateness? What is its effect on the family and the business?

Another question to ask is: "Does the addiction serve a function?" From a systems perspective, the addiction puts "a buffer between us and our feelings" (Schaef & Fassel, 1988, p. 58). Without those feelings, we are operating with incomplete data. How can we really make a sound action plan if one of the family members is not present or not fully involved?

Another area of research in this arena that seems relevant to family businesses is that of *attachment.* Clients start using addictive substances or processes as "a means of regulating affect and/or connection with others and/or themselves" (Keiley, 2000/2001, p. 23). If the family business is the object of the addictive process, the disconnections over time may lead to the founder's inability to let go. Kaye (1996) describes a situation in which, because the parents' ego development is inadequate, they and their children react to the growing up process with such a high level of anxiety that the business becomes the addiction. This is an example of a system with a *process addiction* that, when treated effectively, can recover. The family members can move on to a "better life" in which they do not require the conflicts and anxieties of their former lives.

The difference between having an occasional drink, gambling once in a while, or working hard and long and an addiction is (1) the control that the individual has over the behavior and (2) the element of choice. If the behavior is out of control and if the person seems unable to choose to stop, then it is an addiction.

What We Can Do

In our role as family firm consultants, we generally are not trained to deal with addiction problems. However, there are a few things that the consultant can do:

- Recognize the extent of the problem;
- Learn the dynamics of the addiction process;
- Become competent at identifying the signs of addiction;
- Take a complete history, as addictions and/or addictive behavior runs in families;
- Not buy into the family's denial;
- Not allow addiction to control the process;
- Help the family deal with the addiction and be ready to follow through on necessary steps—for example, firing the addict or doing an "intervention"; and
- Refer the client for appropriate treatment.

It is important to understand the addictive process. The person with the addiction, the family, and business system have developed, over time, ways of coping with or denying the problem. Once you realize that there is a problem, it is important to confront the family with sensitivity and suggest options for them—referral to a therapist who specializes in addictions or hospitalization. They will be simultaneously relieved, unconvinced, and, perhaps, angry. If they continue in denial, decide whether or not you can be effective while the addiction continues untreated.

Suggested Readings

Bepko, C., & Krestan, J. (1985). *The responsibility trap.* New York: The Free Press.

Cohn, M. (1993, Summer). Anticipating the needs of the grandkids. *Family Business.*

Kaye, K. (1996). When the family business is a sickness. *Family Business Review, 9*(4), 347–368.

Schaef, A.,& Fassel, D. (1988). *The addictive organization.* New York: Harper and Row.

Gender Issues

Introducing the 1990 *Family Business Review* special issue on "Women and Family Business," Salganicoff wrote: "If literature about family business is in its infancy, then literature on women in family business is still gestating. Serious papers can be counted on one hand" (p. 121). Consultants coming from professions such as OD must be aware of the history of women in family business to appreciate how far and fast things have changed in the last decade. The brief history of the coming of age of women as owners, bosses, and visible leaders in family businesses has been slow, but is quickly catching up.

Changing Tides

In a 1996 *Nation's Business* article, "A Coming Sea of Change in Leadership," Sharon Nelton writes, "It amazes me how little attention has been paid to the stunning new figures on women's business ownership in this country. According to the National Foundation for Women Business Owners, women now own 36 percent of all U.S. businesses and bring in annual revenues of $2.28 trillion. That's *trillion.* Just a quarter of a century ago, women owned less that 5 percent of American businesses" (p. 60). She continues: "Will it mean that, in due time, women will own one-third or more of all our family businesses? Probably. Right now, we don't know how many women own family businesses. However, in a survey of 1,029 family business owners and co-owners conducted by Mass Mutual life insurance last year, 16 percent of the respondents were women" (Nelton, 1996, p. 60).

For the first time in history, daughters may have a chance of beating out their brothers as successors to leadership and control. Only a generation ago, founders without sons were inclined to sell their businesses rather than have their daughters own and/or run them. Family businesses have been slow in keeping up with the changes in attitudes toward women, but they are catching up. Women are now holding more seats on corporate boards, and increasingly run or own family businesses. But the truth is that, in corporate America, women at the highest levels are still rare.

Implications for Consultants

It is important to see this as a diversity issue. It is not just about women, but about an untapped resource for the entire business. Here's what you can do:

- Help both women and men identify what they want, based on their skills, talents, and interests, not on their gender;

- In succession planning, help parents pick the best leaders, irrespective of gender;

- Establish fair, equitable pay/compensation and formal pay guidelines (The Bureau of Labor Statistics says women in corporate America still earn 76.3 cents for every dollar earned by men);

- Make sure the founder/owner/management looks at all options for women and men (As recently as 2000, Deloitte & Touche instituted major organizational changes when they found that women were leaving at a significantly greater rate than men. The first steps were to stop assuming that the women were leaving to have children and stay home and to accept responsibility for the talent drain [McCracken, 2000]);

- Remember that job descriptions and formal titles are important (Many women in family businesses don't have either, although they work very hard);

- Encourage parents, especially fathers, to give their daughters positive messages growing up (Women in family businesses have unique opportunities to balance the demands of work and family successfully); and

- Think of women for corporate boards (A 1997 study by the National Association of Corporate Directors showed that 59 percent of companies surveyed had no female directors and 30 percent had only one [*Inc.*, 1999, p. 88]).

Suggested Readings

Cole, P. (1997, December). Women in family business. *Family Business Review, X*(4), 353–371.

McCracken, D. (2000, November/December). Winning the talent war for women: Sometimes it takes a revolution. *Harvard Business Review*, 159–167.

Nelton, S. (1998, September). The rise of women in family firms: Call for research now. *Family Business Review, XI*(3), 215–218.

Nonfamily Managers

We often, as consultants to family firms, find ourselves working with nonfamily managers (NFMs) in the business. Often referred to as "outsiders," these people play the following important roles:

- They can be neutral observers;
- They may assist in the development and training of the next generation and may serve as mentors;
- They may serve as administrators in family foundations;
- They may have special relationship with owners with loyalty and commitment to the firm;
- They may feel like family over time; and
- They may be chosen for positions of leadership, although this may have ripple effects in the family and the business (For example, if the succession is not based on objective criteria, sound business strategies, and attention to the process of leadership transfer, the family members may be angry or hurt. Even if the process is done well, the culture in the business and the relationships in the family will change).

In family businesses, NFMs are often faced with:

- Personalities, rivalries, and family issues;
- Mentoring and training the next generation;
- Lack of formal hiring policies;
- Perceived unfair compensation issues and questions of job security and advancement potential; and
- Requests to "step into the void" during the succession process and "bridge the gap."

The questions for NFMs in the latter case are "For how long?" and "Will I be 'sacrificed'?" Clarfeld (1994) recommends that, for the business to survive a crisis in leadership, "The family should have a contingency plan in place for choosing a nonfamily leader and helping him or her succeed. If the family has decided what type of person it would need and has identified potential candidates to take over, it will be ready to respond should an unfortunate event take place."

Traditionally, family-member managers were contrasted with professional, non-family managers. Aronoff, in his article on megatrends, writes: "That distinction is increasingly seen as irrelevant, at best, and dangerous at worst. Family members are expected more and more to meet or exceed the highest levels of executive professionalism, including educational achievement and career success experienced outside the family business" (1998, p. 183). This does not mean that family firms do not depend on nonfamily executives and managers. Yet, according to Poza and Alfred,* "There is little data or thought regarding the most productive ways to manage relationships between family and nonfamily managers. Yet family businesses of any significant size depend upon the quality and effectiveness of their nonfamily managers for their companies' continuing success and growth" (1996, p. 16–17). Poza and Alfred compared family and nonfamily responses and concluded that NFMs were generally less positive about management practices and succession issues than were their employers and that the "differences we uncovered represent important challenges and significant opportunities for owner-managers to improve the motivation and performance of their top employees" (p. 17). Some other conclusions they drew are listed below:

- Family members in general were relatively more confident that the business would stay in the family after succession;

- CEOs of family firms looked for ways to motivate top-flight executives, who realized that the top leadership positions were likely to go to family members who may be less qualified than they were;

- Confidence in their own future career prospects was important for nonfamily managers but not always easy to maintain in a family business as they often had to earn the confidence of the next generation owner-managers;

- CEOs saw their firms as more innovative than NFMs did; in fact, NFMs were less satisfied than CEOs with management practices and more inclined to see the firm as being "pretty much the same five years from now";

---

*Reprinted by permission of the publisher from Autumn 1996, *Family Business*, Philadelphia, www.familybusinessmagazine.com.

- Family members were more likely to agree with the statement: "People in this organization know what we stand for and how we wish to conduct business." This brings up the question of whether NFMs are left out of the loop when values and philosophies are transmitted;

- The NFMs were less involved in "planning the work and working the plan";

- Owner-managers were more optimistic about the utility of practices and procedures (According to the study, because of the "relatively low dissatisfaction with the status quo, it may not be easy to convince CEOs to take steps to revitalize the firm or engage in succession planning";

- NFMs were generally less satisfied than family managers were with their compensation and benefits;

- In only one important category did the NFMs rate their firms' practices consistently higher than did family managers: they were more satisfied with the performance feedback they received than were the family managers.

Poza and Alfred concluded that nonfamily managers have been taken for granted for too long and that family firms need *to create and maintain a culture that maximizes NFM loyalty and performance.*

Suggestions from this study and from our own experiences are listed below:

- Owners must make an effort to demonstrate that NFMs' contributions are valued;

- CEOs should establish ongoing dialogue with top managers in order to check out assumptions, ask about problems and issues, close perception gaps, and clarify expectations and future planning;

- Outsiders on the board should serve as neutral observers of the agendas of family and nonfamily managers;

- Consultants should adopt benchmarks from policies of public corporations in the industry;

- When and where appropriate, consultants should allow greater participation by NFMs in strategic and operational planning;

- Family-owned businesses should invest in the career development and training of NFMs; and

- Everyone should be clear about the expectations and rewards, if any, for mentoring the next generation.

Keep in Mind

- NFMs are rich sources of information on the family and the organization;
- NFMs, who are not caught up in the drama of the family, play useful and helpful roles in team building, staff meetings, and coaching the family;
- The effectiveness of their roles is related to their position in the hierarchy and to the trust that the family has in them;
- NFMs often feel caught between a rock and a hard place when asked for information about the family and/or the business, so confidentiality of their responses is highly important.

Suggested Readings

Lansberg, I. (1999). *Succeeding generations.* Boston, MA: Harvard Business School Press.

Poza, E.J., & Alfred, T. (1996, Autumn). What the silent majority thinks (but may not tell you). *Family Business,* pp. 16–21.

Family Office/Family Foundations

The family office and family foundation are both structures that allow for the family to continue to work together, give together, and plan together. The following definitions come from Lansberg's (1999) *Succeeding Generations:***

"Family office enables the family to invest, with centralized financial planning, their wealth as a group, thereby enlarging their buying power and lowering the costs of portfolio management. It is separate from the family business, although a few of the same people may participate. Professional managers monitor the investments and oversee tax compliance, group insurance, financial planning, and intra-family transactions such as gifts of stock and estate plans." (p. 306)

"Family foundations channel funds to organizations and causes that are consistent with the family's philanthropic initiatives and social values. Along

---

**Used with permission from I. Lansberg. *Succeeding Generations: Realizing the Dreams of Families in Business.* Boston, MA: Harvard Business School Press, 1999.

with such well-known institutions as the Ford, Rockefeller, and Carnegie Foundations, there are thousands of other private family foundations that support activities. These foundations usually confer tax advantages while enhancing the family's reputation and stature through contributions to the community." (pp. 306–307)

Hamilton (1996) notes that nearly half of the family offices have been founded by business-owning families who have accumulated $30 million or more in liquid assets outside the core business. According to Hamilton, the family office has become virtually a second family business. The size and complexity are determined largely by the family's financial goals and investment objectives. Hamilton notes that the staff may range from one professional to more than one hundred; most family offices are able to save more than they cost each year by developing strategies to help the family avoid unforeseen financial risks or implement wealth-transfer plans that minimize taxes.

In fact, most smaller foundations do not have full-time staff people. Usually a family member can do the work. Hamilton suggests three ways that families can establish a pool of investments outside the business to provide for future financial needs and develop a valuable legacy that is not only financial:

1. The dedicated family office;

2. Multi-client family office for families with more than $10 million but less than $30 million to invest (often a family office that has opened its doors to outside clients); and

3. Bank trust departments and private investing firms that specialize in business families.

Stone (1994) remarks: "In the public's mind, private foundations are billion-dollar money machines funded by America's super-rich families. In reality, most of the estimated 20,000 family-managed foundations have assets of less than $5 million" (p. 41). Stone also notes that in recent years, family foundations have undergone a remarkable democratization and that, although they were once the privileged domain of America's wealthiest families, foundations are currently being promoted by legal and financial advisors as an estate-planning tool appropriate even for those with modest excess wealth.

The keys to an effective family office are threefold:

- Having a strategic financial game plan;
- Recruiting dedicated, experienced professional advisors to implement the plan; and
- Having the commitment and follow-through of the family.

Advantages

Operating a successful family office is similar to running a successful business. The benefits are psychological and philosophical as well as financial; a foundation can be a way to do the following:

- Provide opportunity for family members to come together to make charitable contributions; develop family charitable objectives; encourage values decisions and discussions; and strengthen ties for future generations;
- Create family purpose and spirit and use giving to reflect the family's values;
- Helping older generations to "let go"
- Create opportunities for family members to stay involved, for example, a founder who wants to remain active but let the next generation run the business; and
- Diversify wealth outside the business.

Other financial advantages include (1) providing an opportunity to handle complex financial challenges separately for privacy reasons; (2) relieving the full-time CFO who has been serving as a part-time financial advisor to the family and his or her dual responsibilities have become too much; (3) offering a solution to the need to separate personal financial matters from the business in case the business is sold (Hamilton, 1996).

Gifting Philosophy

To make gifting more effective, Karoff (1992) recommends that the family (1) create a focus for the giving that will reflect the family's values; (2) do their research; (3) be results oriented; and (4) view the recipients of the funds as "partners" and work with them to "enhance their capabilities." Kaplan writes: "Organizing a foundation while the family business leader is still active materially increases the chances that the family will be successful in settling on a philosophy and goals for guiding the family foundation" (1993, p. 30). Von Lossberg (1990) says that the family must be professional in their management and investing and explore hiring a nonfamily administrator (NFA): "The inclusion of NFAs in family management represents a new level of development for the foundation. Family members must share family confidences and some degree of control with the NFA in exchange for a more efficient, accountable, organization" (p. 381).

Tips for Consultants

- Help families to consider family offices or family foundations as an option where appropriate, that is, if there is adequate funding and the family wants to work together in this way;

- Plan ahead and set up the foundation when the owner is fifty to sixty years old and still active so the business will begin to fund the foundation, which may become a second career for the owner;

- Help the family clearly spell out objectives and philosophy;

- Help the family to establish a board with outsiders;

- Help them with the necessary infrastructures, personnel, and resources to ensure permanence;

- Help the family to distinguish personal from social priorities;

- Explain the following risks and challenges (from Ylvisaker, 1990):

  - Foundations can intensify already existing stress and exacerbate differences that arise from determination of social needs and priorities;

  - Governance can become a problem if planning has not been adequate;

  - There may be an inability to agree on the goals and objectives;

  - Resources and commitment may become inadequate with poor planning or economic changes;

  - Personal priorities and agendas may take priority over social ones and affect the ability of the family to work as a team and agree on investment strategies; and

  - The infrastructures that have been put in place may not be fully developed.

Suggested Readings and Resources

Council on Foundations, Washington, D.C. (www.cof.org)

Family Business Review (1990, Winter). Special issue on family foundations.

Sara Hamilton, Family Office Exchange, Oak Park, Illinois
   (http://foxexchange.com/public/fox/welcome/index.asp)

Ethnicity

While we will not discuss the issue of ethnicity in detail, it is important for consultants to remember that they bring with them their own ethnicity along with their biases and assumptions. We have found that, for consultants to be successful in any consulting engagement, they must be attuned to their own values and the values of their clients. For example, clients who are of Asian extraction often have very different ways of handling conflicts than those from Europe or Latin America. We have also found that the religious orientation of the clients may provide the backdrop for what is happening in the client system (for example, Mormons, Jews, and Catholics often have different assumptions about power, authority, decision making, and so forth). The following are a few questions for the consultant to ponder on this issue:

- How does ethnicity influence the consulting engagement?
- How does ethnicity affect the consultant's style and fit with the client?
- How does ethnicity affect the client during the consulting process?
- What is needed in way of training programs and future research?

Suggested Readings and Resources

Family Business Review. (1992, Winter). Ethnicity and Family Enterprise.

McGoldrick, M., Giordano, J, & Pearce, J.K. (Eds.). (1996). *Ethnicity in family therapy* (2nd ed.). New York: Guilford Press.

McGoldrick, M., & Troast, J., Jr. (1993, Fall). Ethnicity, families, and family business: Implications for practitioners. *Family Business Review, VI*(3), 283–300.

9

The Rewards
and Challenges of
Consulting to Family
Businesses

ON THE COURSE OF WRITING THIS BOOK, we interviewed twenty family business consultants whose experience ranged from eight to thirty-two years. They represent a variety of disciplines: law, finance, management, OD, family therapy, and business. Of the twenty, twelve were men and eight were women. They were asked the following questions:

- How is the role of the family business consultant unique?

- What is the biggest challenge of consulting to this group?

- Do you have any suggestions for consultants starting out in the field?

- What attracted you to the field?

- What is the most important lesson you have learned?

- What are the most important skills and competencies required?

- What intervention have you found to be the most effective in your practice with family businesses?

The following is a sampling of their answers to these questions. Their biographies are provided at the end of the chapter.

How Is the Role of the Family Business Consultant Unique?

"You need a diversity of skills; multidisciplinary teams are critical." (J.G. Troast)

"Working with family businesses, you're in much more of a facilitator role. They make the decisions; you work on process issues, resources, and facilitation." (K. Vinton)

"You are working with various domains, family, business, and ownership in a highly complicated system. You have to understand them all and they are intertwined; you can't pull them apart." (W. Handler)

"You must be aware of both family relationships and business relationships; it demands an understanding of more than one discipline. You must have an in-depth understanding of interpersonal relations, roles and responsibilities, shareholder roles, and finances. The combination of the two is *very complex*." (P. Karofsky)

"It crosses and involves understanding the roles of other advisors; it demands a working knowledge of what other disciplines entail; you're more of the quarterback who is coordinating and complementing the work of existing advisors. There has to be collaboration with others working with the client." (M. Cohn)

"The family business consultant needs to have an understanding of multiple fields and multiple systems in the clients' worlds: family, shareholders, and managers. The family business consultant needs to manage ambiguity and complexity more than the traditional business consultant." (B. Brown)

"It is special in that we are dealing with a complex system composed of two typically separate systems that often fall into the professional purview of specialists who do not usually deal with the other system. Thus, the role, when done effectively, requires that the advisor deal with the entire system, be aware of the unique dynamics of this system, and connect to the entire system (that is, all stakeholders). It can become even more special as a relationship evolves with the family and others that lasts decades and involves the opportunity to have a connection of great trust and distributed support." (L. Dashew)

"Compared to the world of consulting in general, family business consulting requires an interesting, complex mixture of process and advisory skills. With an expertise in only one or the other, the professional would have a difficult time consulting to family businesses. The consultant needs to relate to multiple personality types/roles, be perceptive, have strong analytical skills, and be an innate problem solver. It's pretty easy to become overwhelmed." (E. Hoover)

"In the same way that family and business systems overlap, family business consultants must straddle that line as well in advising them. Consultants who are well-versed only in the world of financial statement analysis, or alternatively only in, say, Freudian dream analysis, may come to feel ill-prepared to represent family businesses in all of their dimensions. As an example, while my training as a lawyer often makes me predisposed to focus on business issues, I've also worked with clients who have had to deal with family issues of substance abuse, physical violence, marital infidelity, the unexpected death of a family member, gender issues, and sexual abuse, among other concerns. There's often simply no way to represent a family business and disregard the personal dynamic. You can't have professional blinders on; you need a 360-degree perspective. You also need to know when to bring in other professionals." (J. Wolfson)

"There is a uniqueness in the intensity in the consultation; we are always managing task and relationship processes. Working with family businesses is like 'turning up the burner.' The DNA connects the people in an intense way." (K. Wiseman)

What Is the Biggest Challenge of Consulting to This Group?

"Not getting sucked in by one faction or another; you're the facilitator; you don't take sides and you make sure that each side listens to the other." (K. Vinton)

"Family issues go all the way back to birth so often to hope, think, pray that you can change or have an impact on the family is a dream. It is very frustrating work to get the business to work better because, often, family stands in the way." (W. Handler)

"We need to become aware of our own behavior and what we bring to interventions. We need to be aware that that behavior may be negative and may influence future generations." (T. Zanecchia)

"It is important to help potential clients overcome resistance to address the important issues. Getting the family in a room together to address issues is a challenge. It's often hard to get mom and dad to sit down together with other family members." (P. Karofsky)

"Balancing process and action, that is, getting closure and helping clients move on in the engagement. There is a tendency for either too much process or too much technical advice; traditional advisors and CPAs are action-focused; traditional family business consultants are too much process-focused, with not enough emphasis on behavioral change. Focusing on just one or the other results in failure. We also need to take time to understand finance/technical/valuation issues. Looking at financial statements is critical, and we also need to understand the real value of businesses and what drives their value. What are the tangible and intangible assets? A mistake is not understanding the importance of this. It is also important to push the process forward and keep it moving. If you don't look to an attorney or certified public accountant as 'part of the client universe'—as stakeholders—you miss a very important part of consultation." (M. Cohn)

"To provide clients with sufficient understanding of the various fields, give them value without holding yourself as expert in those areas. It is also important to draw in others and have a good working relationship with other professionals who contribute to joint efforts." (J. Wofford)

"This is a new profession. The family is unsure of what you, as a family business consultant, have to offer, whereas they would have clear expectations of a lawyer. The challenge is helping the family understand what your role is and how you can help." (P. Cole)

"Challenges include finding solutions that are practical and not off the rack; teaching old dogs/lizard brains new tricks; realizing that the problem person, the scapegoat, might be the sanest one and the one most in touch with pain." (I. Bryck)

"Be a good team member. Be willing to understand that the best advice is only partially taken and that positive results may be years in coming to fruition. You cannot do it yourself; you need buy-in from the team, the stakeholders, and the other advisors. You need knowledge of complexity and stress. You need to find ways to build a team of key nonfamily leaders." (B. Brown)

"The issue of integrity is challenged the most; you can get sucked in and must be clear about your own role, boundaries, and values. You need to make sure that you get everyone involved and scheduled! I'm a consultant to *families* in business, and the clients are in integrated systems of family and business. Other challenges include balancing the needs of all stakeholders; emphasizing communication; developing skills, structure, safety; setting personal boundaries; taking a developmental perspective; and building legitimizing structures, such as boards." (L. Dashew)

"Biggest challenges are (1) being able to think, have the tools, act, and work with a multidisciplinary focus, which is not natural for psychologists; (2) working with other professionals: learning other languages, dealing with the professional and cultural barriers; (3) keeping from getting incorporated into the client system: need to know your own history of interpersonal dynamics, as well as the clients'; and (4) knowing self." (E. Hoover)

"For me, the biggest challenge has been not jumping too quickly to a conclusion. Attorneys and consultants in general typically view their role as giving advice. The more quickly and decisively the consultant can filter out the pertinent information and reach his or her recommendation, the better. This method may not produce optimal results with family businesses, however, for several reasons. For one thing, the issues tend to be complex, and there is rarely a 'quick fix.' Perhaps more important, if the attorney or other consultant reaches a unilateral recommendation without involving the family in the decision making, the recommendation may be 'heard,' but often will not be acted on. Borrowing the terminology of those who approach family business consulting from the therapy/relationship side, the 'process' aspects may be just as important as the 'content.' It is hard to hold yourself back from giving advice; sometimes the client is just not ready to hear it." (J. Wolfson)

"Managing myself in the intensity of the process; not providing 'the answer'; being respectful of problems; understanding that the family has enormous capacity to figure out the solutions to their problems. Often technical solutions are implemented more to reduce the consultant's anxiety rather than to help the family. We must understand that there are no quick fixes." (K. Wiseman)

"Knowing yourself; just being there is a very powerful intervention; we need to be objective without making value judgments on the data; we need to be able to take the reactions, put aside, not ignore, but be able to process them, not overreact to them. We need to know where our soft spots are, where unconsciously we may get in our own way. This is why a shadow consultant is a good idea." (G. Ayres)

Do You Have Any Suggestions for Consultants Starting Out in the Field?

"Adopt a transitional strategy for yourself; you can't just hang out your shingle no matter what your original profession is. This is a multidisciplinary practice; you need to broaden your skills and not just rely on expertise in a given field. Plan a marketing transition phase while building a client base. The Family Firm Institute is a step in the right direction; it provides ongoing education." (J.G. Troast)

"Having some good work experience in the field, in addition to education in your own field. Develop listening and facilitation skills; work with someone else; know your limitations and admit to them. Experience and maturity are required. Know when to walk away from a job and what jobs not to take. Know what you want to do and don't get into a position where you feel you have to take everything and then make mistakes; know what you don't know." (K. Vinton)

"Be aware of ourselves; have a strong sense of self in order to know what impact you are making. The greatest consultants are those who work on themselves." (T. Zanecchia)

"Be sure you or your colleagues have in-depth knowledge of the family system and the business system. The most important thing you must know is what you don't know and how to find answers. This is a multidisciplinary team approach, with the best teams offering dual gender/dual discipline combinations." (P. Karofsky)

"Take risks; get into an area where you're pushing yourself and team with somebody more experienced." (J. Wofford)

"Challenge your own assumptions about what a family is, what it means to be a family business. Consider what business issues, gender issues, and other assumptions will block your ability to be effective. For example, an assumption may be that protecting the family is most important; they may, in fact, be asking you to 'protect the business no matter what.' It also may be that cutoffs in family relationships are OK. *My* assumption is to protect the family, but I may be working harder on family than they want." (P. Cole)

"Consider that no one solution or fad works for all or that the company might not have what it takes, either the brains or the talent, to succeed. You may be invited in to 'pull the plug.' Understand that their solution may or may not be better than yours. Sometimes they cannot believe it can get better; it's only a place to go in the morning. Also understand that they may not be willing to do what it takes." (I. Bryck)

"My suggestion would be that, no matter the extent of one's prior education or experience, this is a time for humility. There's a lot of learning out there that's already gone on, so take advantage of it. Join the Family Firm Institute (FFI) and attend its conferences. Read some of the outstanding books and articles that have been published. Consider finding an experienced mentor who's willing to be a resource to you. Finally, and this suggestion applies even to those who have been doing family business consulting a long time, seek professional relationships with other high-caliber consultants from other disciplines."
(J. Wolfson)

"Assume you know nothing. You have to be flexible and a good listener. Each family has unique issues; don't generalize. Don't assume all families have pathologies. In fact, the majority that we see are functional; they just have vulnerabilities that can be managed and worked with." (C. Seligman)

"Patience. I thought that once I announced I was a family business consultant that they would beat their way to my door. Not so! It takes education; it takes a long lead time. To get fully ramped up for a client base requires competence in allied fields, and you need to know enough about the allied fields—accounting, insurance, financial plans, family relationships—to be able to call in experts." (K. Wakefield)

What Attracted You to the Field?

"I became an 'accidental tourist'! I have a family business background, during which time I experienced a lot of issues; perhaps, it was partially processing some of those issues. I developed a professional development path; I knew I couldn't just rely on my experiences." (J. Troast)

"I was working on my Ph.D. dissertation. The research was on "The Small, Family-Owned Businesses: A Unique Organizational Culture," and I came from business in family (my dad owned a business). These both developed my interest." (K. Vinton)

"It was personal therapy in a sense! I came from a family business. It started out as raw research. And then I created research questions from my questions: 'How could situations turn out like mine?' It was very personal. I wanted to understand my history: What I did well and what I could do better."
(W. Handler)

"I fell into it. I completed graduate work at Wharton in corporate finance, and my experience in consulting to family businesses there really got me into the field. While working in Boston before that, I realized that I loved the smaller companies best; it was more personal and rewarding work. I then took a week-long course on human behavior at Menninger. Through that course, I met John Messervy in 1986. John and I have co-consulted together for thirteen years." (T. Zanecchia)

"I've had an extraordinarily successful life: a family business, with the right experiences; love of people; and a love of learning. I'm a lifetime student. In mid-life, I returned to graduate school to focus on families and relationships."
(P. Karofsky)

"I grew up in a family business; my work experience with family businesses began with succession issues, decisions to sell or give to kids, and dealing with family dynamics. In 1989, I attended my first Family Firm Institute conference; I never knew there was such a thing or that there were others out there who were interested in these issues." (M. Cohn)

"I first worked in the corporate world with Fortune 500 companies and was 'very bored.' I knew I wanted to work with family businesses; they were a marriage of my interests and presented a richness of systems. Then I joined the Family Firm Institute and got involved in that community. I also spent time with Leon Danco." (P. Baudoin)

"I grew up in family business. It was sold when it was 112 years old. During that time, I met lots of family business consultants. To 'carry on the tradition,' I invested in a radio station with siblings." (P. Cole)

"I 'fell into' the field as someone who had both a clinical (family therapy) practice and an organization development practice. When I noticed that several of my consulting clients were family-owned businesses and had some unique challenges, I began researching literature on family business. I found little. So I began integrating my knowledge of family systems and organization development and specializing in family business work. That was in the mid-1980s. Soon I let go of my clinical practice and rarely consulted with businesses that were not family-owned. What attracted me to this specialization was the challenge. Family-business consulting is the most difficult work I have done and requires the most creativity and collaboration." (L. Dashew)

"There are several things that attracted me: (1) my personal mission is making a difference in people's lives; (2) in family businesses, everything's at stake—reputation, the family relations, legacy, financial security; and (3) your involvement allows family and business to move to new levels of harmony and high net worth, with an increased sense of legacy and stewardship." (E. Hoover)

"Like a number of other family business consultants, I came from a family business background. My grandparents on my mother's side owned a factory that manufactured women's hats; when they brought their son (my uncle) into the business, tensions multiplied. My grandmother on my father's side had two brothers who were in business together (along with my grandfather, for a while). The two brothers got into a dispute over money and literally didn't speak to each other for thirty years until my father cornered them both at my grandmother's funeral and shamed them into conversation. When I got out of law school and started practicing, I found that some of my cases resisted resolution because the parties were acting in a way that, to me, seemed irrational from any business perspective. It took a while for me to realize that personal rather than business issues were really motivating them, much like with my uncles. I attended my first national FFI conference in 1990 and, shortly after that, with my urging, my firm Goulston & Storrs, became a founding sponsor of the Northeastern University Center for Family Business. I was hooked." (J. Wolfson)

"I stumbled into it. I was in business originally as a dealer representative for Shell and my best work was sitting around the kitchen table with a dealer and his wife. My undergraduate degree is in economics. I then worked with my father-in-law, who trained family therapists. I received my master's degree and license in family therapy in 1976, I got my doctorate degree at USC in 1982 and attended an FFI exploratory meeting in 1985 or 1986." (E. Cox)

"After law school, I went into my wife's family's business after my father-in-law was diagnosed with MS. He went into remission, and my brother-in-law came into the business. I went back to practicing law. I began to attract families with estates that had businesses in them. The time of estate planning proved to be a terrible time to be doing serious strategic planning. I knew there had to be a better way so, with Tom Hubler and Steve Schwarz, I built a family business advising company." (G. Ayres)

"There was an electric connection when I met others at the first FFI meeting: 'These are people who are doing what I'm doing.' It was liberating to discover that there were people doing this kind of work." (K. Kaye)

What Is the Most Important Lesson You Have Learned?

"That there is no quick fix and that the models of other professionals can create unrealistic expectations for outcomes. Family business consultants need to prepare clients for the process, while managing their expectations. The pressing issues will bubble up fast. I've found that a multiphase proposal is appropriate." (J. Troast)

"What *not* to get involved in; it helps to have paradigms regarding what good consulting is. For example, mine is not 'consulting forever,' but it is to move the clients to the point they don't need me. It may be the educator in me, but I'm most comfortable getting them to the point where they don't need me. I do check on them after the engagement is over." (K. Vinton)

"As a bright-eyed new consultant, you think it will be easy, but think again! The assessment is easy; the implementation is very difficult to carry out. It is hard and time-consuming; don't expect it to be easy. The diagnostic stage can be relatively smooth and you may think, 'I'm getting somewhere,' but you have to be realistic. The two phases, assessment and implementation, are very different." (W. Handler)

"*Listening.* Early on in my career, I felt compelled to have the right answer. Clients can come up with answers. The answer will come over time. Also, knowing when I'm caught up in the system is critical. I realize I can't be productive if I'm 'sucked into' the system." (T. Zanecchia)

"Everyone's side of the story has some validity; feelings are facts, but are also fiction. They are a view of one person's reality. People see themselves in the center of the universe, the top of the organizational chart; that little is their fault; problems can only be solved by *other* people changing. You can't assume that the person who brought you in is the 'clear one.' The goal is to get them to function together. For this, the consultant needs to figure out a way to un-demonize everyone and consider whether they can change attitudes enough to make the relationships and business work." (I. Bryck)

"My clients really have the ability and capacity to solve problems; my job is to get them enough information for them to take responsibility to find solutions. I don't have to fix the problems for my clients. I work with clients for a long time. Patience and humility are required so that I don't get in my way or their way." (B. Brown)

"Integrity is often challenged. It is important not to get sucked into just one perception, an alliance with one stakeholder or one group of stakeholders. You need to be clear about your own role, boundaries, and values. You need to be aware of what they need versus what they want. Clients I've fired have had a solution in mind and wanted me to execute it; they didn't want an independent assessment." (L. Dashew)

"Humility. My primary role is to be a catalyst, a facilitator. I don't have the final answer. I have worked with clients who had consultants who had 'the answer' and the results are often disastrous. My job is to provide clients with options and so can pick what is right for them—they have the best answer. That's a win-win situation." (E. Hoover)

"While a family business consultant will find it difficult, if not impossible, to ignore the interweaving of both business and personal issues that clients face, I believe that he or she should remain aware of his or her own limits professionally. Otherwise, you may be opening up potentially explosive issues that you lack the professional training to know how to defuse. Innocently asked questions about relationships may open a Pandora's box! Not surprisingly then, perhaps the most important lesson I have learned is a great appreciation for the value that other types of consultants, particularly but not exclusively those with a therapy background, can bring to the engagement. A multidisciplinary approach to family business consulting, which has been long-touted by FFI, makes a lot of sense." (J. Wolfson)

What Are the Most Important Skills and Competencies Required?

"Family business consultants need to know the four 'buckets of information' (law, finance, management and OD, and behavioral science) from the Body of

Knowledge (BOK) committee of the FFI. Then add to those skills: (1) business strategy: Is there enough money? Is succession compatible with the way you'd evaluate any independent business? Is this a good business model? and (2) career counseling: Is this the right career for the individuals in the business?" (J. Troast)

"You need to be a good listener and good empathizer. You also need to see things from many points of view and to understand business skills and ownership and family systems. Problem-solving and negotiating skills are also very important; the answer is often not black or white, but usually in between, some shade of gray that requires creativity. Other skills needed are team building and understanding leadership and types of leadership models. Diplomacy goes a long way, also. For example, you may need to know how to deal with someone who wants to be chief executive officer before age thirty." (W. Handler)

"Obviously, you need your own profession of origin competencies. I'm also a fan of genograms, as a three-generation perspective, that gives me insight into the behaviors and legacies of the family. Don't assume anything and speak with everyone individually (or at least everyone who's impacted by what they and you are doing); help them to achieve and leave a legacy; develop positive behavior and use structures to reinforce. I'm good at making the complicated simple—it's very useful to be able to translate complicated ideas into simple language." (T. Zanecchia)

"Patience; careful listening; confidence to be competent enough to move clients through the process to make decisions. Family business consultants need to know leading tax and legal strategies to implement ideas. They also need to be able to call on, refer to, or have professionals available, as I do in my firm. I have professionals who review legal documents, do valuation modeling, know the value of business to fully understand the 'hard information' (data, numbers), and then work through family dynamics. As a family business consultant, I am a conceptual architect, setting goals and vision and articulating the process and working with each of the other family advisors toward implementation of the next phase." (M. Cohn)

"Being analytical is important, as are listening proactively, using a creative approach to problem solving, having a willingness to take a nonlinear approach, an ability to work as a team, and being able to 'take the heat' and hold the stress. My use of a supervising therapist is very helpful. Belonging to high-level small professional associations, for example, FFI, PDFB (Psychological Dynamics of Family Business), and AFHE (Attorneys for Family Held Enterprise) is also helpful." (B. Brown)

"Ability to listen, paraphrase, and reframe; ability to connect to the entire system and all types of stakeholders and hold conflicting realities concurrently; ability to effectively use one's 'self' and manage boundaries well; ability to work with a group of people simultaneously and engage them in dialogue, collective problem solving, and planning; skill development; dialogue process; ability to collaborate with colleagues from other disciplines and to work effectively as team with them." (L. Dashew)

"Ability to be a problem solver with street smarts; to trust, have optimism, respect; to use common sense, juggle multiple priorities. You need a level of knowledge in four key areas: behavior dynamics, finance, law, and management sciences. The FFI certificate process is a good place to start. Keep reading. I continue to learn by training and experience. I am proficient in management science (as a healthcare senior vice president) and behavior sciences; I have acquired a competent level of understanding in finance and law through FFI, reading, and the 'school of hard knocks.'" (E. Hoover)

"If you're a true family business consultant, versus other professionals who work with family businesses, you operate in a process environment. Family business consulting is a subset of OD consulting. For this, you need an understanding of the impact of entry into the system, the importance of trust, a good contract, the deliverables, and the rules of multidisciplinary confidentiality; you must have a needs assessment, good interviewing techniques, with intervention following feedback, leadership training and thinking, strategic planning, and change management. You also need to know how to end the consultation." (G. Ayres)

"Being a good therapist. In your own office, you can control most things; with this work, you are working outside your office and with various systems. You have to relate to all political, ethnic, religious groups; you have to be a great listener, combining flexibility and assertiveness." (K. Kaye)

What Intervention Have You Found to Be the Most Effective in Your Practice with Family Businesses?*

"Early prevention and education are best; talk about issues before they've surfaced. This is consistent with strategic planning and counseling." (J. Troast)

"At a family business retreat, separate the senior and junior generation into different rooms. Have them each put on a flip chart the important contributions 'your children/parents (the other) have made to business and family.' Bring the group back together and share." (K. Vinton)

"This depends on the issue. Having more than one consultant is important— one with family expertise and one with business expertise—who each can offer different sides and perspectives of the dueling coalitions. The ideal is to have a man and a woman. Expertise in career counseling is valuable; it provides personal advice around career options. It is impossible to know everything and it is important to know when to pass on or refer out and to know when certain businesses and families can't be helped no matter what you say." (W. Handler)

"The financial security analysis for the older generation can be used to help the older generation get comfortable giving up control. If they really know and feel that they will be well taken care of through their lifetime, then they are more likely to pass ownership, including control, to the next generation. The financial security analysis for the younger generation also helps that generation understand what they need for their own long-term financial security and independence. This then allows them to assess what is reasonable to expect the company may contribute to that financial security and when." (T. Zanecchia)

"All key players need to agree to hire us; it's all or none for a consultation. Interview clients individually to get a general sense; meet all the key players first. Then we put our heads together to discuss what we see, what the underlying dynamics are, and where we go. Other issues that must be worked on include lack of accountability; job descriptions; performance reviews; clear reporting structures; and the abundant family issues. It's often useful to work with dyads or one-on-one." (P. Karofsky)

---

*As we have noted, each family and family business is different. Interventions must be tailored to each situation. We have tried to show the variety of successful interventions techniques available and in use.

"Engaging the next generation in estate planning; attorneys are often reluctant to do so. Tackling the issues of representation in how an estate plan will work by involving the next generation in the discussion of wealth and its impact is important. Also, integrate philanthropy into the process; family businesses often haven't formalized their philanthrophy, and it usually adds important values to the process. Possibilities include setting up a family foundation or a fund for philanthropy, which can provide a focus for a new venture, a process for talking about important issues, and an opportunity for those not working in the business to get engaged. Teamwork with advisors is another important tool." (M. Cohn)

"Having the family look at their financial and family picture over generations. I reflect back to them the reality and risks of their consolidated two, three, and four intergenerational financial position. You can't just look at one generation, and you must involve everyone in the discussions. You also need to have the leader engaged in the process. It is important for the consultant to get the respect of the owner or to be able to say 'no' to the client engagement. In my experience, the typical business owner is very insecure about his or her knowledge of family and business." (P. Baudoin)

"I use and recommend the conceptual framework for negotiation and dispute resolution in *Getting to Yes* (Fisher & Ury, 1991). If you keep pushing for people to clarify their reasons—their needs, concerns, fears, hopes, or 'interests' as *Getting to Yes* names them—then disputing parties have more likelihood of finding common ground. As a mediator, my intentions are focused on getting to these deeper concerns, and then helping the parties create new ways to respond to them." (J. Wofford)

"Normalizing the client's situation is elemental to this work. Before the first session is over, I say, 'It makes sense that you are having problems because combining business and family is very hard to do.' This lowers the older generation's anxiety and calms them down; they really understand and believe it; this makes it much easier to get work done." (P. Cole)

"Getting them to see that endless bickering didn't solve the problem before and won't solve it now. It is important to have a skills and needs assessment combined with strategic planning to give them an experience to think strategically. Giving choices to family members is important, including around issues of personal and professional development and leaving the company.

Help families learn to brainstorm and to think more openly together. I will tell the fairy tale of the king and the goose and the golden eggs to illustrate how all members of the family and business are mere servants of the king (the customer). A family that can agree to serve the needs of the company (golden goose) and the customer (king) can then stop using the business as a war zone." (I. Bryck)

"Start with an initial assessment, and find out where the issues are. Identify which two or three people have the most problem relating and get them to dialogue with an action plan format that establishes accountability, positive reinforcement, and positive feedback." (B. Brown)

"Engaging with the entire system through a preliminary workshop; system assessment; creating a shared vision; collective planning; building legitimizing structures for ongoing dialogue, decision-making, education, and problem solving, including family councils and boards of directors; and developing communication and problem-solving skills." (L. Dashew)

"I use the relationship roadmap in our book, *Getting Along in Family Businesses* [Hoover & Hoover, 1999]. It's a valuable map for neutralizing conflict and dissension. I also use Partnering Covenants, described in the book." (E. Hoover)

"Only rarely do I employ interventions, as I generally am more comfortable leaving this to other professional disciplines. There is one intervention that I have found successful on occasion, however, when the parties are at an impasse. I require one party to listen to the other party's chief grievance or 'hot button' without interrupting and then to repeat it back, in his or her own words, without commenting. Then I have the other party go through the same exercise. The process seems to be useful for two things. First, it gets each side to really listen to what the other is saying. Second, and just as important, even if there is no immediate resolution, each side feels that he or she has been listened to, perhaps for the first time." (J. Wolfson)

"Make the assumption that the family business will continue to be successful; the hopeful attitude you bring to the consultation can reinforce positive results." (C. Seligman)

"Getting all family members involved in the business in the same room at the same time is the first step. That normalizes them and makes them feel that 'there's hope for us.' Get them to express their points of view; get support for what you and they are doing here. Begin an engagement with everybody involved." (E. Cox)

"Really listen; check out what you hear; be competent in your field and also in allied fields. There is no replacement for knowing the tools and techniques and staying current. Know the best of best in your field and know how to get it. Don't assume you know enough. Also, working collaboratively is important; you need to develop skills to lead a team and to follow. Understand it is not about who leads the advisory team but whose work is in the foreground and background at any point in time. Keep the family looking at itself and talking." (K. Wakefield)

"Togetherness is not always the answer; bringing everybody together is often not the answer. Always try to work with the most motivated. They have the most stamina. Don't spend time on convincing someone to do something. Also, 'the client is really me'; how I've handled myself is critical to the process. I always ask myself if I've been over- or under-responsible. It is important to appreciate the long-term nature of work." (K. Wiseman)

"Feedback is powerful; you need to (1) speak the truth as you know it and (2) be nonjudgmental. I use the metaphor of a stained glass window; take the shards of glass to create a story. You need to respect everyone's perspective so that all can relate to the feedback; interventions fall out of the feedback discussion. Visioning is important—like Ivan Lansberg's (1999) 'dream the dream,' in which each generation creates its vision of governance and leadership." (G. Ayres)

"Have them 'visit the future'; check out my book, *Workplace Wars*, or visit my website: www.kaye.com." (K. Kaye)

Our Thanks to the Following Contributors

Glen Ayres *is a family business consultant who teams with family enterprises to help them through the major change initiatives needed to keep their families and businesses economically vital and values driven.*

Peter Baudoin, *along with his associates, has developed a software-based information system for documenting, planning, and monitoring the intergenerational, tangible, and intangible wealth of family enterprises.*

Bonnie Brown *is president of Transition Dynamics Inc. (transitiondynamicsinc.com) and executive director of the FOX Foundation. She advises families and organizations in transition.*

Ira Bryck *is director of the University of Massachusetts Family Business Center, a learning community for entrepreneurial families. His third play about family business life, "Tough Nut to Crack," premiers in the fall of 2002.*

Mike Cohn, *author of* Keep or Sell Your Business, *is a family business consultant. He has served as president and board member of the Family Firm Institute.*

Pat Cole *is a family business member and is also associate professor of family therapy and family business at Nova Southeastern University in Ft. Lauderdale, Florida.*

Ed Cox *and his partners at Doud Hausner Vistar in Glendale, California, work exclusively with family businesses to help them achieve balance among business prosperity, family harmony, and personal well-being.*

Leslie Dashew, *president of the Human Side of Enterprise and a partner in the Aspen Family Business Group, has a background in organization development and family therapy and has specialized in working with family-owned businesses for over fifteen years. Ms. Dashew is co-author of* Working with Family Businesses: A Guide for Professionals.

Wendy Handler *is an assistant professor of management at Babson College where she teaches Family Business Management, which, when she developed it in 1986, was the first class in this area in the country.*

Ed Hoover *is a management psychologist who specializes in the unique challenges faced by families who own and manage businesses and other significant wealth.*

Paul Karofsky *is executive director of Northeastern University's Center for Family Business in Dedham, Massachusetts, a resource to families, businesses and educational institutions worldwide. Mr. Karofsky also runs his own consulting group, Transition Consulting Group, Inc. (transition-consulting.com).*

Ken Kaye *has long been one of the critical thinkers and innovators among family psychologists who specialize in resolving developmental and interpersonal problems in closely held firms.*

Carrie Seligman *is the director of business and estate planning for the Boston Group of Northwestern Mutual Financial Network. In this capacity she advises closely held business owners in the areas of succession planning, retirement planning, executive benefits, and estate planning.*

John G. Troast, Jr., *co-founder of the Cambridge Center for Creative Enterprise, was active in a third-generation family business. He currently serves on the board of the family office. He has also been active in public service, having been appointed to positions in both New Jersey and Massachusetts.*

Karen Vinton, *professor emeritus of business at Montana State University, continues to do research on family businesses and owns a consulting firm that specializes in management and human resource management issues.*

Kay Wakefield, *a lawyer in Portland, Oregon, advises owners of family owned businesses on succession and estate planning.*

Kathy Wiseman *is a faculty member at the Bowen Center for the Study of the Family and president of Working Systems, Washington, D.C. Her practice area is the emotional process in family firms and work organizations.*

Jack Wofford, *a lawyer by training, is a full-time facilitator, mediator, and arbitrator, providing dispute resolution and consensus-building services in a wide range of subject areas, including family-owned and other closely held businesses.*

Jeffrey Wolfson, *a family business attorney with Goulston & Storrs in Boston, serves as chairman emeritus of the Northeastern University Center for Family Business and is the author of a published monograph entitled "Practice Points for the Family Business' Corporate Lawyer."*

Tom Zanecchia *is founder and president of Wealth Management Consultants, Inc. (wealth-manage.com), which provides integrated and objective financial, investment, and tax consulting to high net worth individuals and their families.*

Afterword

AS WE HAVE THOUGHT ABOUT our consulting practice with family firms that we have described in this book, it has become clear to us—and we hope to the reader—that our approach to working with family firms is significantly different from our approach to working with nonfamily firm clients. Systems thinking is crucial to helping family firms, as is possessing both content knowledge to provide specific solutions to their problems and process skills to help family firms move through the change process and deal with the resistance that is frequently encountered. We have found that successfully managing each stage of the consulting process, from first contact to exit, gives the consultant his or her best chance for success.

Providing family firm clients with feedback that they can accept and work with is also a significant challenge for family firm consultants. To provide this feedback in a safe environment requires the consultant to build strong bonds of trust with a client. Without such trust, clients will be unwilling to attempt to change or try solutions that are unsettling to them. Whether through a family retreat or some other forum, the skilled consultant can help the family to see clearly the issues and problems and can then help the client make free and informed choices about the future. Moreover, once the client makes a decision concerning how to proceed, the consultant must be skillful in intervening to help solve a problem, be it succession planning, ownership transfer, or improving communication skills. Consultants become role models, coaches, and teachers to their clients to help them break out of dysfunctional family patterns and solve problems regarding the business. Given the varied skill set that is generally required to help family businesses, we have emphasized the importance of using multidisciplinary consulting teams. It is the rare consultant who has all the skills that a family firm client needs.

Understanding not only our clients, but also ourselves, is critical for our success as family business consultants. We must be able to articulate our own biases, shortcomings, and fears in order to deal with them and help our clients gain insight into their own problems. We encourage all who would like to become family business consultants to complete a personal family genogram and reflect on how their experiences in their families of origin have affected their lives. Moreover, each consultant should have a plan to improve his or her skills and abilities. You can only lift a client higher if you are standing on higher ground yourself.

We have also suggested that, while there are common patterns and issues that one finds when consulting with family firms, each family firm is different, with a unique history and dynamics. Thus we have encouraged family firm consultants to be aware of a variety of special situations they might encounter in order to help them tailor their consultation to the needs of the client. A "cookie-cutter" approach to family firm consulting is a recipe for failure, in our view. The experiences of several family firm consultants that we have shared in the final chapter are testaments to the various pitfalls that await consultants who are not attuned to the needs of their various clients.

Finally, in our practices we have found that, despite our best efforts, we do not always succeed. Husbands and wives divorce, children may remain estranged from parents, and the business may end in failure. But success in working with family firms seems to double the intrinsic rewards for consultants, for not only do we see businesses that turn around and improve, but we see relationships enhanced in the families we work with and renewed commitment by the family to maintain their values and accomplish their goals. Our consulting work with family firms has led us to some of the most satisfying experiences that we have had in our professional careers. In most cases, our clients are not just clients, but they become our friends as well. And there is no richer reward than seeing someone that you care about improve his or her own life as well as the health of the business and the family.

In this book, we have outlined the knowledge and skills that we believe it takes to succeed in family business consulting. We hope that this book will inspire a new generation of consultants to help family firms, and we hope that it will improve the practice of those of us who are more seasoned consultants. From our vantage point, consulting with family firms is certainly not easy, but it's definitely worth it.

References

Adams, J.S., Taschian, A., & Shore, T. (1996, Summer). Ethics in family and non-family owned firms: An exploratory study. *Family Business Review, IX*(2),157–170.

Adizes, I. (1979, Summer). Organizational passages: Diagnosing and treating lifecycle problems of organizations. *Organizational Dynamics,* pp. 3–25.

Argyris, C. (1991, May-June). Teaching smart people how to learn. *Harvard Business Review,* pp. 99–109.

Argyris, C., & Schön, D. (1974). *Theory in practice.* San Francisco, CA: Jossey-Bass.

Aronoff, C.E. (1998, September). Megatrends in family business. *Family Business Review, XI*(3), 181–185.

Baldwin, J. (1977, December 19) Every good-bye ain't gone. *New Yorker.*

Barnett, F., & Barnett, S. (1998). *Working together: Entrepreneurial couples.* Berkeley, CA: Ten Speed Press.

Beckhard, R., & Pritchard, W. (1992). *Changing the essence: The art of creating and leading fundamental change in organizations.* San Francisco, CA: Jossey-Bass.

Becvar, D.S., & Becvar, R.J. (1996). *Family therapy: A systemic integration.* Boston, MA: Allyn and Bacon.

Bennett, L., Wolin, S., McAvity, J. (1988). Family identity, ritual, and myth: A cultural perspective on life cycle transitions. In C.J. Falicov (Ed.), *Family transitions: Continuity & change over the life cycle* (pp. 211–234). New York: Guilford Press.

Bepko, C., & Krestan, J. (1985). *The responsibility trap.* New York: The Free Press.

Bork, D., Jaffe, D. Lane, S., Dashew, L., & Hersler, Q. (1996). *Working with family businesses: A guide for professionals.* San Francisco, CA: Jossey-Bass.

Bowen, M. (1976). The theory in the practice of psychotherapy. In P.J. Guerin (Ed.), *Family therapy: Theory and practice.* New York: Gardner Press.

Bridges, W. (1980). *Transitions: Making sense of life's changes.* Reading, MA: Addison-Wesley.

Brown, F.H. (1993, Spring). Loss and continuity in the family firm. *Family Business Review, VI*(2), 111–130.

Burke, W.W. (1994). *Organization development: A process of learning and change.* Reading, MA: Addison-Wesley.

Carlock, R.S., & Ward, J.L. (2001). *Strategic planning for the family business: Parallel planning to unify the family and business.* New York: Palgrave.

Carter, B., & McGoldrick, M. (Eds.). (1989). *The changing family life cycle: A framework for family therapy.* Boston, MA: Allyn and Bacon.

Carter, M. Practice paper. [Available online: ffi.org/members/bok/index.html]

Clarfeld, R.A. (1994, Summer). Preparing a non-family leader for emergencies. *Family Business,* pp. 64-66.

Cliffe, S. (1998, May-June). Family business: Facing up to succession. *Harvard Business Review,* pp. 17–18.

Cohn, M. (2001). *Keep or sell your business.* Chicago, IL: Dearborn Financial Publishing.

Cole, P. (1997, December). Women in family business. *Family Business Review, X*(4), 353–371.

Collins, J., & Porras, J. (1997). *Built to last: Successful habits of visionary companies.* New York: Harper Business.

Danco, L. (1982). *Beyond survival.* Cleveland, OH: The Center for Family Business, University Press.

Danes, S., Zuiker, V., Kean, R., & Arbuthnot, J. (1999, September). Predictors of family business tensions and goal achievement. *Family Business Review, XII*(3), 241–252.

Davis, J., & Tagiuri, R. (1989, Spring). The influence of life stage on father-son work relationships in family companies. *Family Business Review, II*(1), 47–76.

Davis, P. (1990, October). Saving your company by building consensus. *Family Business,* pp. 14-17.

De Shazer, S. (1991). *Putting differences to work.* New York: W.W. Norton.

Drucker, P. (1999, March-April). Managing oneself. *Harvard Business Review,* pp. 65–74.

Duhl, B.S. (1983). *From the inside out and other metaphors: Creative and integrative approaches to training in systems thinking.* New York: Brunner/Mazel.

Duhl, B.S. (1993, November-December). Metaphor in action. *Networker.*

Dyer, W.G., Jr. (1986). *Cultural change in family firms: Anticipating and managing business and family transitions.* San Francisco, CA: Jossey-Bass.

Dyer, W.G., Jr., (1992). *The entrepreneurial experience: Confronting career dilemmas of the start-up executive.* San Francisco, CA: Jossey-Bass.

Dyer, W.G., Jr. (1994, Summer). Potential contributions of organizational behavior to the study of family-owned businesses. *Family Business Review, VII*(2), 109–131.

Dyer, W.G., Jr. (1997, June). Organization development in the entrepreneurial firm. *Journal of Applied Behavioral Science, 33*(2), 190–208.

Erickson, E. (1963). *Childhood and society.* New York: W.W. Norton.

Erickson, E. (1976). *Adulthood.* New York: W.W. Norton.

Editors. (2001, Spring). America's oldest family businesses. *Family Business,* pp. 41–59.

Editors. (2001, Summer). The family business hall of shame. *Family Business,* pp. 53–54.

Feldman, L.B., & Pinsof, W.M. (1982). Dysfunctional marital conflict: An integrative interpersonal-intrapsychic model. *Journal of Marital and Family Therapy, 8,* 295–308.

Fisher, R. & Ury, W. (1991) *Getting to yes (2nd ed.).* New York: Penquin Books.

Flamholtz, E.G. (2000). *Growing pains: Transitioning from an entrepreneurship to a professionally managed firm.* San Francisco, CA: Jossey-Bass.

Forer, L. (1977). *The birth order factor.* New York: Pocket Books.

Gallo, M.A. (1998, December). Ethics in personal behavior in family business. *Family Business Review, XI*(4), 325–336.

Gersick, K. (1994, Summer). Reflections on the family business literature: Pioneers look to the past and future. *Family Business Review, VII*(2), 199-205.

Gersick, K., Davis, J., Hampton, M.M., & Lansberg, I. (1997). *Generation to generation: Life cycles of the family business.* Boston, MA: Harvard Business School Press.

Gilligan, C. (1982). *In a different voice.* Cambridge, MA: Harvard University Press.

Goleman, D. (1995). *Emotional intelligence.* New York: Bantam Books.

Goleman, D. (1998). *Working with emotional intelligence.* New York: Bantam Books.

Goodman, J. (1998, December). Defining the new professional: The family business consultant. *Family Business Review, XI*(4).

Gottman, J. (1994a). *What predicts divorce.* Mahwah, NJ: Lawrence Erlbaum.

Gottman, J. (1994b). *Why marriages succeed or fail.* New York: Simon & Schuster.

Graham, K. (1998). *Personal history.* New York: Vintage/Random House.

Green, R. (1988, October). Impasse and change: A systemic/strategic view of the therapeutic system. *Journal of Marital and Family Therapy,* pp. 383–395.

Greiner, L. (1972, July-August). Evolution and revolution as organizations grow. *Harvard Business Review.* [Reprinted in *Family Business Review, X*(4), 397–409.]

Habbershon, T., & Astrachan, J. (1997, Spring). Research note perceptions are reality: How family meetings lead to collective action. *Family Business Review, X*(1), 37–52.

Hamilton, S. (1996, Autumn). Everyone in the investment pool. *Family Business,* pp. 35-40.

Handler, W.C. (1994, Summer). Succession in family business: A review of the research. *Family Business Review, VII*(2), 133-157.

Harrison, R. (1970). Choosing the depth of organizational intervention. *Journal of Applied Behavioral Science, 6*(2), 182–202. [Reprinted in *Organization development and transformation: Managing effective change* by W. French, C. Bell, & R. Zawacki. 1994, pp. 413–424.]

Hilburt-Davis, J., & Senturia, P. (1995, Fall). Using the process/content framework: Guidelines for the content expert. *Family Business Review, VIII*(3), 189–199.

Hofman, M. (1989, September). Famous splits. *Inc. Magazine,* p. 89.

Hoover, E.A., & Hoover, C. (1999). *Getting along in family business.* New York: Routledge.

Inc. Magazine. (1999, March). The new girls' club (p. 88).

Jacobson, N.S. (1987). Component analysis of behavioral marital therapy: Two-year follow-up and prediction of relapse. *Journal of Marital and Family Therapy, 13,* 187–195.

Jaffe, A. (1996). *Honey, I want to start my own business.* New York: Harper Business.

Jaffee, D. (1990). Married to the business and each other. In *The Best of the Family Firm Institute Conference Proceedings: Vol. III: The Best of Behavioral Science* (pp. 20–26). Boston, MA: Family Firm Institute.

Jonovic, D. (1984). *Someday it'll all be yours. . .or will it?* Cleveland, OH: Jamieson Press.

Kaplan, M.S. (1993). Advice for a successful family foundation. In *The Best of the Family Firm Institute Conference Proceedings: Vol. II: The Best of Law* (pp. 30–33). Boston, MA: Family Firm Institute.

Karoff, H.P. (1992). Philanthropy for the wise investor: A primer for families on effective giving. In *The Proceedings of "Family Business at the Crossroads"* (pp. 158–168). Boston, MA: Family Firm Institute.

Kaye, K. (1991, Spring). Penetrating the cycle of sustained conflict. *Family Business Review, IV*(1), 21–44.

Kaye, K. (1994). *Workplace wars and how to end them.* New York: American Management Association.

Kaye, K. (1996, Winter). When the family business is a sickness. *Family Business Review, IX*(4), 347–368.

Keiley, M. (2000/2001, Winter). Making new attachments. *AFTA Newsletter,* pp. 23–25.

Krasnow, H.C., & Wolkoff, R.L. (1998, September). Three proposals for interdisciplinary study. *Family Business Review, XI*(3), 267–274.

Lane, S.H. (1989). An organization development/team-building approach to consultation with family businesses. *Family Business Review, 2*(1), 5–16.

Lansberg, I. (1983, Summer). Conversation with Richard Beckhard. *Organizational Dynamics,* pp. 29–38.

Lansberg, I. (1988). The succession conspiracy. *Family Business Review, 1*(2), 119–143.

Lansberg, I. (1992, Fall). The family side of family business: A conversation with Salvador Minuchin. *Family Business Review, V*(3), 309–321.

Lansberg, I. (1999). *Succeeding generations: Realizing the dreams of families in business.* Boston, MA: Harvard University Press.

Lederer, W.J., & Jackson, D.D. (1968). *The mirages of marriage.* New York: W.W. Norton.

Leman, K. (1992). *The birth order book.* New York: Dell Paperback.

Lerner, H.G. (1985). *The dance of anger.* New York: Harper & Row.

Lerner, H.G. (1990). *The dance of intimacy.* New York: Harper & Row.

Le Van, G. (1990, March). The secret weapon of family business. *Family Business,* pp. 60-61.

Levinson, D.J. (1978). *The seasons of a man's life.* New York: Ballantine.

Lewin, K. (1951). *Field theory in social science.* New York: Harper & Row.

Marshack, K.J. (1993, Winter). Coentrepreneurial couples: A literature review on boundaries and transitions among copreneurs. *Family Business Review, VI*(4), 355–369.

Marshack, K.L. (1994). Copreneurs and dual-career couples: How different are they at balancing love and work? *The Best of Behavioral Science,* in *The Best of the Family Firm Institute Conference Proceedings* (pp. 27–34). Boston, MA: Family Firm Institute.

McClure, S. (2000, Winter). Leading a team of advisors. *Family Business,* pp. 51–55.

McCracken, D.M. (2000, November-December). Winning the talent war for women: Sometimes it takes a revolution. *Harvard Business Review,* pp. 159–167.

McCracken, K. (2000). The family business client: Managing the complexity. *The Family Business Client,* pp. 7–25.

McGivern, C. (1989, Winter). The dynamics of management succession: A model of chief executive succession in the small family firm. *Family Business Review, II*(4), 401–411.

McGoldrick, M., Gerson, R., & Shellenberger, S. (1999). *Genograms: Assessment and intervention.* New York: W.W. Norton.

McGoldrick, M., & Troast, J.G., Jr. (1993, Fall). Ethnicity, families, and family business: Implications for practitioners. *Family Business Review, VI*(3), 283–300.

Middleberg, C.V. (2001, July). Projective identification in common couple dances. *Journal of Marital and Family Therapy,* pp. 341–352.

Miller, J.B. (1976). *Toward a new psychology of women.* Boston, MA: Beacon.

Nelton, S. (1986). *In love and in business: How entrepreneurial couples are changing the rules of business and marriage.* New York: John Wiley & Sons.

Nelton, S. (1995, February). The shape of things to come. *Nation's Business,* pp. 52–53.

Nelton, S. (1996, April). A coming sea change in leadership. *Nation's Business,* p. 60.

Nelton, S. (1998, September). The rise of women in family firms: Call for research now. *Family Business Review, XI*(3), 215–218.

Neubauer, F., & Lank, A. (1998). *The family business: Its governance for sustainability.* New York: Routledge.

Notarius, C., & Markman, H. (1993). *We can work it out.* New York: Putnam.

O'Hara, W. (2000, Summer). Building the Durtnell dynasty. *Family Business,* pp. 49–55.

Olson, E., & Eoyang, G. (2001). *Facilitating organization change: Lessons from complexity science.* San Francisco, CA: Jossey-Bass/Pfeiffer.

Paul, N., & Paul, B.B. (1974). *A marital puzzle.* New York: Norton.

Petzinger, T., Jr. (1999). *The new pioneers: The men and women who are transforming the workplace and the marketplace.* New York: Simon & Schuster.

Pirsig, R.M. (1984). An author and father looks ahead at the past. *The New York Times Book Review.*

Pittman, F. (1987). *Turning points: Treating families in transition and crises.* New York: W.W. Norton.

Ponthieu, L.D., & Caudill, H.L. (1993, Spring). Who's the boss? Responsibility and decision making in copreneurial ventures. *Family Business Review, VI*(1), 3–17.

Poza, E.J., & Alfred, T. (1996, Autumn). What the silent majority thinks (but may not tell you). *Family Business,* pp. 16–21.

Poza, E., Johnson, S., & Alfred, T. (1998, December). Changing the family business through action research. *Family Business Review, XI*(4), 311–323.

Quade, K., & Brown, R. (2001). *The conscious consultant: Mastering change from the inside out.* San Francisco, CA: Jossey-Bass/Pfeiffer.

Reps, P., & Senzaki, N. (Eds.). (1994). *Zen flesh, Zen bones.* Boston, MA: Shambala.

Roberts, J. (2000, Fall). Couples in today's world. *AFTA Newsletter,* pp. 10–12.

Roizen, M. (1999). *Real age: Are you as young as you can be?* New York: HarperCollins.

Salganicoff, M. (1990, Summer). Clarifying the present and creating options for the future. *Family Business Review, III*(2), 121–124.

Schaef, A.W., & Fassel, D. (1988). *The addictive organization.* New York: Harper & Row.

Schein, E.H. (1983). The role of the founder in creating organizational culture. *Organizational Dynamics, 12*(1), 13–28. [Reprinted in *Family Business Review, 8*(3), 221–238.]

Schein, E. (1988). *Process consultation: Its role in organization development.* Reading, MA: Addison-Wesley.

Senge, P., Kleiner, A., Roberts, C., Ross, R., & Smith, B. (1994). *The fifth discipline fieldbook.* New York: Currency/Doubleday.

Sheehy, G. (1977). *Passages: Predictable crises of adult life.* New York: Bantam.

Sherman, H., & Schultz, R. (1998). *Open boundaries: Creating business innovation through complexity.* New York: Perseus.

Sloane, P. (1994). *Test your lateral IQ.* New York: Sterling.

Stone, D. (1994, Summer). Glue to bind generations. *Family Business,* pp. 41-46.

Stone, D. (1998, Spring). How high is your E.Q.? *Family Business,* pp. 48-54.

Tagiuri, R., & Davis, J.A. (1982). *Bivalent attributes of the family firm.* Working paper. Harvard University Press, Cambridge, MA. [Reprinted in *Family Business Review, IX*(2), 199–208.]

Tifft, S., & Jones, A. (1991). *The patriarch: The rise and fall of the Bingham dynasty.* New York: Simon & Schuster.

Toffler, A. (1990). *Powershift.* New York: Bantam.

Toman, W. (1976). *Family constellation: Its effects on personality and social behavior.* New York: Springer.

Trollinger, A. (1998, May 18). Couples in business can't ignore issues of titles, power, and need for written agreements. *The Business Journal of Kansas City.* Kansas City, Missouri.

Velasquez, J.D. (1998). *When robots weep: Emotional memories and decision-making.* Cambridge, MA: MIT Artificial Intelligence Laboratory.

Vinton, K. (1998, December). Nepotism: An interdisciplinary model. *Family Business Review, XI*(4), 297–303.

Von Lossberg, A. (1990, Winter). The role of the nonfamily administrator in family foundations. *Family Business Review, III*(4), 375-382.

Walton, R. (1987). *Managing conflict: Interpersonal dialogue and third-party roles.* Reading, MA: Addison-Wesley.

Ward, J. (1987). *Keeping the family business healthy: How to plan for continuity, growth, profitability, and family leadership.* San Francisco, CA: Jossey-Bass.

Ward, J. (1997). *Creating effective boards for private enterprises: Meeting the challenges of continuity and competition.* Marietta, GA: Business Owner Resources.

Watkins, C. (1985). *The American heritage dictionary of Indo-European roots.* Boston, MA: Houghton-Mifflin.

Weiner, J. (1995). *The beak of the finch.* New York: Vintage Books.

Weisbord, M., & Janoff, S. (2000). *Future search: An action guide to finding common ground in organizations & communities.* San Francisco, CA: Berrett-Koehler.

Weiss, A. (2001). *The ultimate consultant: Powerful techniques for the successful practitioner.* San Francisco, CA: Jossey-Bass/Pfeiffer.

Wheeler, E.W. (1936). The winds of fate. In H. Felleman (Ed.), *The best loved poems of the American people.* New York: Doubleday.

Whiteside, M.F., & Brown, F.H. (1991, Winter). Drawbacks of a dual systems approach to family firms: Can we expand our thinking? *Family Business Review, IV*(4), 383–395.

Winnicott, D.W. (1987). *Babies and their mothers.* Reading, MA: Addison-Wesley.

Ylvisaker, P.N. (1990, Winter). Family foundations: High risk, high reward. *Family Business Review, III*(4), 331–335.

About the Series

THERE ARE WATERSHED MOMENTS in history that change everything after them. The attack on Pearl Harbor was one of those. The bombing of Hiroshima was another. The terrorist attack on the World Trade Center in New York City was our most recent. All resulted in significant change that transformed many lives and organizations.

Practicing Organization Development: The Change Agent Series for Groups and Organizations was launched to help those who must cope with or create change. The series is designed to share what is working or not working, to provoke critical thinking about change, and to offer creative ways to deal with change, rather than the destructive ones noted above.

The Current State of Change Management and Organization Development

Almost as soon as the ink was dry on the first wave of books published in this series, we heard that its focus was too narrow. We heard that the need for theory and practice extended beyond OD into change management. More than one respected authority urged us to reconsider our focus, moving beyond OD to include books on change management generally.

Organization development is not the only way that change can be engineered or coped with in organizational settings. We always knew that, of course. And we remain grounded in the view that change management, however it is carried out, should be based on such values as respect for the individual, participation and involvement in change by those affected by it, and interest in the improvement of organizational settings on many levels—including productivity improvement, but also improvement in achieving work/life balance and in a values-based approach to management and to change.

A Brief History of the Genesis of the Series

A few years ago, and as a direct result of the success of *Practicing Organization Development: A Guide for Practitioners* by Rothwell, Sullivan, and McLean, the publisher—feeling that OD was experiencing a rebirth of interest in the United States and in other nations—wanted to launch a new OD series. The goal of this new series was not to replace, or even compete directly with, the well-established Addison-Wesley OD Series (edited by Edgar Schein). Instead, as the editors saw it, the series would provide a means by which the most promising authors in OD whose voices had not previously been heard could share their ideas. The publisher enlisted the support of Bill Rothwell, Roland Sullivan, and Kristine Quade to turn the dream of a series into a reality.

This series was long in the making and has been steadily evolving since its inception. The original vision was an ambitious one—and involved no less than reinventing OD and re-energizing interest in the research and practice surrounding it. Sponsoring books was one means to that end. Another is the series website (www.pfeiffer.com/go/od). Far more than just a place to advertise the series, it serves as a real-time learning community for OD practitioners.

What Distinguishes the Books in this Series

The books in this series are meant to be challenging, cutting-edge, and state-of-the-art in their approach to OD and change management. The goal of the series is to provide an outlet for proven authorities in OD and change management who have not put their ideas into print or for up-and-coming writers in OD and change management who have new, sometimes unorthodox, approaches that are stimulating and exciting. Some books in this series describe inspirational concepts that can lead to actionable change and purvey ideas so new that they are not fully developed.

Unique to this series is the cutting-edge emphasis, the immediate applicability, and the ease of transferability of the concepts. The aim of this series is nothing less than to reinvent, re-energize, and reinvigorate OD and change management. In each book, we have also recommended that the author(s) provide:

- A research base of some kind, meaning new information derived from practice and/or systematic investigation and

- Practical tools, worksheets, case studies, and other ready-to-go approaches that help the authors drag "theory" to "practice" to make these new, cutting-edge approaches more concrete.

Subject Matter That Will (and Will Not) Be Covered

The books in this series are varied in their approach, but they are united by their focus. All share an emphasis on organization development (OD) and change management (CM). Hence, books in this series are about participative change efforts. They are not about such other popular topics as leadership, management development, consulting, or group dynamics—unless those topics are treated in new, cutting-edge ways and are geared to OD and change management practitioners.

This Book

In *Consulting to Family Businesses: A Practical Guide to Contracting, Assessment, and Implementation,* W. Gibb Dyer, Jr., and Jane Hilburt-Davis draw on their extensive experience to provide a comprehensive roadmap to anyone consulting with family businesses, including change consultants, therapists, lawyers, accountants, and estate planners. In addition, this is a must read for all family members leading a successful business. This book is the first of its kind to offer a practical, integrated change process for increasing organizational effectiveness.

The book is organized into three parts. Part 1 helps readers understand why family businesses are different from other organizations. Part 2 offers how-to-do-it advice on consulting with family firms. Part 3 summarizes the specialized knowledge, skills, and abilities needed by consultants who work with family firms.

This book is a classic. It is most insightful, helpful, and packed with useful stories, examples, hints, and wisdom.

William J. Rothwell
University Park, PA

Roland Sullivan
Deephaven, MN

Kristine Quade
Minnetonka, MN

Statement
of the Board

IT IS OUR PLEASURE TO PARTICIPATE in and influence the start-up of *Practicing Organization Development: The Change Agent Series for Groups and Organizations*. The purpose of the series is to stimulate the profession and influence how organization change is defined and practiced. This statement is intended to set the context for the series by addressing three important questions: (1) What are the key issues facing organization change and development in the 21st Century? (2) Where does—or should—OD fit in the field of organization change and development? and (3) What is the purpose of this series?

What Are the Key Issues Facing Organization Change and Development in the 21st Century?

One of the questions is the extent to which leaders can control forces or can only be reactive. Will globalization and external forces be so powerful that they will prevent organizations from being able to "stay ahead of the change curve"? And what will be the role of technology, especially information technology, in the change process? To what extent can it be a carrier of change (as well as a source of change)?

What will the relationship be between imposed change and collaborative change? Will the increased education of the workforce demand the latter, or will the requirement of having to make fundamental changes demand leadership that sets goals that participants would not willingly set on their own? And what is the relationship between these two forms of change?

Who will be the change agent? Is this a separate profession, or will that increasingly be the responsibility of the organization's leaders? If the latter, how does that change the role of the change professional?

What will be the role of values for change in the 21st Century? Will the key values be performance—efficiency and effectiveness? And what role will the humanistic values of more traditional OD play? Or will the growth of knowledge (and human competence) as an organization's core competence make this a moot point in that performance can only occur if one takes account of humanistic values?

What is the relationship between other fields and the area of change? Can any change process that is not closely linked with strategy be truly effective? Can change agents focus only on process, or do they need to be knowledgeable and actively involved in the organization's products/services and understand the market niche in which the organization operates?

Where Does—or Should—OD Fit in the Field of Organization Change and Development?

We offer the following definition of OD to stimulate debate:

> Organization development is a system-wide and values-based collaborative process of applying behavioral science knowledge to the adaptive development, improvement, and reinforcement of such organizational features as the strategies, structures, processes, people, and cultures that lead to organization effectiveness.

The definition suggests that OD can be understood in terms of its several foci:

First, *OD is a system-wide process.* It works with whole systems. In the past, the bias has been toward working at the individual and group levels. More recently, the focus has shifted to organizations and multi-organization systems. We support that trend in general, but honor and acknowledge the fact that the traditional focus on smaller systems is both legitimate and necessary.

Second, *OD is values-based.* Traditionally, OD has attempted to distinguish itself from other forms of planned change and applied behavioral science by promoting a set of humanistic values and by emphasizing the importance of personal growth as a key to its practice. Today, that focus is blurred and there is much debate about the value base underlying the practice of OD. We support a more formal and direct conversation about what these values are and how the field is related to them.

Third, *OD is collaborative.* Our first value commitment as OD practitioners is to bring about an inclusive, diverse workforce with a focus of integrating differences into a world-wide culture mentality.

Fourth, *OD is based on behavioral science knowledge.* Organization development should incorporate and apply knowledge from sociology, psychology, anthropology, technology, and economics toward the end of making systems more effective. We support the continued emphasis in OD on behavioral science knowledge and believe that OD practitioners should be widely read and comfortable with several of the disciplines.

Fifth, *OD is concerned with the adaptive development, improvement, and reinforcement of strategies, structures, processes, people, culture, and other features of organizational life.* This statement describes not only the organizational elements that are the target of change but also the process by which effectiveness is increased. That is, OD works in a variety of areas, and it is focused on improving those areas. We believe that such a statement of process and content strongly implies that a key feature of OD is the transference of knowledge and skill to the system so that it is more able to handle and manage change in the future.

Sixth and finally, *OD is about improving organization effectiveness.* It is not just about making people happy; it is also concerned with meeting financial goals, improving productivity, and addressing stakeholder satisfaction. We believe that OD's future is closely tied to the incorporation of this value in its purpose and the demonstration of this objective in its practice.

This definition raises a host of questions:

- Are OD and organization change and development one and the same, or are they different?

- Has OD become just a collection of tools, methods, and techniques? Has it lost its values?

- Does it talk "systems," but ignore them in practice?
- Are consultants facilitators of change or activists of change?
- To what extent should consulting be driven by consultant value versus holding only the value of increasing the client's effectiveness?
- How can OD practitioners help formulate strategy, shape the strategy development process, contribute to the content of strategy, and drive how strategy will be implemented?
- How can OD focus on the drivers of change external to individuals, such as the external environment, business strategy, organization change, and culture change, as well as on the drivers of change internal to individuals, such as individual interpretations of culture, behavior, style, and mindset?
- How much should OD be part of the competencies of all leaders? How much should it be the sole domain of professionally trained, career-oriented OD practitioners?

What Is the Purpose of This Series?

This series is intended to provide current thinking about organization change and development as a field and to provide practical approaches based on sound theory and research. It is targeted for full-time external or internal change practitioners; top executives in charge of enterprise-wide change; and managers, HR practitioners, training and development professionals, and others who have responsibility for change in organizational and trans-organizational settings. At the same time, these books will be directed toward cutting-edge thinking and state-of-the-art approaches. In some cases, the ideas, approaches, or techniques described are still evolving, so the books are intended to open up dialogue.

We know that the books in this series will provide a leading forum for thought-provoking dialogue within the field.

About the Board Members

David Bradford is senior lecturer in organizational behavior at the Graduate School of Business, Stanford University, Palo Alto, California. He is co-author (with Allan R. Cohen) of *Managing for Excellence, Influence Without Authority,* and *POWER UP: Transforming Organizations Through Shared Leadership.*

W. Warner Burke is professor of psychology and education in the department of organization and leadership at Teachers College at Columbia University in New York. He also serves as a senior advisor to PricewaterhouseCoopers. His most recent publication is *Business Profiles of Climate Shifts: Profiles of Change Makers*, with William Trahant and Richard Koonce.

Edith Whitfield Seashore is an organization consultant and co-founder (with Morley Segal) of AUNTL Masters Program in Organization Development. She is co-author of *What Did You Say?* and *The Art of Giving and Receiving Feedback* and co-editor of *The Promise of Diversity*.

Robert Tannenbaum is emeritus professor of development of human systems, Graduate School of Management, University of California, Los Angeles, and recipient of the Lifetime Achievement Award by the National OD Network. He has published numerous books, including *Human Systems Development* (with Newton Margulies and Fred Massarik).

Christopher G. Worley is director, MSOD Program, Pepperdine University, Malibu, California. He is co-author of *Organization Development and Change* (7th ed.), with Tom Cummings, and of *Integrated Strategic Change*, with David Hitchin and Walter Ross.

Shaolin Zhang is senior manager of organization development for Motorola (China) Electronics Ltd. He received his master's degree in American Studies from Beijing Foreign Studies University, Beijing, China, and holds a Ph.D. in sociology from York University, Toronto, Ontario.

Afterword
to the Series

ON **1967,** Warren Bennis, Ed Schein, and I were faculty members of the Sloan School of Management at MIT. We decided to produce a series of paperback books that collectively would describe the state of the field of organization development (OD). Organization development as a field had been named by me and several others from our pioneer change effort at General Mills in Minneapolis, Minnesota, some ten years earlier.

Today I define OD as "a systemic and systematic change effort, using behavioral science knowledge and skill, to transform the organization to a new state."

In any case, several books and many articles had been written, but there was no consensus on whether OD was a field of practice, an area of study, or a profession. We had not even established OD as a theory or even as a practice.

We decided that there was a need for something that would describe the state of OD. Our intention was to each write a book and also to recruit three other authors. After some searching, we found a young editor who had just joined the small publishing house of Addison-Wesley. We made contact, and the series was born. Our audience was to be human resource professionals who spent their time consulting with managers in their development through various small-group activities, such as team building. More than thirty books have been published in that series, and the series has had a life of its own. We just celebrated its thirtieth anniversary.

At last year's National OD Network Conference, I said that it was time for the OD profession to change and transform itself. Is that not what we change agents tell our clients to do? This new Jossey-Bass/Pfeiffer series will do just that. It can be seen as:

- A documentation of the re-invention of OD;

- An effort that will take us to the next level; and

- A practical effort to transfer to the world the theory and practice of leading-edge practitioners and theorists.

The books in this new series will thus prove to be valuable resources for change agents to keep current with the new and leading-edge ideas and practices.

May this very exciting change agent series be most creative and innovative. May it give our field a renewed burst of energy and awareness.

Richard Beckhard
Written on Labor Day weekend 1999 from my summer cabin near Bethel, Maine

About the Editors

William J. Rothwell, Ph.D., is president of Rothwell and Associates, a private consulting firm, as well as professor of human resources development on the University Park Campus of The Pennsylvania State University. Before arriving at Penn State in 1993, he was an assistant vice president and management development director for a major insurance company and a training director in a state government agency. He has worked full-time in human resources management and employee training and development from 1979 to the present. He thus combines real-world experience with academic and consulting experience. As a consultant, Dr. Rothwell's client list includes over thirty-five companies from the Fortune 500.

Dr. Rothwell received his Ph.D. with a specialization in employee training from the University of Illinois at Urbana-Champaign, his M.B.A. with a specialization in human resources management from Sangamon State University (now called the

University of Illinois at Springfield), his M.A. from the University of Illinois at Urbana-Champaign, and his B.A. from Illinois State University. He holds lifetime accreditation as a Senior Professional in Human Resources (SPHR), has been accredited as a Registered Organization Development Consultant (RODC), and holds the industry designation as Fellow of the Life Management Institute (FLMI).

Dr. Rothwell's latest publications include *The Manager and Change Leader* (ASTD, 2001); *The Role of Intervention Selector, Designer and Developer, and Implementor* (ASTD, 2000); *ASTD Models for Human Performance* (2nd ed.) (ASTD, 2000); *The Analyst* (ASTD, 2000); *The Evaluator* (ASTD, 2000); *The ASTD Reference Guide to Workplace Learning and Performance* (3rd ed.), with H. Sredl (HRD Press, 2000); *The Complete Guide to Training Delivery: A Competency-Based Approach*, with S. King and M. King (AMACOM, 2000); *Human Performance Improvement: Building Practitioner Competence*, with C. Hohne and S. King (Butterworth-Heinemann, 2000); *Effective Succession Planning: Ensuring Leadership Continuity and Building Talent from Within* (2nd ed.) (AMACOM, 2000); and *The Competency Toolkit*, with D. Dubois (HRD Press, 2000).

Roland Sullivan, RODC, has worked as an OD pioneer with nearly eight hundred systems in eleven countries and virtually every major industry. Richard Beckhard has recognized him as one of the world's first one hundred change agents.

Mr. Sullivan specializes in the science and art of systematic and systemic change, executive team building, and facilitating Whole System Transformation Conferences—large interactive meetings with 300 to 1,500 people. Over 25,000 people have participated in his conferences worldwide; one co-facilitated with Kristine Quade held for the Amalgamated Bank of South Africa was named runner-up for the title of outstanding change project of the world by the OD Institute.

With William Rothwell and Gary McLean, he is revising one of the field's seminal books, *Practicing OD: A Consultant's Guide* (Jossey-Bass/Pfeiffer, 1995). The first edition is now translated into Chinese.

He did his graduate work in organization development at Pepperdine University and Loyola University.

Mr. Sullivan's current interests include the following: Whole-system transformation, balancing economic and human realities; discovering and collaborating with cutting-edge change-focused authors who are documenting the perpetual renewal of the OD profession; and applied phenomenology: developing higher states of consciousness and self-awareness in the consulting of interdependent organizations.

Mr. Sullivan's current professional learning is available at www.rolandsullivan.com.

Kristine Quade is an independent consultant who combines her background as an attorney with a master's degree in organization development from Pepperdine University and years of experience as both an internal and external OD consultant.

Ms. Quade draws from experiences in guiding teams from divergent areas within corporations and across many levels of executives and employees. She has facilitated leadership alignment, culture change, support system alignment, quality process improvements, organizational redesign, and the creation of clear strategic intent that results in significant bottom-line results. A believer in whole-system change, she has developed the expertise to facilitate groups ranging in size from eight to two thousand in the same room for a three-day change process.

Recognized as the 1996 Minnesota Organization Development Practitioner of the Year, Ms. Quade teaches in the master's programs at Pepperdine University and the University of Minnesota at Mankato and the master's and doctoral programs at the University of St. Thomas in Minneapolis. She is a frequent presenter at the Organization Development National Conference and also at the International OD Congress and the International Association of Facilitators.

About the Authors

Jane Hilburt-Davis is a founding principal of Key Resources, a consulting group that specializes in working with both human dynamics and business systems. Recognized as a leader in the field of family business, she has taught the popular course, *Love and Money*, at the Cambridge Center for Creative Enterprise, an award-winning training and research institute, which she founded almost a decade ago. Her clients include family businesses and closely-held businesses of all sizes.

She has authored and co-authored several articles, including "Using the Process/Content Framework: Guidelines for the Content Expert," "Solving Problems in the Family Business System: Five Questions to Ask," and "Advice to Copreneurs: Don't Avoid Conflict . . . Just Keep It Simple," and "Good Fences Make Good Neighbors." She is also asked to present her ideas at organizations and meetings as varied as the Family Firm Institute, Boston Estate Planning Council, Psychological Dynamics of Family Businesses, National Association of Personal Financial Advisors, New England Society of Applied Psychology, National Association of Social Workers, and the Family Business Foundation of New York.

In all her work, Ms. Hilburt-Davis strives to enhance the human spirit and improve the bottom line. With her unique combination of skills and knowledge in individual, family, and organizational dynamics, she seeks to help her clients bridge the gap between what is and what could be in their personal and professional lives. Originally trained as a biologist and naturalist, Ms. Hilburt-Davis believes in the interconnectedness of our lives, in work and in our families. She lives in Lexington, Massachusetts, and Cundy's Harbor, Maine.

W. Gibb Dyer, Jr., is the O. Leslie Stone Professor of Entrepreneurship in the Marriott School of Management at Brigham Young University. He received his B.S. and M.B.A. degrees from Brigham Young University and his Ph.D. in management philosophy from the Massachusetts Institute of Technology in 1984. He has held faculty positions at the University of New Hampshire and was a visiting professor in 1997 at IESE [Instituto de Estudios Superiores de la Empresa] in Barcelona, Spain. He has published widely on the topics of family business, entrepreneurship, organizational culture, and managing change in organizations. His articles have appeared in the *Academy of Management Review, Journal of Applied Behaviorial Science, Journal of Small Business Management, Family Business Review, Sloan Management Review, Human Resource Management,* and *Organizational Dynamics.* He has authored the award-winning book *Cultural Change in Family Firms: Anticipating and Managing Business and Family Transitions,* as well as *The Entrepreneurial Experience: Confronting Career Dilemmas of the Start-Up Executive.* He is also the co-author of *Managing by the Numbers: Absentee Owners and the Decline of American Industry.* He has served as a consultant to numerous organizations representing a variety of different industries. Because of his innovative approach to teaching, Dr. Dyer was awarded the 1990 Leavy Award for Excellence in Private Enterprise Education by the Freedoms Foundation at Valley Forge. Professor Dyer is a recognized authority on family business and entrepreneurship and has been quoted in such publications as *Fortune, The Wall Street Journal, INC., The New York Times,* and *Nation's Business.*

Index